EMPIRE
OF
IDEAS

EMPIRE
OF
IDEAS

THE ORIGINS OF PUBLIC DIPLOMACY
AND THE TRANSFORMATION OF
U.S. FOREIGN POLICY

JUSTIN HART

OXFORD
UNIVERSITY PRESS

OXFORD
UNIVERSITY PRESS

Oxford University Press is a department of the University of Oxford.
It furthers the University's objective of excellence in research, scholarship,
and education by publishing worldwide.

Oxford   New York
Auckland   Cape Town   Dar es Salaam   Hong Kong   Karachi
Kuala Lumpur   Madrid   Melbourne   Mexico City   Nairobi
New Delhi   Shanghai   Taipei   Toronto

With offices in
Argentina   Austria   Brazil   Chile   Czech Republic   France   Greece
Guatemala   Hungary   Italy   Japan   Poland   Portugal   Singapore
South Korea   Switzerland   Thailand   Turkey   Ukraine   Vietnam

Oxford is a registered trademark of Oxford University Press in the UK
and certain other countries.

Published in the United States of America by
Oxford University Press
198 Madison Avenue, New York, NY 10016

Library of Congress Cataloging-in-Publication Data
Hart, Justin.
Empire of ideas : the origins of public diplomacy and the transformation
of U.S. foreign policy / Justin Hart.
p. cm.
Includes bibliographical references and index.
ISBN 978–0–19–977794–5 (hardcover : acid-free paper)
1. United States—Relations.   2. United States—Foreign relations—1933–1945.
3. United States—Foreign relations—1945–1953.   4. United States—Foreign public opinion.
5. Postcolonialism—History—20th century.   6. Propaganda, American—History—
20th century.   7. Public relations and politics—United States—History—20th
century.   8. Educational exchanges—United States—History—20th century.   9. Overseas
information libraries—History—20th century.   I. Title.
E744.5.H37 2013
327.73—dc23
978–0–19–977794–5

3 5 7 9 8 6 4 2
Printed in the United States of America
on acid-free paper

*For my parents
and for Stephanie*

CONTENTS

ACKNOWLEDGMENTS

IT IS TRULY A pleasure after all these years to be able to acknowledge those who played a significant part, directly or indirectly, in creating this book. Thanks, first of all, to the History Department at Rutgers University, where this book began as a dissertation. The university provided generous financial support in the form of multiple fellowships and assistantships; a stimulating, supportive, and diverse educational experience; and, above all, a chance to work with first-rate students, colleagues and mentors. Choosing to do my Ph.D. at Rutgers is one of the best decisions I have ever made. While there, I had wonderful interactions with more people than I could possibly mention, but I would like to note especially the roles that Sara Dubow and Peter Lau played in my personal and intellectual development. Other friends who contributed to my education and significantly enhanced my quality of life during that time include Tim Alves, Kristen Block, Brady Brower, Kate Burlingham, Curt Cardwell, William Jelani Cobb, Gary Darden, Lesley Doig, Kate Elias, Joe Gabriel, Tiffany Gill, Carmen Khair Gitre, Ed Gitre, Sarah Gordon, Joe Groshong, Kate Keller, Sophie Lau, Kelena Reid Maxwell, Mike McDonough, Danielle McGuire, Khalil Muhammad, Amrita Chakrabarti Myers, Lia Paradis, Jennifer Pettit, Aminah Pilgrim, Amy Portwood, Louisa Rice, Adam Rosh, Karen

Routledge, Eric Schanen, Catherine Howey Stearn, Jennifer Tammi, and Stephanie Sims Wright.

The faculty at Rutgers is, as a whole, unfailingly committed to graduate education, and I benefited enormously from the opportunity to work with a number of them. Michael Adas, John Chambers, Paul Clemens, David Levering Lewis (now of New York University), David Oshinsky (now of the University of Texas), and Edward Rhodes (now of George Mason University) each contributed to my professional development in particularly important ways. Of course, my dissertation committee played the most critical role of all. I am profoundly indebted to James Livingston, who gave me the language to say what I really wanted to say; to Warren Kimball, the author of what I consider to be the definitive interpretation of Franklin Roosevelt's approach to foreign policy; and most especially to Lloyd Gardner, who has served as my mentor in ways that far exceed that of the typical dissertation advisor. I have been around academics all my life and I have never met someone who balances a commitment to teaching, to scholarship, to the university community, and to personal relationships as well as Lloyd. He excels in not one or two of these categories but in all of them. If I manage to balance these things even half as well as he does, I will consider myself a great success.

Before arriving at Rutgers, I received an extraordinary introduction to history and the historical profession as an undergraduate at Southern Methodist University. At SMU, no one did more to shape my thinking than Thomas Knock, who remains a model historian, mentor, and friend. After finishing at Rutgers, I spent a year teaching and advising at Purchase College, SUNY, where Lynn Mahoney and Bryan Roberts, along with many others, made my time there a real pleasure. In 2005, I relocated to Lubbock, TX, to take a position in the History Department at Texas Tech University—a move that has worked out better than I could have imagined. My fantastic colleagues provide a challenging, stimulating, and supportive community, and my teaching and research have benefited greatly from their presence. Rather than listing each of them individually, since they all deserve my sincerest thanks, I will simply say that I am incredibly fortunate to work every day with people I respect and admire and whose company I enjoy. I would also like to thank my undergraduate and graduate students at Rutgers, Purchase, and Texas Tech, many of whom helped me clarify my thinking on numerous issues discussed in this book, whether they realize it or not. Two of those students, William Mountz and Autumn Costa Lass, provided research assistance as well.

Over the years, a number of scholars have offered critical feedback on various portions of this work. Even in cases where I may not have incorporated their suggestions as fully as they might wish, their comments have been fundamental to shaping this book, which has evolved considerably over time. For their thoughtful remarks, I would like to thank Laura Belmonte, Mark Bradley, Susan Brewer, Nicholas Cull, Bruce Cumings, Walter Hixson, Michael Krenn, Robert McMahon, Joanne Meyerowitz, Jason Parker, Kurt Piehler, Robert Schulzinger, Anders Stephanson, the members of the Junior Faculty Reading Group in the History Department at Texas Tech, and an anonymous reader for Oxford University Press. Kenneth Osgood (originally the second anonymous reader at Oxford) deserves special mention here for providing an extremely detailed commentary, as well as line edits, on the complete manuscript. I would also like to thank the *Pacific Historical Review*, *Historically Speaking*, Brill, and Fordham University Press for allowing me to use material I previously published with them.

One of the pleasures of doing research is the opportunity to travel to places near and far and, in my case, to reconnect with old friends. Much of the research for the dissertation was conducted in Washington, D.C., where the hospitality provided by Michael Williams, Kelly Wurtz, and, my oldest friend, Corey Johnson made these trips possible; their friendship made them enjoyable. While on the road, I also accrued debts of a different kind to the staffs at the various archives I visited in researching this project: The Library of Congress; the National Archives in College Park, MD; the Special Collections Division at the University of Arkansas in Fayetteville, where the advice of Betty Austin helped me make it through a large amount of material in a short time; the Seeley G. Mudd Manuscript Library in Princeton, NJ, where I benefited from the good cheer of my friend Dan Linke; and the Harry S. Truman Library in Independence, MO, where Liz Safly and Dennis Bilger kept me thoroughly entertained and well supplied with documents. The Harry S. Truman Library Institute financed my stint there with one of their research grants. After I arrived at Texas Tech, the Provost's Office and the College of Arts and

Sciences generously funded an entire summer of additional research in Washington, D.C., which completely transformed the book.

One of the most rewarding aspects of publishing this book has been working closely with Susan Ferber at Oxford University Press. Although this is the first time I have been through this process, I cannot imagine that there are many—if any—better history editors around. Susan carefully shepherded this project through each stage, always providing honest and timely feedback. She then did a terrific job helping me to streamline the final product, refining my voice without changing my meaning.

In the end, the largest debt I owe is to my family. I will always be grateful for their constant support and encouragement as I wrestled with this project for what must have seemed like forever. (It certainly seemed that way to me.) I would like to thank my in-laws—the Celmans, Colemans, Gannaways, Horstmanns, Johnstons, and Patsleys—for their participation in my life and for allowing me to participate in theirs over many years. Thanks as well, on my side, to the Armitages and Gibbses. In my immediate family, my brother Daniel has been an inspiration to me in many ways, but especially through his music, the clarity and elegance of which provides a model for my own writing. Daniel also deserves a lot of credit for bringing the fabulous Rachel Ballard into our family. My parents, Ken and Ellen Hart, raised me in university communities and they made it such a positive experience that I never wanted to leave. More importantly, the same thing can be said of all my experiences with them. Parents can set all kinds of examples; it is a tribute to them that I have always sought to emulate their examples rather than forget them. This book is dedicated to them and to my wife, Stephanie, who has played such an important role in my life for so long that I would not be who I am without her. This is all the more true since the birth of our daughter, Irene. Raising Irene is the most exciting and rewarding of the many great adventures we have undertaken together. I hope that one day Irene will understand how she makes everything I do so much more meaningful.

Thanks again to all. This book would not have been possible without you.

Justin Hart
Lubbock, TX

EMPIRE
OF
IDEAS

INTRODUCTION

Image and the Origins of U.S. Public Diplomacy

ON NOVEMBER II, 2001, THE *New York Times* published a lengthy article on the quest to win "hearts and minds" in the Muslim world. As part of a special section assessing the state of the nation two months after the terrorist attacks that, according to many, had "changed everything," the article stood out for its emphasis not just on new efforts to shape the nation's image abroad but on historical precedents for those efforts. This very old issue in U.S. foreign relations had come to the fore once again as Americans struggled to answer the widely posed question: "Why do they hate us?"[1]

In the immediate aftermath of 9/11, the administration of President George W. Bush announced that it intended to counter the appeal of Osama bin Laden's al Qaeda network by launching a full-scale propaganda offensive in the Muslim world. At the center of this effort was a promise to reinvigorate the practice of "public diplomacy" at the State Department. Public diplomacy encompasses an incredibly broad set of initiatives designed to shape the image of the United States in the world. During the Cold War, it included everything from overt propaganda—delivered via radio, television, film, and print media—to educational exchanges, cultural exhibits, overseas libraries, and even domestic information campaigns. After 1953, these operations were run out of the United States Information Agency (USIA). However, the entire enterprise of public diplomacy had been left mostly moribund since the end of the Cold War in 1991, a process of decline that reached its nadir with the closing of the USIA in 1999.[2]

Two years later, the Bush administration pledged to undertake, as the *New York Times* reported, the "most ambitious wartime communications effort since World War II." At the time, though, no one—including the *Times*—seemed particularly concerned with exploring what actually happened during the 1940s and why it provided a model worth emulating. As it turned out, these comparisons amounted to little more than part of the public relations strategy itself, an effort to link contemporary policies to the "good war," rather than an authentic interest in probing the "lessons of history." Ultimately, a succession of policymakers (including, most notably, the president's trusted advisor, Karen Hughes) tried and failed to reinvigorate public diplomacy at the State Department. Along the way, they stumbled over many of the same obstacles as their predecessors, including those World War II policymakers who provided the ostensible model for what the U.S. government sought to do in the "post-9/11 world." Once again, U.S. officials struggled to explain away unpopular policies, to synchronize words and deeds, to adapt an advertising model to sell foreign policies, and to develop messages that were internally consistent yet sensitive to regional distinctions. Throughout, everyone seemed to agree that perceptions of "America" abroad mattered; the question that remained unanswered was what, if anything, policymakers could do to shape those perceptions.

Empire of Ideas places this question in historical perspective by taking the reader back to the dawn of what *Time-Life* publisher Henry Luce famously dubbed the "American Century," when U.S. officials first began to think of the nation's image in the world as a foreign policy issue. It examines the first phase of U.S. public diplomacy, which lasted from 1936 to 1953, in order to explore when and why the U.S. government decided to incorporate techniques for shaping the image of the United States abroad as an explicit component of the foreign policymaking process. The importance of image to U.S. foreign policy in the postwar period is frequently assumed but rarely explained, too often treated as a reflexive by-product of the ideological struggles of the Cold War. In fact, U.S. officials embraced what historian Frank Ninkovich has termed the "diplomacy of ideas" during the mid-1930s as part and parcel of a postcolonial, imperial strategy to extend the influence of the United States while avoiding the costs of acquiring a large territorial empire.

* * *

This story began at the Buenos Aires Conference in 1936, where the State Department proposed a series of government-sponsored technological and educational exchanges with the nations of Latin America. The initial stab at what policymakers called "cultural relations" grew out of President Franklin Roosevelt's Good Neighbor Policy toward Latin America, the much-ballyhooed effort to expand U.S. influence south of the border while scaling back the sort of "Big Stick" interventionism so common in the past. With these exchanges, the State Department clearly intended to use Latin America as the "laboratory" for honing an approach that it would eventually deploy worldwide.

During World War II, U.S. policymakers laid the groundwork for expanding the fledgling exchange programs into a global project for attracting hearts and minds. At the same time, they came to appreciate the importance of a unified propaganda strategy that capitalized on proliferating access to various forms of mass communications. Before the war, few diplomats considered propaganda part of what they did. By the end of the war, conceptions of diplomacy had expanded to such an extent that the State Department formally institutionalized propaganda and culture as foreign policy tools. In 1944, the Department established the position of Assistant Secretary of State for Public and Cultural Affairs, and Archibald MacLeish—the Pulitzer Prize–winning poet and Librarian of Congress—was appointed to fill it. The following year, President Truman transferred the overseas propaganda operations of the Office of War Information to the State Department as well, noting that "the nature of present day foreign relations makes it essential for the United States to maintain informational activities abroad as an integral part of the conduct of our foreign affairs."[3]

In the postwar period, public diplomats at the State Department worked to piece together a comprehensive approach to this new method for conducting U.S. foreign policy, but they were beset with a multitude of setbacks and obstacles. Some of these difficulties were endemic to their enterprise, such as the challenge of shaping the global image of a pluralistic democracy. They understood better than anyone that the private media and private citizens would always play the predominant role in determining perceptions of the United States. While image may have become an increasingly prominent component of U.S. foreign policymaking, it was a component over which policymakers themselves had very little control. The sheer power of the private media meant that their contribution to what Woodrow Wilson once called the "whispering gallery of the world" ultimately amounted to little more than a few drops in a very large bucket.[4] U.S. officials could not simply say whatever they wanted, lest they destroy their own credibility.

At the same time, their efforts to define the United States for the world provoked an often extraordinary backlash that put public diplomacy at the center of the vicious domestic political struggles of the early Cold War. Policymakers were heavily criticized for their methods, their management, and their messages, as they struggled to establish their legitimacy with skeptical colleagues, hostile legislators, and an indifferent public. Between 1945 and 1953, they continued to fight this battle, notching some successes and many failures. Perceived turning points ultimately made far less difference than expected. Numerous crises—some self-inflicted, some unavoidable—bedeviled every effort to chart a consistent course. Perhaps the most frustrating part of the criticism they endured was that they realized better than anyone how small and weak their megaphone really was. Throughout, public diplomats certainly could have done a better job of running their operation, but they still would have had to cope with the same intractable dilemma: in order to "project America" to the world, they first had to define "America," which was and always will be an inherently political endeavor.

It was hardly surprising, then, when Wisconsin Senator Joseph McCarthy joined the long list of conservative critics of public diplomacy in the early 1950s. Although it is sometimes forgotten, he launched savage attacks on the Voice of America and the foreign exchange programs as part of his relentless assault on the State Department. As with almost all aspects of his anticommunist crusade, McCarthy simply followed trails blazed by others. His contribution to the cause came not from his originality, but from his gift for demagoguery. In the end, McCarthy's barrage delivered the final blow to the public diplomacy shop at the State Department. Looking to defuse the crisis and start anew, the Eisenhower administration transferred control over most of the government's overseas propaganda and cultural programs to the newly created United States Information Agency in 1953. Although public diplomacy lived on and continued to grow, the creation of the USIA marked the conclusion of its first phase.

*   *   *

This book emerges from a literature that includes surveys of the various components of public diplomacy over a broad span of time, as well as more discrete examinations of one particular period or one particular program.[5] Although *Empire of Ideas* draws on these works, it does not attempt to provide a comprehensive institutional history of public diplomacy or any of its component programs. Instead, it explores the philosophical assumptions about foreign relations that led to the creation of these initiatives in the first place. It focuses, in particular, on explaining what the existence of these programs says about the nature of U.S. foreign relations in a rapidly shifting global environment. The decision to adopt the methods of public diplomacy stemmed directly from policymakers' recognition that U.S. foreign relations had entered a new era in which the U.S. government could no longer remain indifferent to perceptions of the United States abroad.[6]

By framing the origins of U.S. public diplomacy as a response to broader global transformations that began before World War II and kicked into high gear after Pearl Harbor, *Empire of Ideas* stresses the continuities between the pre-1945 and post-1945 period. The past, in this case, was much more than prologue.[7] The basic patterns, philosophies, and, in many cases, the personnel for the postwar operation emerged during the late 1930s and early 1940s. So did the blueprint for an "empire of ideas." As much as the Soviet threat amplified and modified these initiatives after the war, the desire to "project America" throughout the world would have existed irrespective of the Soviet

Union's emergence as a geopolitical rival. Of course, the fact that the Soviet Union posed both a geopolitical and an ideological threat made that rivalry all the more intense and, perhaps, all the more likely.

With image as its central organizing concept, this book brings together a number of very different programs that often utilized very different techniques. In fact, one of the perpetual tensions in the practice of public diplomacy is the fact that it contains some initiatives premised on the unidirectional dissemination of information, such as the Voice of America, and some initiatives premised on a mutual exchange of ideas, such as the Fulbright program. Despite their many differences, both the Voice of America and the Fulbright program shared the ultimate goal of improving the image of the United States around the world. U.S. officials only incorporated the methods of public diplomacy—whether in the form of dissemination or exchange—into the foreign policy process because of their concern for how the United States was perceived abroad. The pages that follow generally adopt the language that U.S. officials used in describing themselves and the programs they ran. However, the reader should be aware that, in my view, "cultural diplomats," "propagandists," and "psychological strategists" were all part of the same project and working toward the same end, even when they advocated different methods for achieving their common objective. I do, however, exclude those, such as CIA officials, engaged in covert information warfare, also referred to as "black propaganda" or disinformation. Although a by-product of their work may have been to shape the image of the United States, it was rarely their primary objective.

There were, of course, many precedents for what the U.S. government decided to do during these years. Efforts to deploy cultural artifacts toward diplomatic ends have long served as "the first resort of kings," as the cultural diplomat Richard Arndt argues. So, too, with government propaganda, which has existed as long as governments themselves. In the modern era, World War I represented a particularly important turning point in the history of public persuasion because of new methods of mass communications. Each of the world's major powers developed mechanisms for appealing to populations at home and abroad. Arguably the most successful of these was the Committee on Public Information (CPI) in the United States, run by the Progressive

Era journalist George Creel. The Creel Committee, as it was typically called, used everything from mass circulation print media to emerging motion picture technology to promote a message of wartime unity at home. Abroad, the CPI pioneered many of the techniques that would become staples of public diplomacy, including the distribution of propaganda via wireless transmissions and the creation of foreign "reading rooms" in a comprehensive effort to influence "world opinion."[8]

Even before the war ended, however, the public backlash against the CPI's heavy-handed messaging, particularly on the home front, led Congress to severely curtail the agency's operations. President Woodrow Wilson's abolition of the CPI in August 1919 simply confirmed the obvious: the American people rejected the idea that the U.S. government needed an apparatus to tell its official story at home and abroad, especially absent the exigencies of wartime. Creel himself expressed a "deep conviction that the [CPI] was a *war organization* only, and that it was without proper place in the national life in time of peace."[9] The idea that a nation's image could function as an independent force in the international arena was still too new to achieve widespread support, even in the halls of government. This dismissive attitude prevailed in the United States throughout the 1920s and early 1930s. The U.S. government stood still as various European nations developed increasingly sophisticated propaganda operations for projecting their ideas abroad—whether to communicate messages to their colonial populations (Britain and France), to expand their imperial reach (Germany and Italy), or to promote proletarian revolutions (the Soviet Union). However, the American reluctance to communicate an official story to the world started to change during the mid-1930s, as U.S. officials imagined themselves assuming the mantle of global leadership. The events of the 1940s only solidified the sense that the U.S. government needed new techniques to respond to changed realities.

The government's decision to develop programs in public diplomacy during the 1930s and 1940s is often portrayed as a weak and largely inept response to the formidable operations of Nazi Germany and, later, Soviet Russia, or as an inevitable, almost unconscious, reaction to the evolution of communications technology. There is, of course, something to both of these interpretations. Throughout World War II and the Cold War, policymakers and pundits worried about how to compete with propaganda from closed societies where governments exerted so much control over the media. This concern undoubtedly led U.S. officials to reverse previous patterns and explore the potential uses of communications technology to counter the powerful propaganda machines of their enemies, not to mention their allies. But to emphasize the reactive aspects of the origins of U.S. public diplomacy minimizes the ways in which these policies functioned as an affirmative response to the fundamental transformation of U.S. foreign relations during this period.

U.S. officials stood at the crossroads of four intersecting phenomena that came together to fundamentally reconfigure the global environment and the place of the United States therein. The first was the arrival of the United States as the world's dominant power by every conceivable measure; the second was the emergence of geopolitical and ideological threats to American dominance, first from Germany and Japan and, later, from the Soviet Union; the third was the continuing proliferation of access to the technologies of mass communications; and the fourth was the disintegration of European empires (particularly the British Empire) and the concomitant explosion of newly autonomous actors onto the international stage. All of these forces combined to render the image of "America" relevant to foreign policy in a way that it never had been before.

U.S. policymakers rightly regarded World War II as a watershed moment, both for their nation and for all nations and aspiring nations. They fervently believed, almost from the moment the country entered the war, that it would emerge not just victorious but a hegemonic force unrivaled in the world, if not in the history of the world. While they tended not to use the term "empire," they clearly thought that the United States would soon be as powerful as any empire in modern memory.[10] But if the United States had, finally, by 1941 reached the point where it might plausibly supplant Great Britain as the world's dominant power, it would not do so solely through mimicking the tactics of the British Empire. Although the United States was itself a colonial power, Roosevelt and many of his principal theorists blamed European methods of territorial colonialism for the violence and destruction that, ironically, created the void they hoped to occupy.[11] Convinced that colonialism could not last much longer in the face of mounting worldwide resistance, they faced the rather interesting dilemma of how to fashion an imperial strategy different from the European model they hoped to succeed. This quandary called for novel strategies to attract the loyalties of millions of newly or potentially autonomous people.

The solution to this dilemma—how to manage without ruling, or perhaps how to rule without managing—lay in the realm of ideology. Converting people to an "American" way of life—the holy grail of U.S. foreign policy from the 1940s forward—held the promise of extending the influence of the United States while avoiding costly, atavistic exercises in military conquest. Simply put, Americanization became the antidote to colonization. Obviously, ideological crusades had always been at the center of popular understandings of America's role in the world. But, during the 1940s, that sense of ideological mission became not only the rationale for a predetermined set of foreign policies but an actual component of foreign policy itself, as image became a critical tool of empire.[12]

This was the basic point, although it is easy to miss amid his jingoistic and xenophobic prose, that Henry Luce tried to convey in his much-cited "American Century" article in the February 17, 1941 issue of *Life* magazine. Primarily concerned with vanquishing the continuing resistance to U.S. entry into World War II, Luce encouraged his fellow Americans to march forth and seize the mantle of global preeminence from the beleaguered British Empire. Although more of a propagandist than a philosopher, Luce laid out a blueprint for how the United States could bring an end to what historian Bruce Cumings has called the "hegemonic interregnum"—the period between 1914 and 1941 "in which England could no longer lead and the United States was not yet ready to do so."[13] In one of his most memorable passages, Luce argued that the global dissemination of jazz, Hollywood movies, and American slang meant that the world already spoke America's language. Policymakers simply had to decide how to capitalize upon this propitious circumstance. The development of public diplomacy was the primary expression of their desire to do so. Although public diplomacy obviously did not cause this evolution in the nation's role in the world, nor was it the only example of the new environment in which policymakers operated, it was the clearest indication of the way in which considerations of image became a factor in the foreign policy process.

Examining the theoretical underpinnings of the decision to embrace public diplomacy reveals that U.S. policymakers, like Luce, were well aware of the central role that individual people would play in the implementation of the American Century. "We think today in terms of peoples rather than nations," said the World War II propagandist and Pulitzer Prize–winning playwright Robert Sherwood. For public diplomats and policymakers more broadly, the proliferation of mass communications and the heightened mobility of individuals and ideas had effectively made "people"—at home and abroad—not just an external influence upon the formation of policy, but an organic component of a broadened conception of what constituted foreign relations.[14]

In contrast to the traditional notion of public *opinion* as a factor for policymakers to accommodate or manipulate, the theoretical foundation of public diplomacy reflected a growing awareness of public *participation* in U.S. foreign relations. Archibald MacLeish offered the clearest articulation of this idea with his observation at a State Department meeting in 1945 that "electric communications has made foreign relations domestic affairs." MacLeish's radical perspective on the relationship of people to the foreign policy process suggested that people not only expressed opinions on policy, but that their actions constituted a critical component of the nation's relations with the external world. This is not to say that policymakers did not also pay attention to, and try to shape, public opinion. Rather, the idea of public participation simply meant that ordinary people played the defining role in creating the image of "America" projected to the world, and policymakers could only do so much to massage or mold that image. This was a sobering realization for the officials charged with monitoring that image.[15]

*   *   *

The purpose of analyzing why U.S. policymakers thought it necessary to create programs in public diplomacy is not to produce a mimetic account of what they said and did, but to understand the changes occurring in the world around them. Their statements are evidence of their participation in a much broader dialogue that occurred, in many cases, over and against their own interests. In fact, the principle protagonists in this story, unlike many of their more powerful superiors, never assumed their own power to shape the world in which they lived and worked. On the contrary, they constantly remarked upon their own impotence in the face of increasingly powerful transnational social, cultural, and political forces. Although the globalization of American society did not begin during the World War II era, the decision to start engaging the conversation over that process did. Regardless of whether policymakers ever actually operated in an environment insulated from larger social, cultural, and political dialogues, their desire to fulfill the terms of the American Century through building an empire of ideas required them to rethink the notion that they could or even should remain insulated.

Needless to say, some responded better than others to these developments. Then, as now, self-styled "realists" inside and outside of government generally belittled the importance of what is known today as "soft power." Their emphasis on power politics relegated images and ideas to the status of ephemeral trivialities, of no real significance compared to the tangible reality of military or economic force. Many others acknowledged the importance of image, but disagreed over how the government should deal with it from a policymaking perspective: Was public diplomacy an organic response to the emergence of "soft power" as a major factor in the nation's relations with the external world, or was it just a mechanism for promoting the decisions of those typically deemed the custodians of U.S. foreign relations? Most importantly, should concerns about the nation's image influence which policies to implement, or did image only matter to the extent that it could be applied as a gloss to enhance unpopular choices?[16]

Public diplomats, too, wavered on these sorts of questions about how to define their role. Sometimes, they insisted on being included in the policymaking process; at other points, they demurred, restricting their job description to advancing the existing objectives of U.S. foreign policy. In some cases, they argued that "words without deeds" counted for very little, that the actual foreign policies mattered far more than anything they could say about them. In other cases they argued that policies could not "speak for themselves," that all policies needed to be framed in a favorable light in order to be fully effective. These two positions were not necessarily irreconcilable, but the struggle to balance them reflected the inherent difficulties of navigating complex global terrain, especially in the realm of images and ideologies.

In this sense, *Empire of Ideas* sheds light on one of the under-recognized paradoxes of the American Century: The same phenomenon that awarded such extraordinary power to the policymakers who presided over the creation of the national security state simultaneously precipitated an astonishing dispersal of authority over U.S. foreign relations more generally. In contrast to their vast accumulation of power in the political, economic, and military realms, U.S. officials exercised comparatively little control over the cultural realm despite their realization that perceptions of America mattered more than ever before.[17]

To resolve this paradox requires thinking carefully about the distinctions between diplomacy, foreign policy, and foreign relations. If "diplomacy" refers to the high-level contacts between the officially designated representatives of various nations (typically ambassadors or statesmen), and "foreign policy" encompasses all aspects of a government's formal approach to the external world (including diplomatic relations, but also incorporating military, economic, legal, and cultural affairs as well), then "foreign relations" signifies the sum total of a nation's contacts with governments and peoples of other nations. During the 1940s, the State Department launched several major reorganizations to accommodate the fact that its responsibilities increasingly extended beyond the parameters of classic conceptions of "diplomacy." Policymakers continually dealt with issues that did not fit neatly into the model of state-to-state negotiations, as conducted by official government representatives. This problem posed topical and geographical challenges to the existing framework. Not only did the State Department deal with a much broader array of subject matter, such as economic affairs and international organizations, but its long-standing institutional structure of geographical "divisions" could no longer accommodate the policymaking needs of a nation committed to thinking in global terms. As a result, "diplomacy" in the traditional sense became just one aspect of an expanded conception of "foreign policy."

The decision to develop the various components of public diplomacy, which also emerged from these reorganizations, followed this pattern to some extent. Just as foreign policymakers found themselves engaged with economic affairs and international organizations, they also confronted cultural and ideological questions that required them to take technologies of mass communications more seriously than ever before. Yet public diplomats also had to deal with the profound limitations on their ability to shape cultural relations or the nation's image in the world. Consequently, they realized, sooner than most of their State Department colleagues, that just as "diplomacy" now comprised only one part of U.S. "foreign policy," "foreign policy" now constituted only one (rapidly shrinking) part of U.S. "foreign relations." Obviously, not everyone in Washington embraced, or even accepted, these conclusions. However, they were virtually unavoidable for those officially tasked with shaping perceptions of the United States throughout the world.

Typically, the question asked about the importance of public diplomacy to early U.S. Cold War policies has been how much of a role it played in the decision-making process. Because of a lack of funding, not to mention the sustained hostility to these programs inside and outside the U.S. government, the answer often seemed to be "not much." However, if the question is reframed to ask why the government adopted the methods of public diplomacy in the first place, why it had such difficulty getting its message out, and why the process of projecting "America" to the world proved so contentious, then we get much closer to understanding the real significance of this story: the way the American Century redefined the nature of U.S. foreign relations and, in turn, reconfigured its domestic affairs as well. As George Marshall remarked in an early television program designed to advertise the State Department to the public, "foreign policy has entered the American home and taken a seat at the family table."[18]

Here lies the explanation for an aspect of public diplomacy that has never been adequately explained: why it repeatedly provoked a level of vituperation so disproportionate to the actual amount of time and money spent on the effort. Arguably, no single government program or set of programs during this period consistently generated greater scrutiny or even apoplexy. Most of the criticism did come from conservative legislators—in a potent and increasingly consequential alliance between Republicans and southern Democrats—who relished the opportunity to blast liberals in the Executive Branch. However, the sustained intensity of the attacks makes it difficult to dismiss them as routine political gamesmanship.

In 1947, several members of the House Appropriations Committee offered an unintentionally revealing insight into some of the deeper sources of their discomfort with the very idea of the government trying to "project America." Justifying their decision to defund the vast majority of the State Department's public diplomacy operation, one of many such efforts through the years, they branded the entire project a "radical departure in the methods of conducting our foreign relations."[19] On this point they were right. The "radical departure" of public diplomacy emerged in direct response to truly radical transformations in the nature of U.S. foreign relations—transformations that reverberated at home as well as abroad. Just as domestic events resonated throughout the world, playing a critical role in defining U.S. foreign relations, America's arrival as a global hegemonic power completely reconfigured the domestic social, political, and cultural landscape.

This development goes a long way toward explaining why it has been so difficult to build and sustain an active and vibrant program in public diplomacy. Dealing with image as a component of foreign policy turned out to be far more complicated than most people anticipated. In this aspect, perhaps more than any other, the "lessons" of the first phase of U.S. public diplomacy remain relevant to contemporary challenges, although *Empire of Ideas* offers no easy answers for how to resuscitate public diplomacy today. Given the intense polarization spawned by the culture wars of the past two decades, Projecting America in a way that allows public diplomats to maintain both their credibility and their viability has probably become more difficult, not less. The mobility of people and ideas across national boundaries has only accelerated over the last half-century, further complicating government efforts to shape the nation's image abroad. Nevertheless, the questions that U.S. officials confronted in setting up these programs between 1936 and 1953 have resurfaced time and again. Even in the many cases where the policy-makers of that generation failed to provide adequate answers, including when there were no answers to be found, their theories and methodologies remain relevant to thinking through what is and is not possible, and what is and is not wise, in doing this sort of work. In that way alone, their story deserves far more attention than it has received so far.

I

"Down with Imperialism"
The Latin American Origins of U.S. Cultural Diplomacy

DECEMBER 1, 1936 WAS A cloudless, sunny day in Buenos Aires. The vibrant, mauve flowers of the jacaranda trees had just begun to flower. Thousands lined the streets that beautiful day, taking advantage of the weather and the national holiday the Argentine government had declared in honor of the opening of the Buenos Aires Conference. As the motorcade slowly wound its way downtown, U.S. President Franklin Roosevelt and his Argentine counterpart, Augustin Justo, waved to the jubilant crowd. Roosevelt had arrived the day before, after an exhausting two-week, 6,000 mile voyage aboard the cruiser *Indianapolis*. His appearance, to give the keynote address to the conference, marked the first official visit by a U.S. president to South America.[1]

As the limousine approached the magisterial white marble palace of the Argentinean legislature—the building "resembles the Capitol in Washington," gushed the front-page coverage in the *New York Times*...but "on a smaller scale"—FDR gathered his thoughts. Aided by the arm of his son James, Roosevelt entered the hall and hobbled to the podium in the massive Chamber of Deputies. He received a standing ovation that lasted several minutes. As the crowd quieted down, eager for Roosevelt to begin, a voice bellowed from near the back of the hall: "Down with imperialism!" FDR paused as police removed the heckler, then proceeded with his speech.[2]

Nearly a year earlier, when Roosevelt first proposed this gathering of what U.S. officials liked to call the "American republics," the president had emphasized hemispheric affairs. Eleven months later, his focus had changed. A shocking series of incidents around the globe led him to recast his original agenda within an international context. As FDR's Secretary of State Cordell Hull later recalled: "Japan had won a war in China, Italy in Ethiopia; Spain, the mother country of most of the Latin American Republics, was in civil war, with Italy, Russia, and Germany intervening; Germany and Japan were linked in a virtual alliance; Hitler was violating one treaty after another; Britain and France were vacillating; the League was limping toward its end; and the United States was set in a concrete mold of isolation."[3]

Having to balance his instinctive call to action with his nation's hostility to involvement in European affairs, Roosevelt began cautiously. He spoke of "events elsewhere" that "have served only to strengthen our horror of war." Gradually, he grew more assertive, suggesting vaguely that "the Republics of the New World" do something to help the "Old World to avert the catastrophe which impends." The longer he spoke, the more forceful he became. By the end, FDR had made an eloquent appeal for the internationalist agenda his administration had tried to pursue, with limited success and great resistance, for most of the past four years. He concluded with a comprehensive accounting of the relationship between democratic forms of government, the free exchange of commerce, greater security, and "a wider distribution of culture, of education, of thought, and of free expression." The audience responded enthusiastically to the speech, which was broadcast on three separate radio networks in Argentina. FDR was interrupted several times by "tumultuous applause," much like a State of the Union address back home.[4]

The next day, thousands once again gathered outside, this time in heavy rain, to watch as the *Indianapolis* began its long journey back to the United States. The trip represented a thorough triumph, yet there was one thing that bothered FDR as his cruiser sailed out onto the open seas: It was the heckler. "Why was I so slow?" the president complained, lamenting the lapse in his usually quick wit. "I should have answered… 'That's right! Down with imperialism. That's why we are meeting in this conference.'"[5]

Although not widely remembered as such, the Buenos Aires Conference stands as one of the more significant achievements in U.S. foreign policy during the mid-1930s. Both in rhetoric and reality the Buenos Aires Conference epitomized the Roosevelt administration's prewar approach to foreign policy. The proposals of the U.S. delegation espoused multilateralism—politically, culturally, and economically. Furthermore, these proposals bucked the popular mood within the United States by requiring both a spiritual and a practical commitment to greater U.S. involvement in world affairs.[6] And the conference took place in Latin America, where the New Dealers first tested many of the initiatives they would later deploy on a global basis.[7]

By far the most significant proposal in this regard—the only one introduced by the United States to make it into the final treaty—was the modest provision for a series of multilateral cultural exchanges between the nations of the Western Hemisphere. This agreement called for each of the twenty-one governments that signed the treaty to pay for the exchange of two graduate students per year, per country. It was not much. But it put the U.S. government in the business of "cultural diplomacy"—that is, the deliberate attempt to deploy cultural affairs in pursuit of foreign policy objectives. By the end of World War II, these simple exchanges had grown into a comprehensive program to shape the nation's image abroad, as U.S. officials combined cultural diplomacy with overseas propaganda, domestic information campaigns, and technological modernization initiatives to form the matrix of what became known as public diplomacy. Thus began the massive postwar project dedicated to winning "hearts and minds" around the world.

"Give Them a Share"

That these efforts started in Latin America was no accident. In fact, they must be understood as an essential expression of the Roosevelt administration's Good Neighbor Policy. FDR actually introduced the idea of the "good neighbor" in his first inaugural—the address better remembered for "we have nothing to fear but fear itself..."—when he pledged to "dedicate this Nation to the policy of the good neighbor... the neighbor who respects his obligations and respects the sanctity of his agreements in and with a world of neighbors." The president did not initially apply this idea to any particular region. Soon, though, the Good Neighbor Policy became the catchall label for the Roosevelt administration's much publicized attempt to scale back the arrogance of attitude and action that had prompted many Latinos to label his nation "El Coloso del Norte" ("the Colossus of the North").[8] The United States officially renounced the sort of Big Stick diplomacy that had resulted in perpetual interference in the domestic politics of Latin American states over the past several decades. To back up his words with action, the president repudiated the Platt Amendment of 1901 (used repeatedly to justify intervention in Cuba), ordered the removal of U.S. marines from Haiti, and generally encouraged greater input from Latin American leaders about policies affecting their own countries. "Give them a share" was how Roosevelt described his administration's attitude towards Latin America. "They think they are just as good as we are, and many of them are."[9]

This sort of tongue-in-cheek remark helps to explain why the Good Neighbor Policy has sometimes been viewed as a sham—as lofty rhetoric designed to facilitate a shift from military domination to economic hegemony. There is some truth to that accusation. However, critics of the Good Neighbor Policy have failed to address why a politician as skillful as Roosevelt would create, in the words of historian Bryce Wood, a "huge red, white, and blue target" for potential critics. The answer to that question lies in the role that Latin America played within the overall scope of U.S. foreign policy during the 1930s.[10]

Led by Cordell Hull, FDR's long-standing Secretary of State, the president's foreign policy team entered office with a philosophical commitment to U.S. involvement in the world—economically and, in most cases, politically as well. Hull differed personally in many ways from the president, yet his background as a respected congressman and his commitment to free trade and Wilsonian internationalism made him an effective advocate for the president's views. Unlike his boss, the New York patrician, Hull's roots extended deep into the foothills of the Cumberland Mountains in central Tennessee where he grew up among yeoman farmers during the Reconstruction Era. Much like Wilson, his personal experiences during that tumultuous period stayed with him and shaped his worldview throughout his long career. In his memoirs, written nearly eighty years later, he still expressed admiration for his father's resistance to "Yankee guerillas" and vividly recalled his family's "outrage" at federal taxes on whiskey revenues. One might say that his hostility to government restrictions on unfettered commerce became ingrained at an early age.[11]

During his first year at the State Department, Hull set out to reverse the protectionist foreign policies of the previous administration. In 1931, a desperate Herbert Hoover had allowed Congress to talk him into signing the Smoot-Hawley tariff, which raised the average tax on certain "protected" imports to a breathtaking rate of 59 percent. Sadly, but predictably, this measure virtually extinguished trade with Europe, exacerbating rather than alleviating the Depression at home and abroad. Hull advocated a return to the Open Door ideology that had served as the animating principle of U.S. foreign policy since the turn of the century. But he found that he had to wait out the early New Deal's focus on the domestic economy. In 1934, Hull finally managed to advance his agenda by securing the Reciprocal Trade Act and the creation of the Export-Import Bank. The former authorized the president to negotiate lower tariffs and most favored nation status on a country-by-country basis; the latter supplied easy credit to boost foreign purchases of U.S. goods. Both played an important role in counteracting Smoot-Hawley and redeveloping overseas markets, earning Hull the enmity of a select group of protectionists and unilateralists in Congress.[12]

For the remainder of the decade and well into the next, the Executive Branch battled legislators determined to insulate the United States from the political and economic chaos spreading across Europe and Asia. These legislators both contributed to and capitalized on the prevailing popular disillusionment with World War I and its failed promise "to end all wars." Led by Republican Senator Gerald P. Nye of North Dakota, Congress conducted investigations during 1934 and 1935 designed to show that multinational bankers and munitions manufacturers, reviled as "merchants of death," had dragged the nation into World War I. With Europe again on the brink of war, anti-interventionists in Congress used the publicity from the hearings to bolster their case for a series of neutrality acts designed to prevent the United States from becoming embroiled in European disaster. Between 1935 and 1937, Congress passed three separate pieces of legislation that restricted American shipments of munitions or money to any nation at war.[13]

For the Roosevelt administration, Latin America represented something of a safe passageway between the Scylla of international crisis and the Charybdis of domestic unilateralism. In Europe and in Asia, unilateralists objected to almost any involvement whatsoever.[14] Latin America, on the other hand, called forth memories of the Monroe Doctrine's brand of backyard diplomacy, and Congress extended the White House greater latitude within the Western Hemisphere. Before Pearl Harbor, U.S. policy toward Latin America thus became, as historian Warren Kimball points out, "the 'side door' for Roosevelt's internationalism"— the testing ground for what the administration eventually hoped to do in the rest of the world.[15]

The Buenos Aires Conference followed squarely in this tradition. There was no mistaking the extent to which Buenos Aires served as a proxy for a broader agenda. The U.S. delegation pushed aggressively for agreements on collective security and multilateral trade.[16] More generally, the specter of German rearmament and territorial expansion hung over the proceedings. Thinking back in his memoirs to the major forces shaping the agenda at Buenos Aires, Hull focused primarily on the "Axis penetration" of Latin America: "The German Lufthansa airlines and the German steamship companies were utilized to the utmost in spreading Nazi philosophy. German radios were beamed to Latin America, and German news services, purveying news with a strong Nazi slant were set up."[17]

For Hull to frame the conference in these terms suggests the emphasis of the U.S. delegation upon the mobility of people and ideas. During the conference itself, the U.S. delegation endorsed the "use of radio broadcasting in the service of peace, an association of writers and artists, bibliographical exchange...and protection of intellectual property." The conference's Committee on Intellectual Cooperation produced nearly half of the "conventions" eventually adopted. Even the Committee on Economic Problems promoted the mobility of peoples through sessions on sea and air transport, as well as planning for the construction of a Pan-American highway. In the assessment of Samuel Guy Inman, the Disciples of Christ minister Hull appointed to shepherd the student exchange proposal through committee hearings: "The Hitler movement had demonstrated to the democracies the tremendous power of propaganda."[18]

Understood within this context, the convention on cultural relations seems less an afterthought than an organic expression of the principal rationale behind the conference. After all, Roosevelt himself had opened with a plea for "a wider distribution of culture, of education, of thought, and of free expression." And the U.S. commitment to an actual exchange of ideas reinforced the general premise behind the Good Neighbor Policy while continuing to use Latin America as a "testing ground" for bigger ideas.[19]

In hindsight, the agreement on inter-American cultural relations meant more than anything else that came out of the Buenos Aires Conference because of what it said about the future trajectory of U.S. foreign relations. At the time, it might have seemed a relatively inconsequential provision on a peripheral matter. However, as U.S. cultural diplomacy became over the next decade a key component of a strategy to extend the influence of the United States throughout the world without incurring the costs of territorial conquest, its true importance emerged. In his "American Century" piece of February 1941, the quintessential expression of U.S. imperial ideology, Henry Luce predicted that Americanization could provide the antidote to colonization—if only the nation could harness the power of its "culture." No wonder FDR could not get that heckler out of his mind: "Down with imperialism," indeed. Or was it?

Foreign Relations "Under Modern Conditions"

Despite its potential for transforming the methods of conducting foreign policy, U.S. cultural diplomacy did not exactly get off to a roaring start. Over a year after the Buenos Aires Conference, the State Department had done little to implement the proposed exchanges of professors and students. Some even questioned if the Office of Education, not the State Department, should assume responsibility for the new exchange programs.[20] At that point, Sumner Welles and Laurence Duggan stepped forward to demand that any government-sponsored exchanges be run through the government department officially charged with the conduct of the nation's foreign affairs.

Welles, the senior of the two, had by the late 1930s developed a formidable reputation as FDR's "global strategist." At times, his advice to the president outweighed even that of his boss, Secretary of State Cordell Hull, with whom he often had a strained relationship. A close, personal friend of the Roosevelts, Welles had served as a groomsman at their wedding. He was also a veteran diplomat, having worked his way through various lower-level State Department posts to become, in 1933, the first Assistant Secretary of State for Latin American affairs. In 1937, his work earned him a promotion to Undersecretary of State. At that point, he tapped his young deputy, Laurence Duggan, to succeed him as the head of what was known as the "Division of the American Republics." It was no accident that the two principal pioneers of U.S. cultural diplomacy both had backgrounds in Latin American relations.[21]

In addition to his expertise on Latin America, Duggan also had the benefit of an extensive apprenticeship with the nation's foremost expert on educational exchanges: his father, Stephen. A self-described Wilsonian liberal internationalist, the elder Duggan had served as the director of the Institute of International Education (IIE) since its founding in 1919. The IIE owed its existence to the leadership and the largesse of the Carnegie Endowment for International Peace (CEIP)—the massive foundation established by the steel magnate and philanthropist, Andrew Carnegie, a decade earlier. Both the CEIP and the IIE espoused the principle that mutual understanding between people from different cultures and nations could advance the cause of international peace.[22]

The Carnegie Endowment, with its broad portfolio of initiatives, took a fairly abstract approach to "cultural relations." Led by former Secretary of State Elihu Root and Columbia University President Nicholas Murray Butler, the CEIP brought diplomats from various countries together for a series of chummy gatherings outside of official channels. The relatively relaxed atmosphere of these meetings was supposed to promote better dialogue. The IIE, in contrast, worked more systematically, facilitating and funding educational exchanges

around the world. Together, these two organizations played a critical role in helping to refine the formal practice of cultural relations.
They functioned, in the words of one historian, as a sort of "halfway
house" between the laissez-faire approach of the 19th century and the
government-sponsored initiatives of the 1930s and beyond.[23]

Over the next several years, Laurence Duggan teamed up with
Welles to press the case for integrating cultural diplomacy into the
unapologetically traditional agenda at the State Department. In this
case, the pupil, having far more experience with educational exchanges,
tutored the mentor. Welles had actually expressed some interest in the
plan to run the exchange programs out of the Office of Education, but
Duggan lobbied hard for "final policy decisions in all matters directly
affecting conduct of international relations to rest with the Secretary of
State." This was about more than shipping a few people here and there,
he told Welles: "Because of the increasing importance of the promotion
of cultural relations to the improvement of general relations with the
other American republics, it was thought wise to formulate a proposal
that would permit greater control by this Department."[24]

Duggan tried to convince Welles that cultural relations should not
only be considered part of foreign policy, it should transform the very
conceptualization of foreign policy. According to Duggan, "carrying
out the provisions of the Buenos Aires Cultural Convention" would
inevitably require action in fields that, "while not classically associated with foreign affairs, under modern conditions [are] very directly
related to foreign affairs." In other words, the State Department should
develop a new brand of "cultural diplomacy," by using "cultural relations" to pursue foreign policy objectives.[25]

Eventually, Welles endorsed Duggan's position. Within a couple of
months, the two of them convinced Cordell Hull to create a Division
of Cultural Relations at the State Department—theoretically on par
with the more traditional geographic offices, such as the Division of the
American Republics or the Division of Near Eastern Affairs. Less than
two years after Buenos Aires, the modest educational exchanges inspired
by the Good Neighbor Policy had prompted the Secretary of State to
elevate "cultural" matters—symbolically, at least—to the equivalent of
a cabinet-level position within the State Department. Appropriately,
the offices for the Cultural Division were located immediately adjacent

to those for Duggan's Division of the American Republics in the old State Department building.[26]

To head up the new division, the State Department tapped Ben Cherrington, who ran the respected International Relations program at the University of Denver. The author of a book on the uses of education in forming international attitudes, Cherrington was a pioneer in the theory and practice of intellectual exchange. His appointment highlighted one of the tensions that would emerge from government sponsorship of international cultural exchanges. Although Hull apparently assured Cherrington he would not "be expected to deal in propaganda"—that these exchanges would not "force any ideologies down the throats of listeners in other nations"—this assurance begged the question of why a national government would engage in these sorts of activities in the first place.[27] Was it even possible to develop techniques of cultural diplomacy that would not, at some level, turn into propaganda? What about Laurence Duggan's prediction that "cultural" matters would occupy an increasingly prominent position within the formulation of the nation's foreign policies? Even if these foreign policies sought to promote greater international cooperation, as they often did during the Roosevelt administration, that overall goal served as an expression of certain nationalist objectives. Simply put, Cherrington owed the existence of his job to the desire of U.S. policymakers to improve the image of the United States in Latin America within the context of the Good Neighbor Policy. Maybe government-sponsored cultural activities did not amount to propaganda in the strictest sense, but they were separated by a line in the sand just waiting for high tide.

The debate that would emerge over the next several years pitted purists, who viewed intellectual exchanges as an almost post-national exercise in reducing strife through a meeting of minds, against policymakers, who sought to deploy "culture" as a tool of U.S. foreign policy. The former insisted that the exchanges remain strictly intellectual, uncorrupted by a political agenda; the latter responded that governments could no longer afford to ignore the impact of "culture" upon U.S. relations with other countries. The purists wanted the Division of Cultural Relations to continue and extend the philanthropic programs of the CEIP and the IIE, now with government funding. Ironically, they would lose this argument to people who subscribed to the logic of IIE product Laurence Duggan. "Modern conditions" required the State Department to account for the role of culture in advancing U.S. objectives abroad.

Accounting for the political implications of cultural relations was not the same as trying to control the process. On the contrary, policymakers were well aware that the dissemination of American culture abroad, whether through educational exchange or Hollywood movies, would always remain a predominantly private endeavor. At most, the government could attempt to channel or supplement existing networks. For practitioners of cultural diplomacy, understanding what is and is not possible requires a sophisticated assessment of the relationship between public and private sources of "culture." This explains why one of the first moves by the newly minted Division of Cultural Relations was to organize an all-day seminar in late spring 1938 between public and private leaders in the field of educational exchange. The assembled audience included representatives from the Guggenheim Foundation, Johns Hopkins University, the Rockefeller Foundation, the Pan American Union, the Foreign Policy Association, the American Library Association, and, of course, the Carnegie Endowment and the IIE. The presence of both of the Duggans— Stephen representing the IIE and Laurence the State Department— aptly symbolized the public-private partnership the State Department sought to promote.[28]

Cordell Hull gave the seminar's opening address. As he had at Buenos Aires, Hull made clear that the State Department's interest in the exchange process was more than academic; in fact, it had the broadest possible geopolitical implications. The rumors of war from December 1936 had been confirmed through the full-blown Japanese invasion of mainland China and the German Anschluss in Austria. Yet Hull still regarded Latin America as critically important. He worried about the "striking lack of understanding" of the United States and its "aims and purposes" in the nations to the south. He placed much of the blame on U.S. citizens, whose apathy and "ignorance" of the "conditions and problems" of their nation's foreign relations made them less than effective emissaries for U.S. values and traditions. Without decisive action, Hull intoned, *Latinoamericanos* "will never be able to preserve and operate a system of popular government.... They can take our Constitution and our bill of rights, but it doesn't operate because the people themselves haven't caught up with the spirit of the thing."[29]

Hull's speech contained several important insights into the nature of U.S. cultural diplomacy and its evolving position as a component of foreign policy. Most glaringly, the crude paternalism of his analysis highlighted the ambiguous quality of the State Department's intervention into the cultural field. It made his assurances to Cherrington about the United States not forcing "ideologies down the throats of listeners in other nations" seem more than a little disingenuous. At the same time, his conclusion—that "political stability to the south of us" could not be promoted "merely by valuable and indispensable trading"—should not be overlooked. For the past five years, Hull had been the nation's preeminent apostle of trade as a panacea for all social and political ills, but here he was saying that trade was not enough. Almost equally remarkable was his emphasis upon private networks, in which he effectively acknowledged the limited influence of U.S. officials over a critical area of foreign relations. The U.S. government, he said, could provide part of the assistance, but 95 percent would have to come from "those in this country who see eye to eye with us as to the significance of what we have in mind."[30]

How Broad, How Far?

What did the U.S. government "have in mind"? It was clear from the moment the State Department created a Division of Cultural Relations that this involved more than funding a few educational exchanges within the Western Hemisphere. But how far would that mandate stretch, and how broad would it be? The geographical part of that question could be easily answered. In fact, it had more to do with time than space. As with other aspects of the Good Neighbor Policy, policymakers always intended to extend the cultural programs worldwide. It was just a matter of how soon they could convince others (namely, Congress) to let them do it. Laurence Duggan was quite clear about this in his initial efforts to sell the project. "Under the present circumstances," he said, "it is probable that the activities of the office, if established, would be concentrated primarily upon cultural relations with the other American Republics." However, "the activities may well be extended to other parts of the world at some future time."[31] Veteran diplomat George Messersmith addressed this issue even more directly a few months later at one of the Cultural Division's early planning sessions. In response to a question from Stephen Duggan, who asked whether the Department expected the programs to "work over the whole world," Messersmith replied that the new division "is to take care of all of these matters so far as they affect our cultural relations everywhere, but... in the beginning we want to very largely concentrate on this hemisphere."[32]

The question of scope was a great deal more complicated. It required, first and foremost, a definition of "culture." For example, would the State Department restrict itself to facilitating the exchange of "high" culture, such as fine art, classical music, literature, and, presumably, formal education? Or should it also try to cash in on the appeal of American "popular" culture exemplified by Hollywood and jazz? Virtually everyone recognized the importance of popular culture to the U.S. image in the world. Long before Henry Luce's articulation of the "American Century," the *Saturday Evening Post* memorably declared that "the sun... never sets on the British Empire and the American motion picture."[33] But could the State Department really turn "soft power" into a tangible diplomatic asset? Should it even try? And did that not fall more under the heading of propaganda than of cultural exchange?

At one early gathering of U.S. officials and educational leaders, Professor Herbert Bolton, the famous historian of the Spanish Borderlands, encouraged the State Department to think as broadly as possible. "A nation's culture," Bolton said, "comprises the whole body of its civilization, its way of life, its modes of thought, its religious mold, its social structure, its manner of artistic, spiritual and intellectual expression. It embodies the sum total of the nation's heritage from the remote and the less remote past... a people's culture is the sublimation of its history." Bolton had a point, and there certainly were U.S. officials—especially the Secretary of State—who conceptualized "cultural relations" in this way. But to export "the sum total of the nation's heritage from the remote and the less remote past," if not by definition propaganda, certainly seemed to head in that direction.[34]

An equally complicated set of questions about the scope of "cultural relations" emerged in response to a proposal for the United States to provide various forms of technical assistance to various Latin American countries. This "technical assistance" included everything from high-way engineering to immigration policy, methods of municipal administration, and agricultural techniques. The idea was that the U.S. government would loan experts in these fields to participating countries to help "modernize" their economic and political infrastructure. The complication was that, while "technical assistance" qualified as "education" (broadly construed), it could not plausibly be described as an exchange. The flow of information clearly went in only one direction. So the State Department created a separate but parallel agency, the Committee on Cooperation with the American Republics (CCAR), which operated in conjunction with the Division of Cultural Relations for the next several years.[35]

One direct connection between the two groups was the presence of Sumner Welles, who chaired the Committee on Cooperation with the American Republics. And the CCAR shared with the Cultural Division an emphasis on improving the image of the United States in Latin America. However, the former group cast its net much wider than the latter. A typical meeting brought together representatives from an astonishing range of fields, including the Departments of Agriculture, Treasury, Commerce, Interior, and State, as well as the Smithsonian Institution, the Federal Communications Commission, the Library of Congress, the U.S. Maritime Commission, and the Export-Import Bank.[36]

In general, the CCAR focused much more specifically upon the economics of inter-American cooperation. Certainly, the members of the Cultural Division understood that good cultural relations could lead to good trade relations, but the initial emphasis upon the higher intellectual purpose of the educational exchanges muted the commercial aspect of the program. The CCAR, on the other hand, discussed quite openly the potential economic benefits of providing assistance for technological development in Latin America. As one report on Haiti concluded, "because of the steamship, airplane, and other forms of communication, the United States supplied Haiti with most of its items of import, the principal one of which is cotton goods. As a result, Haiti is a fine customer of the United States, and anything contributing to the prosperity of that country helps in selling American products and particularly cotton goods."[37] In theory, technical assistance would fuel a boom in trade within the Western Hemisphere through a kind of multiplier effect. If successful, the resulting growth would produce an economy at once more capable of purchasing U.S. goods and also more inclined to do so—perhaps because of gratitude, or perhaps because its industries had been calibrated to U.S. technical specifications.

In practice, however, CCAR administrators ran into a series of difficulties. For one thing, the demand for U.S. experts far exceeded the number the U.S. government could supply. The logistics of negotiating leave time for each government official became quite complicated. An obvious solution would have been to hire additional personnel. However, there was no doubt that if they did so "Congress would certainly object."[38] On a broader strategic level, decisions about when to intervene often forced officials to choose between conflicting priorities. One proposal called for the Department of Agriculture to assist several countries in growing rubber plants with the goal of developing "a self-sustaining rubber industry" to supply the growing U.S. demand. The ensuing debate pitted the Department of Agriculture against an official from the Tariff Commission, who worried that this plan might "prove to be a boomerang to the Good Neighbor Policy." What would happen after the war, the tariff official wanted to know, when rubber producers from Latin America would have to compete with the low-cost rubber traditionally supplied by the Dutch East Indies, not to mention the synthetic rubber production the War Department had started to develop for the war effort? The Department of Agriculture maintained that a Latin American rubber industry would "be able to compete...if developed on the most modern lines." Discussions like these made clear that supplying technical aid was not as simple as it might have seemed.[39]

Another challenge emerged as U.S. officials recognized that the perception of their policies would play an important role in the success of those policies. There was, after all, the ever-present danger that U.S. "assistance" would be regarded as an unwelcome imposition. Welles worried about this enough that he gave an extended speech at one meeting on the need to avoid "indulging in propagandizing." Technical assistance should be nothing more, he said, than a "helping hand to our neighbors to the south of us, in order that they may be in a better position...to make a fairer evaluation of us and have a better understanding of our ways, means, and methods of life." He even went so far as to argue that this assistance would lead to an exchange, of sorts: "In turn our contacts with them cannot but serve to enrich our own knowledge of their problems and principles of life and pursuit of happiness."[40]

Despite rather grandiose long-term ambitions, the CCAR and the Cultural Division worked off a shoestring budget throughout 1939 and 1940; their first run through the appropriations process netted them $370,500 and $75,000, respectively.[41] These amounts would suffice if they were to do nothing more than facilitate the efforts of others, but it clearly would not cover much, if anything, beyond staff salaries and a few stipends. The CCAR and the Cultural Division remained separate before World War II, despite the fact that their missions overlapped. They emerged at the same time, they were staffed by many of the same people, and the work of the CCAR clearly represented another aspect of what Laurence Duggan described as the transformation of foreign policy "under modern conditions." In 1942, Welles decided to bring the CCAR under the control of the Cultural Division. But it took a war and a challenge from another agency to make it clear to the State Department that "cultural relations" could not stop with educational exchanges.[42]

Rockefeller's Role

The German invasion of Poland on September 1, 1939, gave a startling clarity to the abstract debate over the role of "cultural relations" in U.S. foreign policy. The war soon moved at a frighteningly quick pace. In April 1940, the German armies took all of a day to seize Denmark and set their sights on Norway. By May, they had added Belgium and the Netherlands. Then, France, whose stalwart opposition to Germany during World War I had produced a devastating level of carnage on the Western Front, collapsed within a matter of weeks. By July, Axis powers controlled practically the entire European continent. With the potential elimination of the European market, U.S. officials nervously envisioned a growing surplus and an alarming lack of trading partners.

Under these circumstances, U.S. relations within the Western Hemisphere became even more important than they had been just a few years before. As U.S. officials made clear at the Buenos Aires conference, they regarded German cultural influence in Latin America as a critical barometer of German "penetration" of the Western Hemisphere. They saw shrinking dollar signs with every new German cultural center, athletic club, movie release, and radio station that opened in Latin America. Roosevelt, increasingly alarmed, started to look for solutions.[43] Maybe if he had combined the Cultural Division with the CCAR, he could have gotten close to what he wanted. But that possibility had not yet occurred to anyone in a position to make it happen. Besides, FDR loved bureaucracies—the more the better.[44] So when Harry Hopkins, the president's right-hand man, slipped him a memo with the vague title "Hemisphere Economic Policy," Roosevelt thought he had the solution to his problems.

The author of the memo was Nelson A. Rockefeller, the thirty-two-year-old grandson of John D. Rockefeller, the billionaire scion of Standard Oil. A brilliant young philanthropist and international financier, Rockefeller had already built an impressive resume. After graduating from Dartmouth, he worked in the Foreign Department at Chase National Bank, served as the president of the Museum of Modern Art, and played a critical role in the construction of Rockefeller Center in New York City. FDR was far more interested in Rockefeller's expertise in Latin American affairs. During the 1930s, Rockefeller took two extended trips south of the border—one to survey modern art on behalf of the Modern, the other to tend to the affairs of Creole Oil, the Venezuelan subsidiary of the family empire. He also worked closely with the International Division of the Rockefeller Foundation, which, among its many projects, dealt with health work in Latin America.[45]

Rockefeller's experiences led him to many of the same conclusions as Roosevelt about Latin America. As Rockefeller wrote in his influential memo, "[r]egardless of whether the outcome of the war is a German or Allied victory, the United States must protect its international position...it must take economic measures at once to secure economic prosperity in Central and South America." The government must step in, he said, "where private agencies are unable or unwilling to act." It would have to respond decisively to the problems posed by surplus commodities, restrictive tariffs, a shortage of direct investment, and the refinancing of foreign debt. Interestingly, he also called for programs in culture and education to be "pursued concurrently with the economic program."[46] Roosevelt liked Rockefeller's suggestions so much that on August 16, 1940 he created an office to coordinate "Latin American commercial and cultural Relations" and asked Rockefeller to run it.[47]

Rockefeller's outfit, the Office of the Coordinator of Inter-American Affairs (OCIAA), went to work in the fall of 1940 with little more than a vague mandate and the energetic and charismatic leadership of its director.[48] Roosevelt showed his commitment to the new agency by appropriating $3.5 million out of the President's Emergency Fund, which meant that Rockefeller reported directly to him rather than to Congress. As the State Department's Charles Thomson recalled, "it was familiar gossip in Washington that the White House favored creation of the [OCIAA] as likely to exhibit greater imagination and drive than the Department of State."[49]

Rockefeller rewarded the president's faith by devising an innovative approach to inter-American relations. His techniques, in most cases, were not unprecedented, but he had the imagination and willingness to pull them together in interesting ways. Rockefeller's most important contribution, from a conceptual standpoint, was his insistence that economics, information, and culture would be "continually interrelated and tied together" at the OCIAA.[50] The "information" programs, for example, made use of radio, motion pictures, and publishing, all of which could be considered part of a "cultural" outreach. The Coordinator's Office also dealt with certain kinds of economic development, including the kinds of technical assistance the State Department had begun under the CCAR. In this aspect alone, the OCIAA pushed well beyond the boundaries of anything the State Department had been willing to try up to that point.[51]

Rockefeller well understood the novelty and the potential significance of the OCIAA agenda. Like Laurence Duggan, he believed that a "new world situation" demanded "a new conception of diplomacy," and the OCIAA had a responsibility to produce one. For Rockefeller, this meant expanding the very definition of foreign policy, so that "diplomacy is not so exclusively preoccupied with the legal and commercial problems of its traditionary field of action but is fully alive to...the cultural problems of peoples living in dangerous and difficult times under democratic institutions."[52]

This line of thinking led Rockefeller, like his counterparts in the State Department, into complex debates over definitions of "culture." "What we call 'culture,'" he suggested, "is merely the convenient term for summing up succinctly the way people live and feel and think; and cultural influences are, of course, those that affect life and thought among large numbers of people." He regarded the instruments of mass communications as "outstandingly important instruments of popular culture"; "their usefulness for generating sympathy between peoples, causing them to understand each other... [is] a fact of deep significance in current international relations."[53]

These sorts of broad formulations led the OCIAA to focus on the role of image in foreign relations. Although Rockefeller often denied that he was running a propaganda agency, his willingness to use any available medium to "generate sympathy" and to convey "the way people live and feel and think" certainly sounded like propaganda. The theme of ideas united all the projects he pursued at the OCIAA. "Activity in the field of communications," he told FDR, "is preeminently activity in fields of ideas." He viewed the relationship between intellectual and material change as dialectical. He saw "ideas as springs of action," but also thought of "action as a precipitant of a deposit of favorable ideas." In the context of U.S.–Latin American relations during the early 1940s, this meant that cultural, political, and economic initiatives constantly reinforced each other.[54]

In its cultural programs, OCIAA officials borrowed a page or two from the State Department book, touting the importance of education for ensuring "tolerance and understanding among the peoples of all the republics." In some cases, they simply duplicated the efforts of the State Department, such as asking Stephen Duggan and the IIE to supervise the OCIAA educational exchanges. In other cases, they went much further. One striking example was the plan to feed information on Latin American affairs to elementary and secondary schools within the United States. Both Rockefeller and the OCIAA invested a lot in the idea of education. Not only was education supposed to serve as the "[foundation] of neighborly good citizenship," but it also held the key, according to Rockefeller, to ensuring that, "this time," the citizens of the "New World" would not "shrink from their responsibility" as they had after World War I.[55]

Many of the "economic" programs at the OCIAA also resembled State Department initiatives—those of the CCAR rather than the Cultural Division. OCIAA officials provided technical assistance to nations throughout the Western Hemisphere, including how to market products for sale in the United States and how to "produce goods that are non-competitive with goods produced in this country."[56] Other schemes included hiring advertisers to conduct "surveys of the purchasing habits" of people throughout Latin America to maximize the efficiency of trade flows.[57] At one point, Rockefeller estimated that North American concerns of one kind or another purchased 44 percent of advertising linage in Latin American newspapers.[58]

The OCIAA's greatest contribution to the diplomacy of ideas came through its work in the "information" field. Here is the clearest example of how Rockefeller's operation became the model and the impetus for the integrated approach the State Department would pursue in the postwar period. Through extensive use of radio, motion pictures, and print media, the OCIAA spread its message to anyone who cared to see or hear it. In the Radio Division, Rockefeller hired Don Francisco, the former president of the National Broadcasting Corporation. Francisco used his extensive connections to organize a meeting of top industry executives to brainstorm how to improve their audience in Latin America. Eventually, the OCIAA hired J. Walter Thompson, the top Madison Avenue advertising agency, to conduct listener surveys. When overseas broadcasting still proved unprofitable, Rockefeller offered NBC and CBS $250,000 each to subsidize their short-wave programming. Since the more listeners there were, the more successful the broadcasts, Rockefeller pressured the radio industry to produce 750,000 sets that he could sell at cost throughout Latin America.[59]

The OCIAA also worked closely with Hollywood. To run the Motion Picture Division, Rockefeller hired the venture capitalist and motion picture pioneer John Hay Whitney—the man responsible for raising the funds to produce *Rebecca* and *Gone with the Wind*.[60] At the OCIAA, Whitney encouraged studios to film south of the border. He also pushed for greater coverage of Latin America in U.S. newsreels, and then distributed projection equipment to U.S. missions to make sure they could screen these newsreels and films.[61] In another creative use of resources, Whitney convinced Will Hays to install an OCIAA official in Hays's Production Code Office to "read every script dealing with Latin America" and to warn producers of potentially offensive storylines. One apparent success was convincing Louis B. Mayer to remove Clark Gable from the starring role in *Bolivar* after complaints about his lack of authenticity as a Hispanic revolutionary.[62]

The OCIAA's interventions in the realm of print media were as varied as the medium itself. One proposal called on the U.S. Postal Service to lower the book rate to Latin America, which—at approximately eight times the domestic book rate—severely restricted the amount of business U.S. publishers were willing to do in Latin America. OCIAA officials also worked with the Associated Press, United Press International, and the International News Service, as well as an individual who represented approximately one hundred Latin American newspapers. They used these liaisons for everything from publicizing their own activities to lobbying against the reporting of information they considered inaccurate. The OCIAA also took steps to increase purchases of advertising copy in Latin American newspapers, especially those in dire financial straits.[63]

Although Rockefeller set the tone for the innovative approach to cultural policy at the OCIAA, credit also belongs to the extraordinary group he brought in to work on these issues. Frank Jamieson, the Associated Press reporter who won a Pulitzer Prize in 1933 for breaking the story about the death of the Lindbergh baby, was charged with running the Public Relations Division. The Pulitzer Prize–winning historian Carl Van Doren and the publishers Alfred Harcourt and Richard Simon sat on the Publications Committee. For the Music Committee, Rockefeller hired acclaimed composer Aaron Copland and promptly sent him on a Latin American tour on behalf of the OCIAA.[64]

While these luminaries gave the OCIAA cultural programs their credibility, their philosophical consistency came from a less-heralded, but far more influential, group of policy intellectuals. The members of this latter group took the lessons they learned at the OCIAA and, over the next several years, fundamentally shaped the debates over the role of image in foreign policy. George Gallup and Hadley Cantril, the two most influential public opinion theorists of their day, were hired to conduct surveys—a role they would later reprise with both the

Office of War Information and the State Department. The Librarian of Congress and Pulitzer Prize–winning poet Archibald MacLeish ran the OCIAA's Literary Committee before becoming the principal architect of U.S. public diplomacy. The brilliant Madison Avenue advertising executive William Benton served on Rockefeller's Cultural Advisory Committee, an early introduction to the kind of work he would later do for the State Department. Perhaps the most notable member of this group was Benton's colleague on the Cultural Advisory Committee, Time-Life Publisher Henry Luce.[65]

Luce used the early meetings of the Cultural Advisory Committee in the fall of 1940 to work through the arguments he would lay out a few months later in his "American Century" article. Echoes of that piece appear numerous times in the minutes of meetings at the OCIAA, such as the moment when Luce bluntly stated that it was time for "us to spread our way of life." Until World War I, he said, "the development of the world was not our job," but now with the world "closing in on us," things had changed. For Luce, this was about more than defeating Germany: He regarded "a positive philosophy of our own... more vital than the negative anti-Nazi one which this country has at present." Over the next decade, U.S. propagandists would repeatedly make the same point. The United States was not just "against" the Germans and then the Soviets; the nation had its own philosophy well worth spreading whether the United States faced an external enemy or not.[66]

Nelson Rockefeller welcomed the effort to take these conversations onto more grandiose terrain. He responded to Luce's proposition with the equally provocative suggestion that such a "philosophy would meet a natural psychological urge of this country." William Benton, too, endorsed this idea and argued that the OCIAA should accelerate the spread of U.S. cultural artifacts. In fact, he believed that the "culture" of the United States provided a better reflection of the nation's values than did its "business." This was a remarkable, if telling, statement coming from the master pitchman. The final word, though, came from Luce, who wondered if "it might be more important to flood South America with five-cent copies of Emerson than with issues of the [heavily propagandistic] *March of Time.*" How best to export "America"?

Now that was an interesting question—a question that would continue to occupy each of these men in the coming years.[67]

Who Speaks for US?

The OCIAA's importance lay in the way that it served as a model for what the State Department decided to do in the postwar period: integrate economics, culture, and information into a comprehensive, worldwide strategy for public diplomacy. So too did it bring together many individuals who would shape subsequent debates about the importance of image. Rockefeller made a significant contribution to conceptualizations of image and the subsequent evolution of public diplomacy through his aggressive use of "information" policy. Simply put, "information" was a euphemism for propaganda. The OCIAA walked a fine line between promoting dialogue and simply promoting the United States. The office received heavy criticism, for example, for the $600,000 it poured into advertising in Latin American newspapers in 1942—not so much for the plan itself, which provided the newspapers with financial relief, but for the gauche advertisements touting the beauty and grandeur of the United States.[68]

In a telling article that appeared shortly before Pearl Harbor, James Reston, the foreign affairs columnist for the *New York Times*, tried to explain how the work done by the OCIAA differed from William Donovan's Foreign Information Service, the newly created overseas propaganda bureau. According to Reston, Donovan engaged in "psychological war," whereas "Rockefeller has no such program for Latin America." However, when he tried to explain what the OCIAA did do, his attempt to draw distinctions between the two agencies seems murky, at best. According to Reston, the OCIAA pursued four principal objectives:

1. To convince the people of Latin America that the "good neighbor" policy is not a temporary expedient designed to gain their cooperation for the duration of the war, but a sincere and permanent reversal of our nineteenth century policies of "dollar diplomacy" and "manifest destiny."

2. To convince them that we have no desire nor intention to inter-
   fere with their independent sovereignty.
3. To convince them that we cas [*sic*] and will defend them from the
   economic imperialism of the Germans, and that we can and will,
   if necessary, implement the Monroe Doctrine by force of arms.
4. To convince them that we are engaged in a sincere attempt to
   bring about a lasting friendship between the peoples of this hemisphere through the conduct of a long-range commercial and cultural program which will be beneficial to every country.[69]

Each of these categories, as defined by Reston, called for the U.S.
government to "convince" Latin American peoples and governments
of one thing or another. The reciprocal part of the process had entirely
dropped out of his analysis. Furthermore, even if "they" could be convinced of these four things, it was not at all clear that "they" would be
reassured by them. The distinction between the "Monroe Doctrine,"
on the one hand, and "Manifest Destiny" and "Dollar Diplomacy,"
on the other, may have seemed clear to someone like Reston, but
probably not for people on the receiving end of these policies over a
long stretch of time. In fairness to Rockefeller and the OCIAA, this
was Reston's interpretation of their mission, not necessarily how they
would have described it. Nevertheless, Reston's assessment exposed
the inevitable ambiguity of the government's interest in cultural relations and the way that interest was understood by the media, the public, and people abroad. Moreover, if a prominent reporter like Reston
had gotten the message so wrong, then it obviously needed quite a bit
of clarification.

The blunt truth was that the U.S. officials who embraced the methods
of public diplomacy during the late 1930s did so because they began to
care about the image the nation projected to the world. And if image
mattered, then reason—to say nothing of national security—demanded
that policymakers use every mechanism at their disposal to try to shape it.
Whether they were ready to admit it or not, they would have to do more
than place their faith solely in the long-term benefits of increased "mutual
understanding" through cultural exchanges. This undertaking meant a
full-fledged commitment to the diplomacy of ideas in a package that
combined the use of mass communications, popular culture, educational

exchanges, and technical assistance. This was the logical outcome of the position articulated by Hull, Welles, Duggan, and FDR himself—first at Buenos Aires and then through the creation of the Division of Cultural Relations at the State Department. However, when State Department officials moved slowly in implementing a policy that reflected the full implications of their assumptions, Rockefeller preempted them.

Perhaps recognizing the importance of what the OCIAA was doing, perhaps motivated by simple jealousy, State Department officials eventually moved to steal back some of Rockefeller's thunder. They focused particularly on the need for, and initial lack of, coordination between the two groups. After all, who really "spoke" for the United States abroad? As Laurence Duggan complained, the OCIAA engaged in a "wide range of activity that will cut across the jurisdiction of a number of Divisions within the Department." Stanford historian Harley Notter, an advisor to the Cultural Division, argued that mixing informational with cultural operations threatened to discredit the entire enterprise of cultural diplomacy. Notter even linked the OCIAA to the World War I–era Creel Committee, an apt, but loaded, comparison to the agency whose heavy-handed techniques sullied the reputation of government information programs for at least a generation.[70]

In April 1941, with resentment building at the State Department, Sumner Welles used his personal connection to Roosevelt to ask the White House to clarify the relationship between State and the OCIAA. Together, FDR and Welles drafted a letter to be sent out to Rockefeller over the president's signature. Referring to the "delicate inter-weaving of the various phases" of foreign relations, FDR suggested to Rockefeller that "it is now more than ever essential that the Secretary of State be apprised of all Governmental undertakings, whether carried on directly by Governmental agencies or indirectly through private agencies, related to foreign countries. The Department of State is charged with responsibility under the President for the conduct of the foreign relations of the country." He further ordered the OCIAA to make sure that all projects were discussed "fully with, and approved by, the Department of State."[71]

Later that year, the State Department responded to Rockefeller's challenge, taking the first steps to broaden its approach to "cultural relations." After the United States entered the war, the Cultural

Division annexed the CCAR and its technical assistance programs and eventually won control of the OCIAA's cultural activities as well. In 1944, the State Department snagged Rockefeller himself, when FDR appointed him Assistant Secretary of State for Latin American Affairs.

By the time Rockefeller moved into the State Department, the U.S. government had already adopted the strategic logic of the Good Neighbor Policy, accepting that the nation's image abroad would be one of the keys to achieving its geopolitical objectives. However, recognizing the importance of image was not the same as developing a new conception of foreign relations that accommodated the full range of cultural and ideological forces shaping the relations between nation states. That came only through the transformative experience of World War II, which forced policymakers to rethink the entire foreign policy-making apparatus as the nation prepared to emerge as perhaps the most dominant power in the history of the world.

2

"The Drift of History"

War, Culture, and Hegemony

IF 1941 DID NOT change everything about the U.S. posture toward the outside world, the events of that year certainly came very close. First remembered, of course, is the "infamous" date of December 7, 1941, when the Japanese attack on Pearl Harbor propelled the United States into World War II. That date mattered not only for what it started but for what it ended: the Great Debate that Americans had waged over the future of U.S. foreign policy ever since Germany had invaded Poland over two years earlier. This debate turned out to be one of the most consequential in U.S. history—the last time that the national dialogue on a foreign policy issue began with the question of whether, rather than how, the United States should exert a global presence.

Behind closed doors at the State Department, the Great Debate provided the essential backdrop for the complete reconceptualization of cultural diplomacy that took place during 1941. U.S. policymakers operated from the assumption that World War II had upended the existing global order and transformed the role of the United States in the world—even before the United States entered the war. For cultural diplomats, this meant broadening their vision and their job descriptions to develop new strategies to deal with changed realities and eventualities. In response, they took the first concrete steps to expand the cultural programs from a series of limited, bilateral educational exchanges with various Latin American countries to a comprehensive global initiative explicitly designed to advance the overall objectives of U.S. foreign policy.

Going back to 1938, U.S. officials had made no secret of the fact that they viewed Latin America as but a starting point for cultural diplomacy. In September 1939, six days after Germany invaded Poland, representatives of the Cultural Division began a blunt and revealing discussion about how to capitalize on the European crisis in order to expand America's cultural influence. According to one analysis, "the retirement of the principal European states from many phases of cultural relations in this hemisphere gives the United States an extraordinary opportunity." If handled properly, "this country has an opportunity culturally which can only be compared with the remarkable economic opportunity of 1914–1918." In other words, if the destruction of Europe during World War I had allowed the United States to emerge as the world's dominant economic power during the 1920s, then World War II offered the chance for it to become a political and cultural hegemon as well.[1]

By the time the United States entered the war, the Cultural Division had adopted a more expansive view of cultural relations that incorporated economics and politics, high and low culture, all within the scope of an increasingly global vision. New faces also brought new perspectives, as the Division added members and established an advisory board that drew participants from a diverse array of backgrounds. The original idea of bilateral educational exchanges became one small part of a much larger package explicitly wrapped up in discussions of an emerging American empire. Increasingly, the field of "cultural relations" involved not just the export or exchange of a specific intellectual product but also efforts to shape the nation's image in the global arena—the sort of work that moved cultural diplomacy ever closer to the propaganda end of the dissemination-exchange spectrum.

For the cultural programs, the focus on image grew organically from their roots in promoting the objectives of the Good Neighbor Policy. At the same time, the global crisis of World War II added new dimensions to the project of capitalizing culture for foreign policy purposes. With the massive propaganda machines of Germany and Japan providing a daily demonstration of the power of the mass media, finding ways to communicate directly with the "masses" took on new significance. Moreover, the prospect of a power vacuum in so many areas left the identities of millions of people potentially in flux, raising the question of which ideas and ideologies would rise to prominence. For cultural diplomats looking to sell their operation to skeptical bosses higher up in the State Department and across the federal government, the nature of the war provided a powerful case that cultural relations had moved to the heart of foreign relations. During the years of the Great Debate, cultural policymakers laid the groundwork for expanding the scope of cultural diplomacy to reflect the growing ambitions of the Roosevelt administration's foreign policy; all that remained was for the United States to actually enter the war.

The End of the Great Debate

Between 1939 and 1941, Americans divided sharply on the question of whether the nation could afford to treat the European crisis as just something "over there." Proponents and opponents of intervention each recruited prominent politicians, pundits, and policymakers to lobby for their position in Washington and to sway public opinion nationwide. Advocacy groups flooded the editorial pages of newspapers as fervently as they swarmed the hallways of Capitol Hill. Anti-interventionists unified under the slogan "America First" and drafted famed aviator Charles Lindbergh to serve as their public face; interventionists countered with a committee headed by William Allen White, the "sage" of Emporia, Kansas, whose widely syndicated newspaper columns had established him as the voice of smalltown Middle America. Complicating matters further, White's outfit was known to be coordinating its message with White House officials who wanted to publicize the administration's policy of providing Great Britain with "all aid short of war."

In the early months of the war, despite widespread revulsion against the Nazi onslaught, the foreign policy attitudes of the 1930s still predominated among many segments of the U.S. population.[2] Only in retrospect did it become clear that, throughout 1941, public attitudes toward U.S. foreign policy had begun to change. In March, Franklin

Roosevelt convinced Congress to pass the Lend-Lease Act by a wide margin. Lend-Lease provided military assistance to Great Britain, which was at that point struggling mightily to withstand the nightmarish blitz of the German *Luftwaffe*. Although sold as a means of keeping U.S. forces out of the war, the aid package nevertheless signaled a growing belief that the United States could not remain neutral about Britain's fate.

In July, the interventionist film *Sergeant York* opened in theaters across the country to tremendous critical and commercial success. The movie told the story of Tennessee farmer Alvin York, the real-life World War I hero who famously set aside his religious pacifism to fight on the Western Front, where he managed in a single battle to kill twenty-five Germans and take another 132 prisoner. In one sense, the film represented just the latest in the string of pro-war films to come out of Hollywood. The studios, which depended on the European market for their profit margin, rarely even bothered with the pretense of neutrality in the Great Debate. At the same time, *Sergeant York* differed from other classics of that genre, such as *Confessions of a Nazi Spy* and *The Great Dictator*, which focused on the evils of Hitler and Nazism. *Sergeant York* spoke clearly to those who might be reconsidering their previous opposition to war; it provided a masterful object lesson in reluctant belligerence.[3]

In September, the members of the America First Committee became so alarmed by the growing popularity of films like *Sergeant York* and the general decline in support for their position that they convinced their allies in Congress to launch an investigation of Hollywood's role in the production of pro-war propaganda. America First and its Congressional allies demonstrated beyond any doubt that Hollywood had taken a side in the Great Debate, but in general the anti-interventionists embarrassed themselves with their buffoonish behavior and the hearings fizzled out three months before the United States entered the war. Their inability to generate widespread outrage suggested that the 1930s narrative of devious "merchants of death" conspiring to trick the United States into war no longer raised the same level of public alarm.[4]

A number of public opinion polls offered additional evidence for this proposition.[5] During 1941, internal government surveys noted a sharp increase in the percentage of Americans who believed that, regardless of whether the United States ultimately went to war, the nation should play a substantial role in the construction of the postwar order. Most striking was the reversal of previous patterns of opposition to U.S. participation in an international organization along the lines of the League of Nations. Just four years before, two-thirds of Americans opposed such an idea; in 1941, polls showed a 50–50 split; one year later, a solid majority came out in favor; by the end of the war that figure reached 80 percent.[6] Nothing symbolized a commitment to Wilsonian liberal internationalism more than support for an international organization, because nothing had symbolized the defeat of Wilson's ideas after World War I so much as America's refusal to participate in his beloved League of Nations. 1941 marked the turning point in the nation's openness to what the historian Robert Divine has called a "second chance" for Wilsonianism. It also signaled a willingness to take up Henry Luce's challenge to the American people to accommodate themselves "spiritually and practically" to the pursuit of an "American Century."[7]

In the February 17, 1941 issue of his magazine, *Life*, Luce called upon the American people to embrace their nation's destiny and step forward to succeed the declining British Empire as the world's hegemonic power. Most notable was his prediction that U.S. dominance would not occur through the sort of territorial expansion that had provided the foundation for the age of European high imperialism; rather, it would come through the extension of ideological influence. After all, Luce surmised, the groundwork for that process had already been laid through the worldwide dissemination of American cultural forms. The piece was prescient, but pure propaganda. In the short run, he hoped to defeat the forces opposed to U.S. involvement in World War II; in the long run, he sought to push the nation toward adopting a posture of global dominance.[8]

By the time Pearl Harbor was bombed ten months later, millions more Americans had bought into the logic of the American Century. Many of those people had probably never even heard of Henry Luce, whose article generated little contemporary coverage. By the end of the war, however, analyses of the American role in the postwar world often referred to the prospect of an "American Century," as though everyone knew what that meant. Used by public figures in the United States and abroad, the phrase had become ubiquitous.[9] What Luce accomplished, then, was akin to what John O'Sullivan did a century before when he coined the term "Manifest Destiny": He articulated in a clear and concise manner a number of ideas percolating within the culture at large. Only in retrospect is it clear just how well his article captured the truly profound shift in popular attitudes toward U.S. foreign policy that occurred over the course of that year—a trend that the war solidified. As John Adams famously said of the American Revolution, "the revolution was effected before the war commenced. The Revolution was in the minds and hearts of the people."[10]

"There Is No Sharp Line of Division"

As the country gradually moved toward acceptance of the eventuality of U.S. intervention in the war, State Department officials developed a concrete plan of action to realize the long-standing goal of broadening the cultural program. The wartime emergency, if not exactly the *raison d'être* for expansion, certainly assisted in the process by throwing matters of perception and image into sharp relief. A substantially larger Congressional appropriation contributed to this endeavor by providing the funds necessary for the Cultural Division to move beyond the activities specified in the Buenos Aires Convention. Before long, the exchange of students and teachers turned into just a small portion of a comprehensive agenda that treated culture as the key to unlocking the sort of economic prosperity that could expand America's influence and prestige on the global stage.[11]

The specific mandate for expanding conceptions of cultural diplomacy came from a series of high-level meetings of the General Advisory Committee for the State Department's Division of Cultural Relations. The Advisory Committee served as the primary forum for policymakers to define the agenda for the long-term development of the cultural programs. As a result of these recommendations, the Cultural Division expanded its purview beyond the Western Hemisphere, as well as its very definition of culture. At their most expansive and illuminating, the meetings of the Advisory Committee exhibited an extraordinarily frank engagement with the relationship between culture and empire and the ways that cultural relations would shape perceptions of the United States in the postwar world. These gatherings attracted a remarkable collection of intellectuals and policymakers from inside and outside the government. But no one did more to shape the tone and the approach outlined in these meetings than Henry Wallace, the Vice President of the United States.[12]

During his long and distinguished political career, which included stints as Secretary of Agriculture and Secretary of Commerce, Wallace was accused of being many things: a mystic, a zealot, a tireless advocate of "globaloney," and—especially during his 1948 run for President on the Progressive Party ticket—a communist. The "New Dealingist of New Dealers," as one newspaper profile put it, Wallace is probably best described, like his intellectual compatriots in the Roosevelt Brain Trust, as a redistributive capitalist. For all of them, the crisis of world capitalism in the 1920s and 1930s fundamentally shaped their view of economics, politics, and society. It led Wallace, in particular, to fixate upon finding policy solutions to address economic inequality, which he saw as the principal cause of political instability at home and abroad.[13]

Wallace made his first appearance before the Advisory Committee on Cultural Relations on February 2, 1941, two weeks before Luce's call for an "American Century." Although Wallace certainly would have protested the comparison, the Vice President and the publisher shared a commitment to expanding the American presence in the world through a consensual form of U.S. ideological hegemony.[14] Wallace hated Luce's brand of arrogant nationalism; he also accused him of shamelessly advancing the interests of big business. But Wallace's own economic ideas were hardly anticapitalist. As his contributions to discussions of cultural diplomacy made clear, his goal was to grow the economic pie in such a way that more people in more places could get a slice. For that, he saw culture as key.

Although Wallace played no role in the day-to-day operations of the Cultural Division, his participation in the Advisory Committee meetings has been widely credited with redefining the State Department's approach to cultural diplomacy.[15] He introduced himself to the Advisory Committee by reporting that he had just returned from a trip to Mexico. Advancing a line of analysis he would continue to refine over the next couple of years, the Vice President encouraged the State Department to think of culture much more broadly than it had up to that point, targeting not only the "high classes" but also "representatives of the people." While the United States should certainly continue to pursue "cultural rapprochement," he said, the "emphasis should be placed upon improving the economic condition of the [other] country, principally through assistance in increasing its agricultural efficiency."[16]

As Wallace would later put it, "there is no sharp line of division between...the economic action programs and the Cultural Relations Program.... One must supplement the other." He was essentially calling for the State Department to combine its cultural relations program with the initiatives in technical assistance it had already developed through the Interdepartmental Committee on Cooperation with the American Republics. His suggestion, if adopted, would refashion the State Department cultural programs along the model established by Nelson Rockefeller at the OCIAA. Technical assistance and cultural relations should be thought of as two sides of the same coin in Wallace's view.[17]

In fact, the State Department had already started to move in this direction. The previous year, the Cultural Advisory Committee voted to expand its membership beyond the fairly small group of educators and diplomats who dominated the early meetings. By late 1940, influential policy intellectuals, such as Archibald MacLeish and Waldo Leland of the American Council of Learned Societies, began to make frequent appearances. Along with Wallace, these individuals launched a remarkable series of discussions, beginning that fall and continuing for several years, on the topic of "planning for the cultural relations program on a long-term basis."[18]

Charles Thomson, who had replaced Ben Cherrington as the head of the Cultural Division the previous year, opened the September 1941 session with a request to consider "the kind of world which will come out of the present conflict." Wallace began by expanding on the ideas he had outlined in February. He again criticized the existing cultural programs for being "largely directed towards the elite of the Americas." Long term, he argued, "it is also necessary that we establish helpful relations with the remaining 90 percent of the people, who are for the most part engaged in agriculture. Unless we help them to improve their economic lot, thus making it possible for health and education to develop, there will be no dependable basis for democracy.... In a truly democratic system, cultural and economic cooperation are largely interdependent. The one cannot thrive long without the other."[19] Along these lines, he advocated the extension of such initiatives as the Pan-American Highway and the Inter-American Tropical Institute. He also called for the United States to provide technical assistance on ways to maximize agricultural production through exploiting comparative advantages and developing more effective "practices of investment." Although both the State Department and the OCIAA had already experimented with all of these techniques, Wallace insisted that these activities be included within the scope of cultural relations.[20]

The committee responded very favorably to these suggestions. Records from the meeting note agreement that "the future cultural relations program should be economic and social as well as intellectual and artistic." The committee also agreed upon broadening the program to "include (as cultural fields)...the contributions which educational interchange, publications, and other media can make to public health, engineering, agricultural and industrial development." Some traditionalists, such as Waldo Leland, worried that Wallace's suggestions were "so far-reaching that they would radically change the program of cultural relations as heretofore understood." Leland also worried that the programs, as an "instrument in the hands of the Government...for the achievement of social and economic (and by extension political) objectives in other countries," would be denounced as propaganda. Indeed they might. This had been a concern ever since the State Department first decided to establish a government-sponsored educational exchange program. After all, governments rarely pursue policies for apolitical purposes.[21]

The question of how, or whether, to separate cultural diplomacy from propaganda would remain a contentious one over the next several years. Some committee members would continue to insist on the need to maintain a firewall between the two operations. But the discussion at the September 1941 meeting signaled growing acceptance of the idea that both cultural diplomacy and propaganda had an important role to play in government attempts to shape perceptions of the United States. As one participant put it:

> Cultural relations have become a concern of national policies. All major governments now engage in one or more phases of cultural relations as generally conceived. Propaganda, for example, is a preoccupation of nearly all major and many minor powers. Because the potential advantages in the realm of cultural relations are seen by governments to be powerful supports to national aims, they represent a force which government cannot leave alone to private foundations and organizations. Cultural relations have become an obligation upon government.[22]

Even purists like Ben Cherrington, who remained involved as a member of the Advisory Committee, had to acknowledge that "cultural and intellectual relations" would be a "permanent and increasingly important aspect of modern government." While Cherrington stopped short of calling for a full-scale propaganda program, his concession that governments could no longer ignore the realm of ideas led logically to such a conclusion.[23]

Of those in attendance, no one articulated the role of cultural relations within the grand sweep of U.S. foreign policy more effectively than Stanford University historian Harley Notter. During World War II, Notter worked in several capacities at the State Department, serving on the Advisory Committee for Cultural Relations and also on the Committee on Postwar Foreign Policy Planning. The author of a weighty volume on Woodrow Wilson, Notter brought to the table a sense of the evolution of America's role in the world and its position within the rise and fall of empires throughout history.

Like Luce, Notter focused on the need to seize the mantle of global hegemony from the fading British Empire. In his words, "[a]s England a century ago began to export its manufacturing secrets of industrial processes, tools, and methods to the incidental benefit of other nations we now must export the cultural equivalents deliberately for advancement of peoples." Over time "cultural influence has corresponded with the rise and tide of national power." By the end of the war, the United States would be the only country left to serve as "a world cultural magnet." Cultural policymakers had a duty to "contemplate the whole great expanse of the earth which has bearing upon world stability, in the interest of our own national hopes and in behalf of western culture." If the nation were to shirk this responsibility, "this war agony will be only a prelude to greater troubles...our own national interest in world stability leads in the same direction of duty." According to Notter, "the drift of history" decreed that the United States would emerge from the war as the next dominant empire. Although the United States had not even entered the war, he saw nothing that could "deflect those forces."[24]

Culture and the Open Door

In the end, Pearl Harbor did little to change the consensus philosophy of cultural relations that emerged in the final months of the Great Debate. If anything, it gave greater urgency to the pursuit of already accepted premises. At the Advisory Committee's first meeting after the United States entered the war, Charles Thomson erased any doubts about a change in direction when he stated that "to assure the people of the American republics and of the United Nations of the sincerity of our friendship, it is fundamentally important to continue the program and to intensify certain phases of it during the war."[25] This seemingly innocuous statement raised two critically important questions: First, which aspects of the program would be intensified? Second, why had Thomson expanded the purview of the Cultural Division to include not just Latin America, but the entire "United Nations," which, at this point, referred to all the nations allied against the Axis powers?

The first question had an easy answer: Over the last several months, the State Department had moved aggressively to implement the broader program of cultural relations outlined by Henry Wallace and endorsed by Harley Notter, Archibald MacLeish, and others. This meant a greater emphasis on technical assistance, specifically, while also working towards the more general goal of improving the image of the United States in the world. The widespread acceptance of these new policy objectives was confirmed by the Secretary of State's decision in April 1942 to award the Cultural Division control of the Interdepartmental Committee on Cooperation with the American Republics. The very existence of the

Interdepartmental Committee stemmed from the initial urge in 1938 to separate the technical assistance programs from "cultural relations," but that distinction no longer seemed to make sense.[26]

The same conclusion may be drawn from the expansion of the Cultural Advisory Committee and its agenda. These gatherings now routinely attracted high-powered intellectuals throughout the Executive Branch and across the private sector. By February 1942, the group had swelled to fifty-two members from the nine attendees at the first meeting less than two years earlier. The Cultural Division supplied eighteen of those members while the OCIAA sent thirteen representatives. Despite their diverse backgrounds, they all managed to zero in on how they and their expertise could contribute to the new goal of reaching out to Wallace's fabled "ninety percent." Some talked about the role of public opinion in hemispheric defense; others addressed the need to design an art program that made use not just of the "fine arts," but of "industrial arts, folk art, [and] architecture."[27]

Although the Cultural Division would continue to focus primarily on Latin America, 1942 marked the long-anticipated expansion of the programs beyond the Western Hemisphere. Early that year, the State Department established a formal cultural exchange program with China. There was something apropos about taking a cultural strategy designed to facilitate non-territorial imperialism and applying it to the birthplace of the U.S. Open Door Policy. Dating back to John Hay's Open Door Notes of 1899–1900, China had served as the model for the general quest to secure unfettered access to overseas markets—an "open door" for trade—without incurring the costs of acquiring formal colonies. Only a tiny fraction of U.S. exports actually went to the Far East, but the prospect of reaching hundreds of millions of new consumers made Asia supremely attractive as a possible cure to the chronic ills of overproduction.[28]

By the interwar period, China had come to occupy a romantic place in the American imagination. This can be attributed, as much as anything, to the Christian missionaries of the late 19th and early 20th centuries, who brought back hackneyed but nevertheless uplifting stories of a hearty, industrious people. The two most influential voices in perpetuating this narrative were both children of Christian missionaries—Pearl Buck, author of the best-selling novel *The Good Earth*, and Henry Luce. Sympathetic accounts of an "ancient" and "noble" culture resonated more forcefully during the 1930s after the Japanese invasion of Manchuria in 1931. When Japan moved into mainland China in 1937, occupying most of the major port cities and engaging in numerous atrocities such as the horrific "rape" of Nanking, Franklin Roosevelt delivered an emotional, belligerent address that labeled Japanese aggression a "disease" in need of a "quarantine."

To make China the first location outside the Western Hemisphere where the U.S. government tested its new theories of cultural diplomacy thus made sense for historical and contemporary reasons. President Roosevelt formally launched the China program in January 1942, when he authorized $150,000 from his wartime emergency fund as seed money for the operations in China. Most of the arrangements had already been made before the war, so the exchange program started with a small, but distinguished staff, which included Wilma Fairbank—the wife of Harvard Professor John King Fairbank, the dean of American East Asianists—and Haldore Hanson, who began an extended association with the cultural programs that would continue throughout the decade.[29]

Unlike in Latin America, U.S. officials never had any ambivalence about linking technical assistance to cultural relations in China. At a meeting in November 1941, they agreed that providing technical training to Chinese doctors, engineers, and other professionals would, in fact, be their first priority, with the more traditional cultural component, including radio and motion pictures, to follow.[30] China held the distinction of having been the recipient of the very first educational exchanges ever sponsored by the U.S. government. During the early 1900s, the United States used the Boxer Indemnity fund (the money the Chinese government paid to the United States to reimburse losses suffered during the Boxer Rebellion) to sponsor a limited, ad hoc exchange program that lasted several years. The long-term ties between the United States and China also meant that U.S. officials had a ready supply of private foundations to draw on for assistance. Several groups volunteered immediately: The American Bureau of Medical Aid to China helped to organize conferences that brought together Chinese and American doctors; and the United China Relief, the largest American foundation devoted to Chinese affairs, raised over seven million dollars in 1942 alone for humanitarian relief.[31]

Despite these advantages, the China program got off to a rocky start. The Cultural Division applied many of the same principles used in Latin America, which transferred well in some cases but poorly in others. For one thing, the Japanese occupation of so many key areas created a level of infrastructural disarray in China. The capital of "Free China"—the nationalist government led by Chiang Kai-shek—had moved to Chungking, an isolated internal port city on a tributary of the Yangtze River. To stay out of the way of frequent Japanese bombings, the United States Embassy was located on the outskirts of the city, down a steep cliff and across the river from the seat of government. The chaotic situation also hampered the use of the principal methodologies of cultural diplomacy. The lack of reliable transportation made the logistics of an exchange program exceedingly difficult. Furthermore, radio transmitters were in short supply, limiting access to the most powerful tool of mass communications. When added to the Chinese government's interest in keeping its skilled professionals in the country, it meant that "America's cultural experiment" in China, as Wilma Fairbank called it, never progressed beyond the trial stage.[32]

In the postwar period, China received the first of the Fulbright exchange scholars and benefited from a number of scientific and technical assistance efforts that directly foreshadowed the modernization projects of the Cold War.[33] Yet the ultimate significance of the China program probably lies more in its symbolism than its accomplishments. During its short tenure from 1942 to 1949, the "cultural experiment" in China managed to encapsulate most of the major themes of 20th-century U.S. foreign policy: the fascination with China as the great untapped resource of the future; the desire to use culture and ideology as a means of expanding U.S. hegemony without incurring the costs of traditional territorial imperialism; and, ultimately, the attempt to counteract the appeal of revolutionary communism through winning hearts and minds.

All of those lofty goals came to a decisive end in 1949, when the Chinese Communist Party led by Mao Zedong defeated Chiang's Nationalist Party and exiled Chiang and his supporters to Taiwan. The United States immediately cut off all relations with mainland China, including the cultural programs.[34] Although the Chinese Revolution was the product of a long internal struggle, most Americans were not interested in taking the long view—or, really, any view—of Chinese history. Instead, the rather demonstrative conclusion to the fifty-year struggle to maintain an Open Door in China provoked solipsistic accusations about how the Truman Administration "lost" China to communism. At the same time, through the prism of cultural relations, it seemed the United States had clearly failed in its appeal to the Chinese masses.

"The Method of Dealing with Such Peoples"

Among the reasons why cultural policymakers placed so much emphasis on improving the image of the United States among ordinary people was their deep concern about the growing strength of independence movements in what became known, in the language of the Cold War, as the Third World. Policymakers recognized that the United States was poised to become the world's dominant empire amid the decline of the traditional imperial form, and they sensed the explosive possibilities of decolonization. However, the problem for them was both broader and more abstract. Their primary reference point was not the failing European empires in Africa, Asia, and the Middle East, but rather the U.S. experience in Latin America, most of which had not been under the yoke of European colonialism for more than a century. Charles Thomson picked up on this theme in an important memo he circulated in anticipation of the Advisory Committee's first meeting following Pearl Harbor. Forecasting a "social revolution" among people who no longer saw "insecurity and poverty... [as] inevitable or necessary in a day of practically unbounded scientific advancement," Thomson called for cultural diplomacy to address the "social-economic demands of people in all nations for protection against insecurity and poverty."[35]

The clearest expression of this attitude came from Henry Wallace, whose statement at the February 1942 meeting of the Cultural Advisory Committee surely ranks as one of the most revealing articulations of U.S. strategic objectives in the 20th century. The United States, Wallace suggested, had arrived at the height of its power at a "time in [the] world's history... when the so-called backward or inferior races, or underprivileged portions of such races, are coming into their own.... And therefore the method of dealing with such peoples successful in past centuries was no longer feasible or suitable." In Latin America, "the underprivileged constitute at least 90 percent of the people.... We must therefore direct our program toward the mental and moral encouragement of that 90 percent, for in the final analysis it is the people who will decide the success or failure of our efforts in these countries."[36]

Policymakers saw two paths—at least within the realm of cultural relations—for reaching out to that 90 percent: The first was the technical assistance programs designed to share the "ideas embodied in inventions and machines." Yet there was a danger in wedding these modernization programs, as they would come to be known, to the more traditional intellectual exchanges. With technical assistance, the flow of knowledge only traveled in one direction, which put U.S. officials in the position of "teaching" other countries how to run their economies. Policymakers repeatedly cautioned against adopting a "patronizing" or "chauvinistic" tone or an "attitude of some superiority." But they also assumed that "the masses" sought Western-style "economic development" and, in the words of one of Nelson Rockefeller's OCIAA emissaries, that "it is the fundamental function of the United States to accelerate the evolutionary process."[37]

The second method for reaching out to the "masses" involved a return to promoting mutual understanding through an exchange of ideas. Unlike the original plan back in the 1930s to exchange a handful of educators and students, the new proposal called for promoting connections between groups within the United States and abroad. The idea was to take advantage of American pluralism ("a fusion of peoples," Harley Notter called it), which many policymakers saw as one of the nation's greatest strengths. Within a few months, developing a comprehensive strategy for drawing on the experiences of "minority groups" within the United States had become a major priority for the Cultural Division.[38]

At the June 1942 meeting of the Cultural Advisory Committee, Hunter College President George Shuster led a lively discussion on the role of "minority groups" in shaping U.S. foreign policy. The journalist Louis Adamic immediately pointed out that even to speak of "minority groups" created certain problems, "since to do so presupposes a particular notion of what a 'real' American looks like." Even more problematic was the tendency to think of "minority groups" as foreign nationals and their descendents, while ignoring the influence of African Americans—the largest and historically most significant "minority" within the United States. Even so, surveys showed that some forty-three million Americans were either foreign-born or had at least one foreign-born parent. Cultural policymakers thought it foolish to ignore the ability of these people to shape impressions of the United States in foreign countries, to say nothing of their potential for helping Americans, generally speaking, to develop a "world point of view." For Shuster, the issue lay at the heart of U.S. leadership in the postwar world: "Current world developments imply an increasingly greater responsibility for the United States in the international picture. Something must be done to develop a broader insight into the cultures, the heritage and the tremendous contribution of those peoples in particular who have had a part in making America and in whose reconstruction we in turn will have to share."[39]

Of course, the key question was what should be done? Policymakers proposed several options: An obvious answer involved working with educational institutions in the United States to promote greater knowledge of foreign cultures and the way they shaped U.S. history. The government could coordinate resources, dole out scholarships, promote foreign language training, and commission better studies of foreign culture and better translations of foreign literature. A more complicated initiative called for reaching out to "minority groups" through the mass media. For advice, the advisory committee itself reached out to the Office of Facts and Figures, the domestic propaganda bureau under the direction of Archibald MacLeish, which had developed a sophisticated operation to monitor and communicate with foreign-language newspapers in the United States. It invited Alan Cranston, who ran the Foreign Language Division for MacLeish, to attend a meeting and speak about his methods. Cranston reported that officials in his office regularly read and catalogued stories in over 1,000 foreign language newspapers published domestically. His team then used this information to develop a propaganda strategy to tell these groups "what they can do to help in the war effort." The Advisory Committee listened to Cranston's presentation but ultimately resolved to adopt instead a more modest proposal by Ben Cherrington that called for promoting intercultural education through already established organizations on the local level.[40]

The important part of this discussion was not the policy decision it produced, but the fact that the State Department, through its work on cultural relations, had moved into another new realm. Because of their interest in connecting to overseas populations through group-based identity politics, policymakers increasingly began to pay attention to the impact of domestic affairs on U.S. foreign policy. As Louis Adamic pointed out, the State Department did not traditionally have any "direct responsibility for problems of a purely domestic nature." Yet, viewed through the prism of cultural diplomacy, the role of domestic issues as "an important factor in our foreign policy" could not be ignored.[41] Even the narrowest conceptualizations of cultural diplomacy insisted on the importance of establishing relationships between peoples at home and abroad. Broadening the definition of culture to include everything that contributed to foreign perceptions of "America" required even greater attention to domestic affairs. Image thus became the point of convergence between the domestic and the foreign, as U.S. officials contemplated how to capitalize upon American ideas and ideology.

This line of thinking also opened the door to unabashedly linking cultural relations to propaganda. By 1942, cultural policymakers spoke openly of the need to consider the role of propaganda in U.S. foreign policy. Four years earlier, Cordell Hull had assured Ben Cherrington, when he became the first director of the Cultural Division, that his work would not involve propaganda. Now, many cultural policymakers stipulated that "anything which is done in the cultural field is in itself propaganda." Their decision to invite a propagandist to address the Advisory Committee spoke to that evolution in thinking, as did the critical role played by Archibald MacLeish, the government's chief propagandist during that period. While most officials still believed that the "distinction" between propaganda and cultural relations "should be maintained," their interest in shaping perceptions of the United States through culture and communications led them to take an ever-greater interest in the means of modern mass persuasion.[42] One could argue, of course, that the cultural programs had never been anything more than a euphemism for propaganda and that policymakers had finally admitted the obvious. But that misses the critical distinction between the cultural purists, who believed in the importance of exchange for its own sake, and the pragmatists, who viewed the exchanges as a starting point for a much broader agenda. Increasingly, the vision of the latter group came to dominate, as the voices of the former receded in the face of American globalism.

The turn toward propaganda was a sharp departure from conventional approaches to foreign policymaking. In mid-1942, top State Department officials thought so little of propaganda that they largely ignored President Roosevelt's decision to create the Office of War Information (OWI) as an autonomous agency outside the control of the Secretary of State. Obviously, the more expansive definition of cultural relations had not yet filtered up to the Department's top level. Over the next several years, opinions on the importance of propaganda as a foreign policy tool slowly began to change, often driven by the issues encountered in cultural diplomacy. By the end of World War II, senior leaders of the U.S. government—including the President—had changed their minds about the role of image in U.S. foreign policymaking. But to reach that point, policymakers first had to rethink their very definition of foreign policy.

"A New Conception of Foreign Policy"

By the fall of 1942, the State Department had reached a crossroads in planning for the future of cultural diplomacy. Over the past year, cultural policymakers had broadened their mission to a stunning degree, redefining their enterprise from something that supplemented the existing objectives of U.S. foreign policy to something that encompassed every aspect of U.S. foreign policy. It was time, Charles Thomson believed, to move beyond thinking of cultural diplomacy as some sort of experiment and to begin thinking of it as a "permanent" component of the foreign policy process. It needed to be understood as "one of the basic instrumentalities for modifying international relations and attitudes, and for maintaining a better stabilized world order."[43]

Looking for clarity on how to proceed, the Cultural Division asked Yale historian Ralph Turner to prepare a prospective analysis of international cultural relations in the postwar world. The author of

a two-volume survey on the place of cultural traditions in the formation of "Western Civilization," Turner had spent much of the past year
directing a wide-ranging research program for the Cultural Division,
as well as serving on its Advisory Board. For his latest assignment,
Turner prepared a remarkable series of memoranda in late 1942 and
early 1943, in which he made the case for the importance of culture
to any postwar reconstruction program.[44] These memoranda formed
the basis of a pivotal meeting of the Advisory Committee on Cultural
Relations in February 1943.

Turner's proposals demanded a complete redefinition of the relationship
of cultural relations to foreign policy. Although Turner did not initiate
this process by himself—Henry Wallace did far more in this regard—he
did force committee members to confront some of the dichotomies inherent to a state-run initiative in cultural exchange. As a result, the February
1943 meeting produced the closest thing to a clearly articulated operational theory that the cultural programs would ever have. In search of
answers to the much-debated question of whether the cultural programs
should be used to implement the objectives of U.S. foreign policy, Turner
argued that the question itself was moot since it was predicated on a false
dichotomy between cultural relations and foreign policy.

Theoretically, "foreign policy" represented a series of decisions conceived as the extension of nationalist imperatives within the global
arena. In contrast, purists regarded "cultural exchange" as an internationalist project to bring the peoples of the world closer together
through intellectual cooperation, meaning that cultural diplomacy
would be corrupted by any association with the selfish aspirations of
one particular nation's foreign policy. Turner urged his colleagues to
move beyond this either/or choice, proposing that "if cultural relations
have in the past been at the periphery of foreign relations, it may be
that in the new situation into which the world is moving cultural relations are at the heart. Possibly this may be revealed only as we acquire
a new conception of foreign policy."[45]

Unsure what to make of Turner's call for a new conception of foreign policy, several critics fell back on old arguments by attacking him
for trying to subordinate the cultural programs to what they saw as
the inherently nationalist aspirations of U.S. foreign policy. Sumner
Welles, unable to attend the meeting, submitted a written critique of

Turner's memoranda to Charles Thomson, who read it aloud: "A true cultural relations program," Welles claimed, "could not be used to implement the foreign policy of any one country." Stephen Duggan, who had done so much to shape the early cultural exchange programs, went a step further: In his view, cultural activities used to carry out foreign policies "ceased to be cultural relations and became propaganda."[46] Looking to advance the discussion, Waldo Leland of the American Council of Learned Societies asked for a clarification of the definition of "cultural relations...in the broader sense in which it seemed to be used in the memoranda." Turner replied that in his view cultural relations encompassed not just the exchange of knowledge for its own sake but also the "problem of its application and utilization," which would seem, inevitably, to shape foreign relations.[47]

In the end, though, the key question was not Leland's ("What constitutes cultural relations?"), but Turner's ("What constitutes foreign policy?"). Time and again, committee members returned to this issue, slowly coming around to Turner's position. Historian Guy Stanton Ford complimented Turner for developing "a new philosophy and a new approach to the whole question of cultural relations" and for accomplishing his goal of working towards a "new conception of foreign policy." Grayson Kefauver, dean of the School of Education at Stanford University, agreed that "in a world growing continually smaller in a physical sense, the influence of the cultural aspect will become greater." Alger Hiss tried to win over some of the skeptics by suggesting that perhaps the committee should draw a distinction between "foreign policy in a limited sense involving temporary and changing objectives" and "foreign policy in a broader sense...[as] the manifestation of the 'personality' of a nation." This seemed to help clarify things for some. Stephen Duggan's colleague, Carl Milam, although initially critical of Turner, ultimately acknowledged that the diffusion of knowledge could create a climate hospitable to the "propagation of the kind of foreign policy...in which the American people believe." Even Harley Notter, who felt that some of Turner's proposals went too far and smacked of cultural imperialism, was forced to concur with the proposition that "to suppose that a cultural program could be conducted unrelated to [foreign] policy is preposterous...nothing that happens without or within a country can be totally divorced from its foreign policy."[48]

Leland, among others, remained unconvinced, arguing that the entire discussion seemed to presuppose a "certain validity of [American] experiences which [is] not necessarily so." However, he also recognized that the attitude of the committee as a whole had evolved and so he agreed to draft a resolution that conveyed something of a compromise position:

> Be it resolved that cultural relations programs may serve a constructive purpose of peculiar significance within the framework of the foreign policy of the United States, insofar as that policy attempts to form a climate of mutual international understanding and to seek as goals to be obtained as rapidly as possible (a) the free exchange of ideas and information, particularly, as these relate to the health, economic and social welfare, and general cultural advancement of the people, and (b) the establishing and maintaining of a peaceful, secure, and cooperative world order.[49]

In the long run, as Turner predicted, the evolution of modern mass communications along with the reconfiguration of national boundaries, in both the physical and the metaphysical sense, elevated the importance of "culture" in the conduct of modern foreign relations. Simply by creating a Cultural Relations Division, even the staid State Department had acknowledged that it would be unwise, if not impossible, to make foreign policies absent a consideration of their cultural manifestations and ramifications. At the same time, the cultural purists' point about the potentially corrupting influence of nationalist priorities, particularly upon the fruits of intellectual exchange, deserved consideration as well. Clouding the entire discussion was the inevitable blurring of the boundary between nationalist and internationalist motives in a nation committed, for admittedly selfish reasons, to worldwide freedom of information.

To be sure, framing cultural relations in such a broad way posed a daunting challenge to the relatively small staff of the Cultural Division. Yet the logic of their enterprise nearly demanded this kind of a response, especially when considered against the backdrop of emerging U.S. hegemony in a world of unstable boundaries and shifting power relations. Top officials in the U.S. government sought a postcolonial imperial strategy for extending the political and cultural influence of the United States throughout the world; cultural policymakers were, first and foremost, employees of the U.S. government, in charge of a realm particularly conducive to this larger agenda.

These debates would no doubt have been aided by a conceptual distinction that seems obvious today but was only hinted at in these discussions: the difference between a nation's foreign policies and its foreign relations. In revealing the necessity of a new theory and a new language, the discussion of Turner's memoranda pointed toward the need for a better understanding of the divergence between the two. To distinguish between America's foreign policies (the official decisions made deep inside the corridors of the State Department and the West Wing) and its foreign relations (the sum total of the nation's contacts with the external world) would have clarified the question of whether cultural exchange could be at once nationalist and internationalist. To the extent that policymakers operated within the overall context of American foreign relations, even the "purest" cultural exchanges helped to shape the environment in which nationalist policies and priorities were set. By the same token, the nation's official policies established certain parameters—via trade, information flow, and travel, among other factors—for nongovernmental exchanges. If a nation's foreign policies impinged upon its foreign relations and vice versa, then to insist upon complete separation between cultural exchanges undertaken for nationalist versus internationalist motives made no sense in theory or in practice.

What ultimately became clear in these discussions was that the purist conception of intellectual exchange sought to use culture, ideas, and education only under very specific conditions: for promoting peace on a global scale. This agenda derived from the approach of the earliest INGOs, such as the Carnegie Endowment for International Peace, which often waged a quest for peace over and against the policies of particular national governments. Turner's formulation did not repudiate the use of intellectual exchanges for peaceful purposes, but it did insist upon appreciating the larger context in which ideas had to be acknowledged as an independent force in the global environment. As such, national governments did not have the luxury of leaving the realm of ideas to international organizations. Increasingly, ideas would shape the setting in which governments made their foreign policies, and as they became a more potent force in international relations, governments would inevitably use them to execute nationalist policies. In the end, what Turner really wanted to convey was that the U.S. government could not afford to abstain from the world-wide marketplace of ideas—even if that meant that cultural relations would increasingly serve the same ends as outright propaganda.

"Making the State Department into a Twentieth Century Institution"

Turner's proposals changed the nature of the discussions at Cultural Advisory Committee meetings, but they did nothing to alter the over-all structure of the State Department. Actually implementing Turner's ideas would require the State Department to reconfigure a badly out-dated framework. Power still flowed almost exclusively through the Department's conventional geographic divisions, a setup that severely constrained policymakers in responding to the ever-broadening array of issues they confronted. Foreign policymakers now had to account not just for the political and diplomatic relations between nation states, but also for the economic, cultural, technological, and informational aspects of foreign policy as well. While these newer components of foreign policy did not transcend geography, they required a different conception of geography—multilateral and transnational in scope, in contrast to the bilateral, nation-centered approach of traditional diplomacy.[50] However, the very structure of the State Department treated these sorts of issues as a subset of the diplomatic relations between individual nation states rather than as transnational forces integral to the conduct of foreign policy in the modern era.

Throughout late 1943 and early 1944, an era when the bureaucratic inner-workings of the State Department routinely made national front-page headlines, coverage of the State Department frequently complained about the outdated structure of America's foreign policy bureaucracy. The famed public intellectual Walter Lippmann offered perhaps the most succinct version of this critique:

The troubles of the State Department are best understood and can be most surely overcome if we realize that they are growing pains. It is an old established department. Its conversion, expansion, and reju-venation to meet the demands of war have been difficult. Yet they are necessary.... At the time when the President created the Board of Economic Warfare, the State Department had neither the organization nor the men for this novel kind of operation. The same was true of relief, of foreign propaganda, of strategic intelligence service, and of finance.... Ultimately, the system of parceling out foreign affairs in many agencies could not work.... Unity of direction and clarity and coherence in policy have become urgently necessary. The country must have one foreign policy. It cannot have several foreign policies.[51]

Neal Stanford of the *Christian Science Monitor* made the same point, a bit more harshly, in calling for the "winds of reorganization" to blow through the "ancient and august pile of Pennsylvania Avenue which houses the State Department."[52]

To preside over the Department's reorganization, Roosevelt tapped Edward Reilly Stettinius, Jr. Appointed Undersecretary of State in October 1943, Stettinius replaced the dashing Sumner Welles, who had been forced out after an ugly, highly public feud with Cordell Hull. Stettinius did not really fit the profile of a diplomat. Mild-mannered and sensible, a lifelong teetotaler, he seemed a rather uninspired choice. Moreover, he brought no traditional foreign policy experience to the second-most powerful position within the State Department. What he did possess was a reputation as an administrator *par excellence*, first at U.S. Steel and then for the Lend-Lease program.[53]

Colleagues described the silver-haired Stettinius as a workaholic who approached his job "with the fury of a fervid immigrant."[54] Roosevelt probably had this image of a relentless taskmaster in mind when he said to Stettinius's wife that "Ed is going to raise Hell in the State Department...and he will do it with my blessing."[55] If that was the goal, then he fell far short of reaching it. But what he did do in terms of modernizing the departmental infrastructure—first as undersecretary, and then as secretary after Cordell Hull stepped down in late 1944—made a far greater impact than a little hell-raising ever could have.

Upon his arrival, Stettinius quickly perceived just how antiquated the internal structure of the State Department had become. Even Roosevelt, who typically favored decentralized bureaucracies in order to maximize his own authority, had begun to consider various proposals for reorganization shortly before Stettinius's appointment; this undoubtedly influenced his choice.

Stettinius carried out two reorganizations—the first in the spring of 1944, the second that winter—that completely transformed the entire structure and chain of command at the State Department. Two aspects of this transformation stand out as especially important. The first was the decision to develop mechanisms for approaching policymaking from a topical as well as a geographical perspective. The Department "flattened out" its bureaucracy by creating twelve "line offices," with "Labor Relations," "Special Political Affairs," "Economic Affairs," and "Public Information" taking positions alongside the traditional "regional" offices.[56] The other major innovation was the creation of an Office of Public Information, which spoke to the increasing importance of public relations as a component of foreign policymaking. Overall, the theme of modernization dominated coverage of the reorganization effort. An editorial in the *Washington Post* predicted that Stettinius "could earn a niche in the country's history by making the State Department into a twentieth century institution."[57]

Cultural diplomats had been at the vanguard of those pushing for a more expansive vision of foreign policy. By illustrating the way in which ideological and economic forces combined to permeate the structure of traditional diplomacy, their work demanded a reconceptualization of the distinction between the nation's foreign policies and its foreign relations. As Neal Stanford noted at the time, Stettinius clearly based his agenda on the theory that "any American interests or activity abroad is *ipso facto* of diplomatic concern to this country."[58]

At the same time, domestic events likely to make it into foreign coverage of the United States were also now "of diplomatic concern to this country." For many commentators, this interest in domestic affairs via public relations was actually the most significant of the many changes of the Stettinius era. It suggested not only that the Department would provide more and better information about its activities to the public, but that it would actually begin to treat the "public," at home and abroad, as an integral component of the foreign policy process. As several observers noted, the Office of Public Information was much more than a public relations bureau. It included several different divisions that covered both "information" functions (such as research and publications), as well as "cultural" activities (such as motion pictures and scientific and artistic exchanges).

The decision to gather all of these operations under one umbrella is especially noteworthy. By 1944, the "domestic" activities of Roosevelt's propaganda bureau, the Office of War Information (OWI), had generated a considerable amount of hostility from Congress. Despite the toxic reputation of the OWI's domestic operation, the State Department quietly adopted many of those same techniques, combining them with the existing cultural programs. With the blurring of the boundary between domestic and foreign affairs, policymakers had to account for the domestic reaction to foreign policy decisions. As the *Washington Post* noted, the creation of an Office of Public Information sent the message that "the era in which our diplomacy could be conducted in a vacuum has gone forever."[59]

This sweeping reorganization, which relocated and redefined the place of cultural relations within the foreign policy bureaucracy, dominated the meetings of the Cultural Advisory Committee in 1944. Not surprisingly, several committee members continued to worry about the corruption of what they saw as the original internationalist mission of the cultural programs. Noting that cultural diplomats now operated out of an Office of Public Information, they pushed their colleagues to adopt a statement distinguishing between the "informational activities of the government in its communications with foreign populations... and the facilitation by the government of communications and interchanges of a cultural nature."[60]

By June, however, the entire committee seemed to have made peace with the reforms. In what became the final meeting of the Cultural Advisory Committee, the members generally moved beyond semantic and theoretical debates on the nature of foreign relations and the importance of maintaining distinctions between culture, education, and information. In a wide-ranging, forward-looking discussion, the members of the committee concentrated on the importance of intellectual and technical exchanges to the process of social and economic reconstruction in the postwar world. They also discussed how better to harmonize the operation of the student exchange programs with the objectives of U.S. foreign policy, since the committee agreed that "the attitudes toward American life and institutions acquired by foreign students living in this country would influence foreign relations."[61]

To close its last meeting, the committee adopted a final set of resolutions on "the essential character, scope and objectives of a publicly supported program of cultural relations." Typed up by Waldo Leland, the resolutions acknowledged the many different points of view and philosophies that emerged during committee meetings yet professed a general consensus on the need for a "publicly supported program of international cultural relations." This statement marked the conclusion to the debate over whether true processes of cultural exchange could ever occur under national auspices. While the committee members believed in "cultural relations at the higher intellectual and aesthetic levels," they agreed that the government would have to formulate its own proactive policy to utilize the dissemination and exchange of culture in conjunction with the growing needs and objectives of U.S. foreign policy.[62]

Over the previous six years, U.S. cultural policy had evolved from the modest effort to sponsor a handful of educational exchanges per year to a comprehensive view of the importance of disseminating American images, ideas, and technical know-how throughout the world. Whether this evolution in thinking represented the negation or the realization of the original vision depended on one's understanding of that original vision. Yet, given the contradictions inherent within that vision, even to pose this sort of either/or question probably distracts from appreciating the real significance of this truly profound shift in conceptions of foreign policy and foreign relations.

Redefining Diplomacy

As 1944 drew to a close, the State Department carried out its second major reorganization that year. The January reshuffling, which broke up the geographical hegemony of the old chains of command, transformed the structure of the department, but had little effect on the overall culture since there were few changes among the top ranks. Some described the first reorganization as "so complete and sweeping as to leave veterans in the department speechless," while others considered it a "fraud," just "phony finagling," in which "only the furniture inside was shifted around." In

general, the Department's fiercest critics were not satisfied. Obviously, neither was Stettinius, who had recently replaced Hull as Secretary.[63]

The second makeover brought wholesale changes to the Department's leadership. Out went veterans Adolf Berle, Breckinridge
Long, and G. Howland Shaw; in came Archibald MacLeish, Nelson
Rockefeller, Will Clayton, and Leo Pasvolsky as new Assistant
Secretaries. Only Dean Acheson kept his position. Political appointees
typically bring in their own people, but what stood out from Stettinius's
selections was his new team's lack of traditional diplomatic experience.
MacLeish was an idea man, a poet and a propagandist. Rockefeller
brought his experience with propaganda and economic modernization in Latin America. Clayton, like Stettinius, was a businessman
with a background in national and international economic planning.
Only Pasvolsky had served previously in the State Department, but
he was a specialist in international organizations rather than coming
through the ranks of the Foreign Service, like many previous Assistant
Secretaries.

The variety in the backgrounds of these appointees was no accident.
On an official level, the two reorganizations had so expanded the scope
of the Department's responsibilities that Stettinius had no choice but to
look for expertise in new places. Stettinius and Roosevelt agreed: "We
have to have some new people, and we have to get rid of some of the
deadwood."[64] Several commentators noted the significance of this shift,
although they disagreed rather emphatically about whether it would
work. An article in the *Christian Science Monitor* complained that several
of the appointees were "untrained in diplomacy" and predicted that this
sort of experimental effort "will not likely succeed because the Foreign
Service has not been adequately developed." The always-critical Arthur
Krock of the *New York Times* expressed support for some of Stettinius's
selections, but he criticized Rockefeller and MacLeish, in particular,
while claiming not to understand the purpose of "cultural relations."[65]

On the other end of the spectrum, several writers immediately grasped
the significance of the nontraditional appointments as a response to the
"absorption by the department of many war and postwar functions now
distributed among distinct agencies." Another article commended the
"desire to find a place within the State Department for certain new
activities of the government which properly belong there." From that

perspective, Clayton, Rockefeller, and MacLeish—with their wealth of experience in such matters as international economics, technological modernization, cultural exchanges, and propaganda—could hardly be described as "untrained in diplomacy." To put it another way, the extent of their qualifications as "diplomats" depended upon how one defines "diplomacy."[66]

* * *

For the cultural programs, the appointment of Archibald MacLeish as Assistant Secretary of State for Public and Cultural Relations represented a major milestone. Symbolically, the creation of that position demonstrated that the diplomacy of ideas had now attained cabinet-level status within the State Department. Practically, the post provided the platform for enacting the theories developed in the meetings of the Cultural Advisory Committee. Since the watershed year of 1941, the scope of "cultural relations" had evolved considerably. From Henry Wallace's interpretation of cultural relations as economic modernization to Ralph Turner's insistence that cultural relations required a reconceptualization of foreign policy and foreign relations, U.S. officials increasingly viewed the cultural programs as a tool of empire to be used to facilitate American hegemony.

MacLeish only occupied the position for a few short months before Roosevelt's death brought a new president with a new foreign policy team, but in that time he embodied the emerging practice of public diplomacy. In addition to his work for Rockefeller's OCIAA and the Cultural Advisory Committee, MacLeish played a seminal role in drafting the propaganda strategy that would be used by the World War II propaganda agency, the Office of War Information. When the State Department then adopted the overseas operations of that office at the end of the war, MacLeish inherited the job of incorporating them into the foreign policy bureaucracy. Propaganda was the final piece of the matrix of public diplomacy. By the time it arrived at the State Department in 1945, foreign policy had already been redefined to such an extent that excluding it was unthinkable.

3

"The Projection of America"

Propaganda as Foreign Policy at the Office of War Information

HISTORY HAS NOT BEEN kind to the World War II propaganda initiatives of the U.S. government. The work of the Office of War Information (OWI)—the best known and most influential of the wartime propaganda agencies—has received very little acclaim, apart from nostalgic appreciation for the iconic images of "Rosie the Riveter" and "The Four Freedoms." During the war, the OWI provoked howls of protest, mostly from conservative critics, who complained about incompetence, waste, and liberal bias. Many assessments since have characterized the organization as mismanaged and ineffective. The OWI story, if not entirely relegated to the dustbin of history, is certainly not regarded as central to the plotline of World War II.[1] This is unfortunate, for the OWI, both in its existence and in its operations, symbolized and precipitated a broader transformation in conceptions of U.S. foreign relations.

Before World War II, overseas propaganda was widely viewed as peripheral to, if not entirely separate from, the foreign policy process. When President Roosevelt issued Executive Order 9182, which created the OWI in June 1942, there was little expectation that it would become enmeshed in questions of foreign policy. Secretary of State Cordell Hull spoke for the relentless traditionalists at the

State Department when he informed the OWI that, in his view, war information did "not include information relating to the foreign policy of the United States."[2] Events soon demonstrated otherwise. By the end of the war, the OWI experience had made it clear that propaganda not only mattered to U.S. foreign policy, but that it *was* a foreign policy—one of several voices speaking for the U.S. government throughout the world.

In demonstrating the importance of propaganda to foreign policy, the OWI played a critical role in laying the groundwork for postwar public diplomacy, reinforcing the conclusions reached around the same time by the State Department's Cultural Division regarding the role of images and ideas in shaping America's foreign policies and its foreign relations. More importantly still, OWI officials grappled with the way that these issues manifested in a world marked by the erosion of traditional imperial structures and the emergence of U.S. hegemony. While cultural diplomats reflected upon the potential for cultural relations to contribute to the goal of securing a postcolonial empire, OWI officials did the same for propaganda. When united in the State Department in 1945, cultural diplomacy and propaganda formed the core of the public diplomacy matrix in the postwar period.

OWI officials identified and confronted most of the dilemmas that would shape government initiatives in public diplomacy for decades to come. They played a seminal role in theorizing the place of propaganda in a democratic society, the proliferation of access to mass communications, the relationship between foreign relations and domestic affairs, the distinction between propaganda and psychological warfare, and the relationship between public and private sources of information. Even in cases where their basic premises echoed those of the World War I–era Committee on Public Information (CPI), OWI officials often brought a fresh perspective that demanded a redefinition of conventional notions of foreign policy and foreign relations, along the lines of what Ralph Turner proposed at the State Department. Wartime propagandists were also the first to confront what became one of the hallmarks of government propaganda in the postwar period: the inevitable backlash against any attempt to define "America" in the world. The significance of the OWI lies less in the agency's actual accomplishments, or lack thereof, and more in its attempts to respond to rapid and dramatic changes in the global environment and the role of the United States therein. Even in its failures—maybe especially in its failures— the OWI experience provides critical insights into the practice of government propaganda in the American Century.

"A Nation of Groups"

In many ways, the evolution of the World War II propaganda apparatus mirrored the nation's haphazard path towards involvement in the war itself. Between 1939 and 1941, the White House set up several propaganda agencies that came close to putting the nation on a war footing with respect to information policy—essentially the unacknowledged bureaucratic embodiment of FDR's growing commitment to U.S. intervention. At the same time, the president feared that a centralized propaganda bureau would recall the lingering antipathy toward the CPI, the much-maligned operation run by George Creel during the First World War.[3]

The "Creel Committee" was the most comprehensive propaganda outfit to emerge from the First World War. It was so successful at mobilizing public opinion that it became a model for the propaganda bureaus that several other countries developed after the war.[4] Among Americans, however, it provoked widespread condemnation for its aggressive messaging designed to inflame hostility toward America's wartime enemies. Few mourned the decision to dismantle it when the war ended. During the 1920s, many of its depictions of enemy "atrocities" were exposed as categorically false.[5] Twenty years later, even to recall the subject of government propaganda still reminded many people of Creel's excesses, as well as Woodrow Wilson's failed quest to make the world "safe for democracy." The last thing that FDR needed was to provide additional ammunition for those who believed that he intended to follow in Wilson's footsteps, guiding the United States toward involvement in another European war.

The president clearly hoped that his decentralized approach to wartime propaganda would create a moving target for his critics. Instead, he generated a bureaucratic snafu of significant proportions. The various propaganda agencies that preceded the OWI were hampered by their overlapping jurisdiction, limited authority, and confusing structure.

Nevertheless, their influence on the eventual trajectory of government information policy should not be underestimated. Many of the debates and theories developed in these agencies—in particular the Office of Facts and Figures (OFF) and the Foreign Information Service (FIS) of the Office of the Coordinator of Information (COI)—laid the groundwork for the production of propaganda during and after World War II. The contributions made by these agencies may be attributed primarily to the highly influential individuals who ran them: in the case of the OFF, Archibald MacLeish, and at the FIS, Pulitzer Prize–winning playwright Robert Sherwood. MacLeish and Sherwood then joined the OWI in June 1942, bringing with them both insights and personnel from their previous assignments.

Over the next several years, MacLeish and Sherwood would shape an emerging philosophy of propaganda as a foreign policy tool. MacLeish was particularly perceptive in analyzing the impact of information technology on the foreign policy process. He moved rapidly around the bureaucratic chain during World War II—the omnipresent voice on the use of information and ideas for the pursuit of foreign policy objectives. In many ways, he was the George Kennan of U.S. information policy in that his thinking would continue to pervade virtually every aspect of the emerging propaganda programs long after his relatively short tenure in government ended.

One of the most prominent Americans of his era, MacLeish was known for being successful at literally everything he tried. As a young man, he was a star football player at Yale University, where he was also elected to the prestigious secret society, Skull & Bones. He went on to pursue a promising career as a lawyer, in which he held simultaneous positions as a litigator at a prominent Wall Street firm and as a professor of constitutional law at Harvard. During the 1920s, MacLeish soured on the law and devoted his life to poetry, which he pursued as an expatriate in Paris. There he wrote several of his best-known poems and rubbed elbows, in many cases becoming fast friends, with Ernest Hemingway, F. Scott Fitzgerald, T. S. Eliot, Ezra Pound, James Joyce, and Gertrude Stein, among others. After returning to the United States in the 1930s, he decided to try his hand at journalism and went to work for Henry Luce at *Fortune* magazine—an interesting pairing of two future advocates for the American Century.[6]

MacLeish's reporting at *Fortune* captured the attention of President Roosevelt, who asked him to serve as Librarian of Congress in 1939. MacLeish, reluctant to take time away from his writing, initially turned down the job, but he relented after FDR sprinkled a bit of his famous charm. Apparently, Roosevelt hoodwinked him into believing that he could wrap up his Library duties in the morning, leaving the remainder of the day to work on his poetry. MacLeish's confirmation hearing in the House of Representatives proved unexpectedly controversial when New Jersey Congressman J. Parnell Thomas became one of the first Americans to use the pejorative "fellow traveler" to attack MacLeish's political outlook. MacLeish overcame these objections, though, and went on to serve what is now considered an innovative and successful tenure as the nation's chief librarian.[7]

In October 1941, FDR added to MacLeish's duties when he appointed him director of the Office of Facts and Figures. Though only in existence for eight months, the OFF constructed a sophisticated propaganda and information policy around the concepts of public opinion and morale. In short, MacLeish sought to use "all the techniques of public opinion research which have been developed in the government, private foundations, business, and industry in the past several years."[8] Although focused primarily on the domestic scene, MacLeish and his colleagues developed ideas that applied to overseas propaganda as well. They established a number of precedents through their effective use of opinion polling, their advocacy for a centralized information agency, their notion of a "strategy of truth," and their insights into navigating the boundaries between domestic and foreign affairs—issues that remain central to any government information program.

MacLeish and his staff saw the purpose of the OFF as facilitating a "widespread and accurate understanding of the national war effort." They worried that, without domestic unity, "we will lose the war of ideas before we have even the opportunity to strike the enemy with our armed fist." The OFF interest in public opinion derived from the fairly traditional notion of maintaining high morale at home as an essential precondition to fighting a successful war abroad. Yet, as with the more general problem of leading a democracy at war, "unity" was hard to measure and even harder to achieve. In one of his most crucial insights, MacLeish recognized that his office could never hope to dictate the flow of information to the public. Unlike the Axis powers, which possessed the technical means for "monopolizing the channels to the mind," U.S. propagandists had to monitor hundreds of radio stations and thousands of national, local, organizational, and foreign language newspapers.[9]

Winning the "word war" required more than just producing glossy government pamphlets: "It is not enough to make the full story available in Washington," warned an early policy directive from the OFF. "The issue is what actually comes to the attention of the people and various sections of the public." Government propagandists had to worry not just about disseminating information but also about propelling it in certain directions. The American people drew their ideas from a remarkably diverse array of what OFF officials called "information channels." The complexity of those "channels" reflected the vast range of interest groups and identity politics in the United States. As OFF analysts recognized, "in this country we do not have a homogeneous society. We have a nation of groups."[10]

The philosophy of the OFF bears a striking resemblance to the principles that George Creel espoused at the CPI. Creel, too, focused on the importance of public opinion in building domestic unity, on the multiplicity of information channels, on capitalizing upon American pluralism, and on the possibilities for using "truth" as a weapon against enemies that told only "lies."[11] Equally striking, though, is the lack of attention that Creel's CPI seems to have received from its World War II successors. Nowhere in the records of the OFF or the OWI is there any sustained analysis of CPI precedents—positive or negative. While it would be logical to assume that many of the philosophical and tactical choices at the OWI and its predecessors were made either because they worked for Creel, or because they did not, there is little evidence for this proposition. Instead, World War II propagandists often reinvented the proverbial wheel.[12]

"Boundaries Are Hard to Draw"

One place where World War II propagandists did move significantly beyond the CPI was in their approach to the global implications of domestic public opinion. The ever-expanding reach of mass communications worldwide infinitely broadened both the sources and the reach of public opinion. Not only did the public have access to information from multiple perspectives (domestic, foreign, urban, rural) and filtered through multiple lenses (religion, race, class, gender, among others), but these channels flowed both ways, as any policymaker concerned with the politics of unity quickly came to appreciate. After all, the machinery used to promote consensus and support for the war could just as easily be used to record the success or failure of those efforts and then intentionally or unintentionally broadcast around the world. Although there were no easy solutions to this problem, this observation in itself shaped future approaches to information policy.

The permeability of boundaries—national and otherwise—posed the most significant dilemma MacLeish and his staff confronted. In theory, the OFF monitored domestic attitudes toward the war. The nature of that work, however, often involved measuring the flow of information and the formation of ideas, both of which prodded policy-makers to look overseas. They could not simply ignore the possibility that American information about the war originated in foreign sources. At this point, limits on the scope of OFF operations became problem-atic since responsibility for overseas propaganda lay not with the OFF but with the other major agency that ultimately fed into the OWI: The Foreign Information Service in the Office of the Coordinator of Information. The ensuing turf war between the OFF and the COI exposed some of the most critical fault lines in the making of U.S. information policy.

The Coordinator's Office was run by the flamboyant international lawyer, William J. Donovan, known as "Wild Bill" by his less ardent admirers. A slick salesman, Donovan personally convinced FDR to augment the U.S. government's woefully inadequate resources for the collection and dissemination of information overseas. U.S. capa-bilities, Donovan rightly argued, lagged far behind those of the major European powers. Amid the isolationism of the interwar period, the U.S. government had stood by as Britain, France, and Germany devel-oped sophisticated broadcasting networks and intelligence services to assist in the management of their far-flung colonial empires. Persuaded by Donovan's appeal, the President decided on the spot to create the COI. As FDR later recalled, it was Donovan who "got me started on this [information business]."[13]

Between June 1941 and June 1942, the Coordinator's Office played a major role in the creation of a worldwide propaganda program. It engaged in both overt and covert activities, though Donovan cared far more about the cloak-and-dagger intrigue of the latter. He regarded straightforward overseas propaganda as fairly mundane and uninteresting, so he delegated most of those duties to Robert Sherwood, who ran the Foreign Information Service for Donovan.[14] Though a shy, retiring, giant of a man, Sherwood was known for his passionate, avowedly political, morality plays. He was at that moment at the height of his fame, having just won his third Pulitzer for *There Shall Be No Night*, a heroic tale of the Finnish resistance to the Russian invasion of 1940. In addition, his speechwriting had helped FDR win an unprecedented third term as president. Sherwood signed up for government service out of a belief that intellectuals could best serve their cause through joining the fray rather than attempting to remain detached social critics. He embodied the activist spirit so integral to the worldview of most New Deal liberals—an attitude that playwright Norman Cousins once characterized as a "disillusion with disillusion."[15]

Temperamentally and philosophically, Sherwood had much more in common with MacLeish than with Donovan. In terms of information policy, the two of them advocated a "strategy of truth"—arguing that the prevalence of "Nazi lies" had created a vacuum, even a hunger, throughout many parts of the world for any sort of credible information. Both MacLeish and Sherwood believed that telling the "truth" helped the U.S. government—partly because of the content of the message itself and partly because it threw into sharp relief the dishonest tactics of America's enemies. While policymakers would, of course, arrange the facts to portray their policies and their nation in a favorable light, they would not, or at least should not, resort to outright falsehoods.[16]

MacLeish and Sherwood differed sharply with Donovan on the type of propaganda the government should emphasize. Sherwood championed propaganda that relied upon public statements and official reports, in which the source of the information was clearly identified. Donovan favored the spread of disinformation, sometimes misleadingly labeled to seem to originate from one government while subtly serving the objectives of another. The distinction between the former approach (often labeled "white" propaganda) and the latter ("black" propaganda) is now generally understood but was far less theorized on the eve of World War II. In fact, the war played a key role in clarifying for subsequent generations the issues and the stakes involved.

Proponents of "black" propaganda viewed information as quite literally a weapon of war, to be used in the same way one would use a tank or a bomb. Social Scientist Daniel Lerner famously referred to "black" propaganda as "sykewar." For advocates, the long-term impact on America's image did not matter, as long as the disinformation accomplished its immediate goal of weakening the enemy in one way or another. The "strategy of truth," on the other hand, approached information policy from the assumption that image itself constituted a critical component of foreign policy, not simply a way to dress up or "sell" a preexisting set of policies. Therefore, disseminating "black" propaganda not only jeopardized the credibility of the U.S. government's "white" propaganda; it also threatened to undermine the larger objectives of U.S. foreign policy.

There was an undeniable tension here: all propagandists claimed that they told the truth while others told only lies. In other words, the U.S. government distributes "information," whereas its enemies produce "propaganda." Yet the divide between the "strategy of truth" and outright disinformation did not simply amount to a distinction without a difference. In fact, there was a fundamental disagreement about the appropriate role for information and ideas in U.S. foreign policy. Proponents of "white" propaganda and the "strategy of truth" took the position that credibility mattered when it came to information policy; proponents of "black" propaganda and disinformation had other priorities.

These differences in philosophies of propaganda underscored the way in which mass communications had contributed to the erosion of boundaries between domestic and foreign. In MacLeish's words, "we do not, like the propaganda bureaus of the dictators, tell one story at home and another abroad." However overstated, MacLeish's boast highlighted the need for a comprehensive approach to information policy that could account for the international ramifications of domestic events. As he observed in a memo to Donovan written a week before Pearl Harbor: "Boundaries are hard to draw. Your people, in their short wave programs aimed abroad, are on the lookout for happenings at home. And happenings at home necessarily affect American opinion in the field assigned to OFF. The result is that OFF is directly concerned with attempts to 'make news' in America and that COI, though indirectly, is also affected."[17] The jurisdictional battle between MacLeish and Donovan, which only intensified after the war began, thus highlighted a problem endemic to the production of government propaganda: synchronizing the message disseminated at home with the message broadcast abroad.

Consolidating "Washington Initialdom"

After Pearl Harbor, Roosevelt's decision to stifle criticism with a decentralized bureaucratic structure came back to haunt him, as politicians and the media complained about the "overlapping authority" of "Washington initialdom."[18] Even supporters of an active propaganda program realized that something had to change. Although nearly everyone recognized the need for greater coordination, the key question was how centralized the whole operation should be. Once again, the specter of the Creel Committee hovered, unacknowledged, over these discussions. Sherwood and MacLeish advocated the creation of a new agency responsible for both domestic and foreign propaganda with a structure closely resembling that of the CPI. MacLeish even came up with the name, suggesting that the Office of Facts and Figures be renamed the "Office of War Information" and then assigned control over the other agencies. Donovan could not see what domestic affairs had to do with the kind of information policy he favored, nor did he like the idea of subordinating his agenda to someone else's. Ultimately, Sherwood and MacLeish convinced the president to side with them. In June 1942, Roosevelt signed Executive Order 9182, creating the Office of War Information.[19]

Suggestions for someone to head the new organization varied. MacLeish would have been a logical choice although he waffled over whether he wanted that level of responsibility. "I don't think I would be much good at the job of actually running the production end of a central government propaganda agency," he wrote presidential speechwriter Samuel Rosenman. He did add that "I have become intensely interested in the broad information job," indicating a greater affection for policymaking than for administration.[20] Sherwood, too, was certainly qualified although his quiet nature made him a less than ideal choice to be the public face of the new agency. Instead, FDR turned to a relative outsider, the charismatic CBS radio personality Elmer Davis.

A plainspoken Midwesterner from Aurora, Indiana, Davis was a journalist's journalist. He had built his career from the bottom up. At the age of fourteen, he joined the staff of his hometown newspaper as a "printer's devil," the jack of all trades in a print shop. After graduating from Franklin College in Indiana and attending Oxford on a Rhodes scholarship, he landed a job as a foreign correspondent for the *New York Times*. Although he left journalism in 1924 to write fiction, he returned as a radio commentator on the eve of World War II. His reputation for fair and balanced reporting made him a popular choice in many quarters to direct the OWI.[21] MacLeish became the OWI's Assistant Director in charge of policy, and Sherwood signed on to run the OWI's Overseas Branch, continuing the work he had been doing at the FIS.

Left out in this new configuration was Donovan, whose intelligence operations were transferred from the civilian to the military sector. For "Wild Bill," who had clashed frequently with the Joint Chiefs, this decision represented an affront. Ultimately, though, the separation worked out far better than he could have imagined, as it led to him assuming command of the newly formed Office of Strategic Services. In addition to its "black" ops, the OSS became America's first comprehensive intelligence-gathering operation, ultimately morphing into the Central Intelligence Agency after the war.[22] By splitting the overseas operations of the Coordinator of Information between the OWI and the OSS, Roosevelt temporarily resolved some of the bureaucratic and jurisdictional issues that had plagued the prewar propaganda agencies. Yet the larger strategic questions about the appropriate role for propaganda and information within U.S. foreign policy remained unresolved.

Comprised of both a Domestic Branch and an Overseas Branch, the OWI mostly followed the outline that MacLeish and Sherwood had proposed. In its structure, the OWI resembled the sort of unified propaganda bureau that FDR had initially tried to avoid. The new agency became the clearinghouse for all official government propaganda at home and abroad (with the exception of Latin America, which remained the responsibility of Nelson Rockefeller's Office of the

Coordinator of Inter-American Affairs). It also had the power to issue directives to other government agencies on how they should release information to the public, although control over the actual process of releasing that information remained with the individual agencies. By locating the OWI within the Office of Emergency Management, FDR ensured that Elmer Davis would report directly to him, theoretically insulating the OWI from undue pressure applied by any individual government department or agency.

Yet, the President made clear that Davis would have nowhere near the power that George Creel had wielded during World War I. The Executive Order failed to specify what would happen in cases where other agencies and departments disagreed or failed to comply with Davis's directives. With the State Department moving into the information business, future conflicts over who really "spoke" for the U.S. government would be hard to avoid. As Creel himself said in a letter to Davis, "I am more sorry than I can say that your control over Army, Navy and State is not real in any sense of the word.... While you may think you have established an arrangement that will permit a free flow of news, just wait until an issue arises."[23]

With MacLeish and Sherwood appointed to high positions, the OWI seemed poised to carry on most of the policies designed over the past year, but now with better coordination and clearer authority. In some cases, this happened; in others, substantial roadblocks soon emerged. Early on, the exuberance that accompanied the creation of the new agency allowed policymakers to articulate their philosophy in grand terms, which Elmer Davis did in his first appearance before Congress. Drawing on his expertise in print journalism and radio, Davis presented a broad vision of the role of ideas in modern foreign relations. He imagined the OWI as an "auxiliary to the armed forces," arguing that it could "pave the way for their operations and make their success easier."[24]

Alluding to the traditions established at the OFF and the FIS, Davis stressed the importance of employing "truth instead of falsehood," which he thought essential not for moral reasons but for strategic ones. As MacLeish and Sherwood had argued before him, the suppression of freedom of speech in many countries made factually accurate information "a more powerful weapon than ever before." After all, "many millions of people" were desperate "for any truthful account of what is going on." All the better, he implied, if that "truthful account" came from the U.S. government. The need for "truthful" information was just as acute on the home front. To keep foreign "news out of the country would be impossible"; there was little point in trying to insulate the American public from foreign affairs. Whether at home or abroad, "bad" information would be countered with "good" information— "falsehoods" with "truth."[25]

Obviously, these sorts of claims were themselves part of the propaganda. Davis essentially conceded this when he noted that, while "'propaganda' is a word in bad odor in this country . . . there is no public hostility to the idea of education," and "we regard [public information] as education." Nowhere, however, did Davis begin to define the content of this "education," which is what tends to provoke disputes. For a short time, though, the urgency of the situation and the flourish of liberal idealism that accompanied the creation of the OWI overwhelmed the critics and naysayers. Davis walked away from his first hearings with an initial appropriation of approximately twenty-six million dollars.[26]

The "Multitude of Voices"

Officials throughout the ranks of the OWI agreed that the agency's primary job would be "educating" people about the rationales for war. In a speech before the American Society of Newspaper Editors in March 1942, Archibald MacLeish provocatively claimed that "the real battlefield of this war is the field of American opinion." MacLeish did not just mean that the American people had to support the war in order for the United States to succeed but that the way people responded to the war and the way the press covered that response helped to determine the context in which the military fought its battles. In other words, it was one thing to simply back the policies of the Roosevelt administration in the polls and at the ballot box; it was another thing for the American people to echo the administration's message for the benefit of an overseas audience.[27]

OWI officials recognized that, compared to the overwhelming power of the private media, their ability to shape opinions about the nation and its war effort was intermittent, at best. Speaking in April 1942 at an Associated Press luncheon, MacLeish told the assembled journalists that while the government "cannot avoid, and would certainly never wish to avoid, its full quota of responsibility, [it] is not the first or even the main line of defense" in the "psychological front." Words are "weapons," MacLeish continued, precisely the sort of "weapons journalists and publishers are trained to use." So, "in a country which puts its reliance on a free and independent press," it was imperative for writers to get it right. This condescending line of argumentation could be interpreted as an attempt to bully the press into seeing things the government's way, but it also reflected the deep concern among propagandists about the constraints upon their own authority.[28]

In an article that appeared in *Public Opinion Quarterly* in 1943, OWI Deputy Director A. H. Feller worried that the "multitude of voices" available in a "free press" could translate into a "serious confusion of the public mind." It was the job of the OWI, then, to eliminate as much "confusion" as possible by making the government's public message as consistent as possible. Feller did insist that the "government will not and cannot tell the press what to print," and OWI officials resisted the temptation to publish a "government column" in newspapers or even a "government newsletter" suggesting which stories the press should run. As Elmer Davis pointed out, Washington correspondents would undoubtedly view both measures as "infringements on their prerogatives." Instead, OWI officials preferred to work more or less closely with top-level executives from radio, newspapers, magazines, motion pictures, and publishing.[29]

The details of these relationships varied from industry to industry. In Hollywood, for instance, the OWI had only limited influence, despite the importance of the medium. Elmer Davis called it "one of the most potent instruments [for creating] the sort of a post-war world we seek," while George Barnes of the OWI's Motion Picture Division described movies as "second only to food [for raising the] morale of peoples whose country we occupy." Realistically, the OWI had the resources to make short, informational films, but the prohibitive cost of producing full-scale features left the government dependent on Hollywood. In the end, this dependence did not present a major problem, since the Hollywood studios—staffed largely with vigorous advocates of internationalism and U.S. intervention in World War II—generally backed the government's position with very little prodding.[30] Furthermore, OWI officials worked closely with the motion picture industry's War Activities Committee to make nonbinding recommendations on the scripts for some feature films. They also collaborated with industry executives on the distribution of newsreels, shorts, and feature films throughout the world for propaganda purposes. In this case, the OWI received a fair degree of autonomy over what went where. As Elmer Davis told Congress, Hollywood "knows how to make motion pictures, but does not always understand the impact of those pictures."[31]

In dealing with the radio industry, the OWI found that it had to assume control of an entire genre of mass communications technology. Unlike motion pictures, the overseas market for radio had not developed sufficiently to make shortwave broadcasting a profitable venture for the commercial radio corporations. In early 1942, the OWI virtually took over U.S. overseas broadcasting, at first by leasing transmitters from the major corporations and later by developing its own. This was not the preferred strategy, to be sure, but there were few alternatives. Even that aggressive measure gave the Voice of America access to a "skimpy fourteen transmitters," as compared to the sixty-plus the Axis powers were rumored to have. As late as 1944, the OWI still complained of the "staggering...mechanical problems of bringing the Voice of America to the continent of Europe," namely the twin forces of technological inconsistency (the Northern Lights, sunspots, electrical storms, the time of day, and the seasons all interfered with broadcasts) and enemy jamming ("developed to a fine point").[32]

The evolving technology of "radiophoto" presented an interesting example of the complicated public-private partnership between the government and the radio industry. A process whereby photographs and other graphic images could be sent around the world via wireless transmitters, radiophoto was so underdeveloped that commercial broadcasters could not begin to meet the OWI's demands. Although the technology dated back to the 1920s, picture quality still varied greatly, depending on the time and wavelength of the particular transmissions. The best way to ensure optimum quality would have been for the Federal Communications Commission (FCC) to assign several exclusive frequencies to transmitters either owned or rented by the OWI for radiophoto purposes. But the FCC was reluctant to undertake such a measure since it would have put the OWI into direct competition with commercial broadcasters who offered the same services, such as the Radio Corporation of America (RCA) and Press Wireless.[33]

Fearing criticism for encroaching on private media outlets, the OWI negotiated contracts with the leading companies to broadcast its materials, even though doing so often meant that the government received less than ideal times and wavelengths, thereby reducing the quality. Furthermore, by supplying these businesses with government equipment and personnel in order to produce the broadcasts, the OWI feared it had, in effect, "subsidized communications companies in a radiophoto venture." Its officials worried about "the potential embarrassment and paternalistic attitude" of such a move, not to mention the "uneconomical" decision to subsidize radio companies that did not reciprocate with reduced rates. The government, in this case, worked so hard to "avoid identifying the OWI as a communicating agency" that it risked going too far toward "the opposite extreme." But, given the general preference for free-market solutions in Congress and the press, the OWI could not afford to be perceived as interfering with private enterprise in any way.[34]

In the more traditional forms of print media, the public-private partnership functioned with greater congruity, largely because of the small degree of overlap in the objectives of each side. The government's interests lay mostly in the publication of informational pamphlets and graphics, which private companies could not have produced profitably. Federal officials did see the benefits of a book distribution program in certain select areas, but they had no interest in becoming a large-scale book publisher. Consequently, a liaison of mutual convenience emerged in which the OWI produced its own informational pamphlets for distribution at home and abroad and contracted with major publishers to provide the books used for overseas propaganda purposes. Believing that books, too, could be "weapons" in the war of ideas, OWI officials set up a "Book Section" to function in the same sort of advisory capacity as their liaison with Hollywood.[35]

Seeking a "voluntary collaboration between government and private enterprise in which the services of the latter can be put to the government's use," OWI officials looked to hybrid associations such as the Book Publishers Bureau. Headquartered on Fifth Avenue in Manhattan, the Book Publishers Bureau brought together representatives from a large number of commercial and university presses to address industry issues. In exchange for OWI data on "the kind of books most needed in various countries," book publishers agreed to make the "U.S. book as freely available in other countries as those of any other foreign supplier." Under the terms of these agreements, groups such as the Book Publishers Bureau received data that amounted to, in effect, a marketing survey of potential consumption patterns in foreign countries. In return, the government received some input on what was sent where, in some cases even "discouraging certain deals." This input never amounted to anything "resembling censorship or police powers," but, in the words of one assessment, the "relationship between the interests of government and the interests of private enterprise...is obvious."[36]

The OWI book program dovetailed nicely with the system of overseas libraries then being developed by the State Department; in both cases, the methodologies developed during World War II would shape the way the government utilized books as a tool in public diplomacy for years to come. The guiding philosophy behind the OWI book program was to maximize opportunities for "other peoples...to become familiar with the purposes, ideals and consequences of our culture."[37] U.S. policymakers minced no words in addressing the potential long-term significance of these methodologies. Like their colleagues in the Cultural Division at the State Department, OWI officials assumed that they were paving the way for future efforts to capitalize on the power of American culture for extending American hegemony in the postwar world. In the words of S. T. Williamson, head of the OWI's Bureau of Overseas Publications, "if, as seems likely, the U.S.A. steps out and this time takes its rightful place in [the] world, American magazines, films, books, etc., are going to be in greater demand than ever."[38] Assuming, in other words, that the United States did not succumb to the sort of political contraction that followed the previous war, policymakers had to be prepared to make use of American ideas and ideologies to advance foreign policy objectives.

Advertising America

In thinking about how to sell a particular vision of "America" at home and abroad, U.S. propagandists turned repeatedly to the techniques of American advertisers. Conceptualizing propaganda as a form of advertising was nothing new; twenty years earlier, George Creel titled his memoir on the work of the CPI, *How We Advertised America*. By World War II, though, this connection had become far more explicit and far better theorized, in part because of the incredible growth of the advertising industry during the interwar period.[39] During the "Roaring Twenties," the industry developed ever-more sophisticated methods for measuring people's wants, needs, and desires—a practice that would become known as public opinion polling when adopted by politicians during the 1930s.[40] U.S. policymakers were also acutely aware that, while the United States might possess the most formidable advertising machinery in the world, it certainly did not have a monopoly. In fact, OWI officials noted that Adolf Hitler's propaganda minister, Josef Goebbels, modeled his operation on "American methods of advertising salesmanship." Yet, while enemy propagandists might absorb American advertising techniques through osmosis, U.S. officials had the luxury of being able to go straight to the source.[41]

Shortly after Pearl Harbor, U.S. propagandists moved to formalize the government's relationship to the advertising industry by reaching out to an organization that billed itself as the War Advertising Council. Composed of the owners and principal figures of magazines, newspapers, radio, and the major national advertising agencies, the War Advertising Council was headed by Chester J. LaRoche, the chairman of Young & Rubicam, the nation's second largest advertising agency. "The United States has at its command the most powerful information mechanism that exists anywhere in the world," LaRoche told Congress in 1943. What it lacked, though, was the sort of central coordination that could give the United States "a weapon of war that makes insignificant anything the enemy has to offer." This was where the War Advertising Council came in. Over the next several years, it provided the liaison between the government and private industry, giving policymakers easy access to top-notch advice on how to sell "America" to the world.[42]

Early on, the OWI added to the board of its Surveys Division two of the country's best-known pollsters, Elmo Roper and former Young & Rubicam executive, George Gallup, who used the techniques he developed on Madison Avenue to become the most famous political pollster of all time.[43] For the OWI leadership, the decision to implement advertising methodologies made perfect sense. As one OWI position paper concluded, "business concerns would not spend hundreds of thousands of dollars a year on marketing research studies if the results obtained from samplings of the public were not trustworthy." If the goal was to understand the beliefs and opinions of various interest groups, "top-flight advertising men know more about the people than they know about themselves," LaRoche claimed. Elmer Davis adapted this line of argument for his appropriations request to Congress, noting in 1942 that the entire budget for the Domestic Branch—about nine million dollars—was "not much more than half as much money as a single American company has spent annually to inform the American people about a single product."[44]

Advertising methodologies received their fullest application in the ambitious, worldwide effort that Robert Sherwood labeled "the Projection of America." Reflecting the slick packaging and catchy sloganeering one would expect from the collaboration with brilliant salespeople, the "Projection" campaign, begun in 1943, served as a catchall directive "to govern the production of all long range media." Sherwood's directive called for defining "central themes which are universal," such as "the overwhelming power and incontestable good faith of the U.S.A.," while remaining sensitive to the "special treatment" required in "certain areas"—a clear precursor to the style and objectives of Cold War propaganda.[45]

Believing that "sympathy, trust and friendliness will grow only through fuller knowledge and understanding," Sherwood insisted that the "projection" had to follow the conventions of the "strategy of truth," which of course had never precluded a little embellishment. He argued that America's propaganda should emphasize the strength of its institutions—its system of education, its culture, its social legislation, and its labor organizations. This was a "land of unlimited possibilities!"

He also emphasized the importance of conveying the nation's credentials for leading in the postwar world: the sheer diversity of its environment allowed the United States to "train troops to fight in the snowy
mountains of Norway, the desert of Africa, or the steaming jungles of
New Guinea."[46]

Gendered images figured prominently in the way Sherwood sought
to "project" the nation's leadership credentials. Surely, foreigners would
want to know as much as possible about "what our kitchens look like"
and "the place of the American woman in war and in peace." Sherwood
worried about widespread perceptions of a sort of "Hollywood America,"
replete with "glamour girls and gangsters." Axis propaganda used such
images, in Sherwood's view, to show "that we are effete." He argued
that, in response, American propaganda should focus on the "hardi-
ness" of the American people to make clear that although "we do not
start fights... we have a habit of finishing them."[47]

One of the most delicate issues in "projecting America" involved
broadcasts to European colonial territories. These messages required
U.S. policymakers to balance their global ambitions with their need
for European alliances, stretching the "strategy of truth" to tell different stories in different places. U.S. propagandists frankly could not
describe America's alliance with Great Britain the same way in India—
where vibrant anticolonial sentiments were brewing—as they did in
Canada or the United States. The problem, as Elmer Davis ruefully
conceded after the war, was that "the selection and emphasis of news
sent to a particular country at a particular time was often determined
by the need to support specific military or political objectives. But any
news published in the United States could, by one means or another,
readily reach foreign countries; and sometimes the task of selection and
emphasis was rendered very difficult thereby." Archibald MacLeish was
right: "boundaries [were] hard to draw."[48]

Another tricky issue was the pressure from the State Department
to toe the line on official U.S. policy, without regard to what OWI
officials might view as the broader long-term interests of the United
States. In the British West Indies, for example, the State Department
demanded that Voice of America broadcasts clearly convey that the
United States was "not interested at all in any change of sovereignty."
At the same time, Davis suggested to Sherwood, the OWI should not

miss the opportunity presented by the fact that U.S. broadcasts seemed "to be more trusted by the natives than . . . the BBC."[49]

The same general problem plagued the OWI response to the British crackdown on Mahatma Gandhi's Quit India Movement in late 1942. Although the British violated the rights of over 100,000 protesters who were arrested along with Gandhi and future Prime Minister Jawaharlal Nehru, MacLeish acceded to the wishes of the State Department and allowed excerpts from speeches by the British Ambassador, Lord Halifax, to stand as the OWI interpretation of the crisis. OWI press releases quoted Halifax to the effect that "we do not regard the Colonies as possessions." They also passed along, unchallenged, his statement that the Indian situation could not be reduced to the "terms of one people struggling to be free and of another people struggling to keep them down." MacLeish and his colleagues struggled to find ways to express "sympathy with the long-range aspirations of the Indian people," but more often than not short-term expediency trumped long-range aspirations. In the end, even the idealistic MacLeish grudgingly accepted the official position. Since "any real opportunity for Indian freedom" hinged on defeating the Axis, the United States had to focus "solely at this time . . . [on] measures which contribute to anti-Axis victories."[50]

The American Century and the American Dilemma

European alliances certainly complicated the position of the United States in the colonial world, but nowhere near as much as the nation's woeful record of racism. For OWI officials, the long-standing and well-known discrimination and violence against African Americans soon became the proverbial elephant in the room. Jim Crow quickly turned into a propaganda nightmare on several different levels, as reflected in the early planning sessions that deemed the "Negro Problem" an "urgent project." German and Japanese propagandists relentlessly hammered away at the hypocrisy of American democracy—aided, in effect, by the American press, which provided the raw data on the tortured story of race in the United States.[51]

At first, questions of domestic unity and morale—would African Americans fight for a nation that treated them as second-class citizens?— took precedence. On some level, OWI officials surely worried that there might be some truth to Josef Goebbels's 1933 pronouncement that "nothing will be easier than to produce a bloody revolution in North America. No other country has so many social and racial tensions." MacLeish himself called for an analysis of "the degree to which Nazi propaganda, and even more Japanese propaganda, was having its effect on the attitude of the Negroes toward the war." The emphasis upon Japanese propaganda reflected what was by then a well-known fact: the Japanese proclaimed themselves the worldwide "champion of the darker races" by advertising their empire-building conquests in China, Vietnam, Korea, and elsewhere as a fight to expel centuries of Western, white colonial rule. As MacLeish warned Roosevelt, "the intensive Tokyo propaganda that Japan is fighting for the cause of all races against the white race...has had some effect on the Chinese; it has had more effect on the Filipinos, Malaysians, and the peoples of India. It even reaches, as you doubtless know, our own Negroes."[52]

Propagandists soon realized, though, that the damage American racism did to the nation's image in the world posed a far greater problem than the imagined crisis of loyalty among African Americans, who had always fought for the United States despite the treatment they received in return. Addressing the image problem created a real dilemma for OWI officials. As Elmer Davis suggested in a letter to FDR, the United States could only counteract Japanese claims "that this is a racial war...if our deeds permit us to tell the truth." MacLeish went even further, declaring in late 1942 that "no agency of the United States Government can be in the position of positively signifying acceptance of the principle of racial segregation." However persuasive their point, the fact remained that the OWI made propaganda, not laws.[53]

Some OWI officials pushed the agency to do more. Theodore M. Berry, a lawyer from Cincinnati who advised the OWI on racial matters, complained that "any program which attempts to improve Negro morale within the framework of the status quo...will be palliative, wasteful and ineffective." Noting that "the problems of Negro morale are inherent within the social and racial concepts of the nation," Berry advised the government to put pressure on industries and organizations to eliminate segregation and discrimination. Berry's activist stance did not go unchallenged. His colleagues George Barnes and Milton Starr shot back that "a direct and powerful Negro propaganda effort" did not necessarily equal "a crusade for Negro rights." Barnes even tried to convince Gardner Cowles, who ran the Domestic Branch, that "we are an information agency and not the bearer of the black man's burden."[54]

Starr and Barnes were obviously indifferent, at best, to the general cause of racial equality, but they were right that the Roosevelt administration faced a genuine political dilemma in dealing with domestic racism. It would either take a hit from enemy propagandists, who relished pointing out instances of discrimination in the United States, or from one of its key constituencies—southern Democrats—who would not simply stand by and allow the Executive Branch to speak out against Jim Crow. As Starr pointed out in his debate with Berry, the Roosevelt administration derived its "strength largely from an unusual coalition of the reactionary south and liberal elements of other sections," meaning that the "loss of southern political support would be serious." It would not be the last time that federal officials confronted that difficult political equation.[55]

In the end, the OWI leadership tried to split the difference. Publicly, the agency avoided any criticism of racism and Jim Crow. It stuck to feel-good stories about African Americans and other racial minorities, which were intended to ameliorate tensions and improve morale on all sides. Robert Sherwood's critical memo on "the projection of America" provides an excellent example of the OWI's approach to this thorny issue. Sherwood suggested that OWI propaganda should try to finesse the issue of American racism by exploiting the racist assumptions of Nazi propaganda. Ignoring the charges of American hypocrisy, Sherwood seized instead on Nazi characterizations of the American people as a "hybrid race." Here was a discussion of race in America that OWI officials might be able to play to their advantage. Rather than refuting the proposition that Americans were a "hybrid race," Sherwood embraced it. He argued that U.S. propagandists should emphasize that "our sympathies are universal because we are ourselves composed of many racial and national strains...and we are proud of it." How better to convince people of "other countries that this really is a people's war and that we are not fighting merely to reestablish the old order?" To suggest that propagandists might actually capitalize upon the nation's diversity certainly represented a novel strategy, although it turned out to be a tough sell both at home and abroad.[56]

Behind closed doors, OWI officials did a bit more than dispense innocuous bromides. They used what little influence they had to try to persuade the Roosevelt administration to take actions that might, at best, improve the image problem and, at worst, stop exacerbating it. Along these lines, Associate Director Milton Eisenhower pushed Assistant Secretary of War John J. McCloy to reconsider the military's exclusion of Japanese Americans from the draft. Elmer Davis wrote to the President to make the same point and to lobby against a congressional bill that, in flagrant violation of the Constitution, proposed to deprive *Nisei* (the children of Japanese immigrants, born in the United States) of citizenship. Around the same time, Gardner Cowles contacted senators in hopes of convincing Congress to repeal the Chinese Exclusion Acts, arguing that this "would be enormously to our advantage as a refutation of Japan's claim that we are fighting a racial war." When the State Department's Far Eastern Division released a memo concluding that "one of the important aspects of our war with Japan is that it *is* racial," Davis fired off an angry letter to the head of that division, Joseph Grew, a man who was infamous for his racist diatribes against the Japanese. Stressing "the unusual opportunity which the United States possesses in its citizens of foreign origin," Davis reminded Grew that such racism prevented the United States from taking advantage of Americans' "knowledge of the languages, customs, and aspirations" of other cultures and nations, which "no post-war planning can afford to overlook."[57]

In their concern with the image the United States projected to the world, OWI officials often saw foreign policy issues in a different light from their colleagues in the State Department—a tension set in sharp relief by the way each group responded to stories of racial discrimination and violence in the United States. During the war, State Department officials generally dismissed protests against Jim Crow and its trappings as "a domestic question" that "does not come within the jurisdiction of this Department." OWI policymakers, in contrast, immediately sensed the explosive power these charges would carry when juxtaposed with plans for postwar American hegemony.[58] In the words of one especially frank memo: "From an international viewpoint, it will be difficult for the United States to maintain the color barriers in this country and lead yellow Asia and black, white and brown South America."[59]

OWI officials were the first U.S. policymakers to grapple with the corrosive effect of domestic racism on America's image in the world precisely because they were the first group to systematically address image as a foreign policy matter. They certainly would have understood, probably better than anyone else in the Roosevelt administration, why Louis Armstrong would later tour the world on behalf of the State Department; why, during the Cold War, federal officials repeatedly felt the need to tout the nation's progress towards racial equality (despite the backlash it provoked from diehard segregationists); and why successive presidential administrations would rally ever-so-cautiously behind the efforts of civil rights activists to topple Jim Crow.[60] The equation, really, was quite simple. Image would be the key to the ability of the United States to extend its influence in the postwar period while avoiding the costs of territorial colonialism. In this context, racial discrimination in the United States was more than an embarrassment; it was a fundamental threat to the promise of the American Century.

"A Philosophy That Is Alien to Us"

Standing at the juncture of transformations in U.S. foreign policy, domestic politics, colonialism, mass communications, and ideological warfare, OWI officials were frequently ahead of the curve in conceptualizing the nature of the postwar world and the demands it would place on U.S. foreign policy. This was often a difficult position to be in. Beginning in 1943, OWI officials confronted a series of challenges that undermined their entire operation and, for a time, threatened its existence. Still unsure of their own arguments and their position within the government bureaucracy, they often failed to respond effectively to their critics. They were not solely to blame, however. Many of their problems stemmed not from their own missteps but from the nature of their work, making these episodes especially important for understanding the dilemmas inherent to the practice of public diplomacy.

The divisions that brought the OWI to its knees in 1943 began from within. Although the agency ultimately faced abundant criticism from politicians, pundits, and even their own colleagues in the Roosevelt administration, the exodus of some of the OWI's own personnel served as the first harbinger of trouble. In January 1943, Archibald MacLeish returned to full-time service at the Library of Congress after complaining to Elmer Davis that he felt marginalized in the decision-making process. His departure followed an internal debate over the essence of a government propaganda agency: Should propagandists make policy or should they serve as nothing more than a highly sophisticated megaphone for the real policymakers?

The disagreement between MacLeish and several of his colleagues had both a practical and a philosophical component. MacLeish and other liberal intellectuals within the agency had strong views on many foreign and domestic policy issues and they wanted a vehicle to convey those views, which they believed would strengthen the war effort. Yet if the OWI was to function in this capacity, propagandists would encroach upon the territory of other government agencies. The way that the OWI spoke about, say, the wartime alliance with Great Britain or the Soviet Union would inevitably affect the work of the State Department. At the same time, MacLeish saw no possible way that propagandists could do their job without making judgments about what messages the public, at home and abroad, needed to hear in order to buy into the U.S. mission. A pragmatist like MacLeish understood as well as anyone that words were deeds, and he often chafed at having to sell bad policy.

Some of the more cautious policymakers at the OWI worried that MacLeish's interpretation of their mission invited a backlash from other government agencies. In particular, Associate Director Milton Eisenhower insisted that "our job is to promote an understanding of policy, not to make policy." MacLeish countered that it would be pointless to have an information agency that served as nothing more than an "issuing mechanism for the government departments." Worried about the tenuous position of his fledgling organization within the government bureaucracy, Davis abandoned his earlier support for a broad vision and sided with Eisenhower; frustrated, MacLeish left shortly thereafter.[61] But the questions he raised did not vanish with his departure. Given the massive scope of the OWI's operations and the breadth of its technological resources, how could OWI officials possibly hope to coordinate their message precisely with that of the policymakers they purported to speak for? The broader issue at stake here was who should speak for the U.S. government.

Although significant internally, MacLeish's exodus generated little public controversy. The same cannot be said for the brouhaha that erupted over the abrupt resignation of fifteen members of the OWI Writers Branch in April 1943. Led by the Pulitzer Prize–winning biographer Henry Pringle and the promising young historian Arthur Schlesinger, Jr., the writers issued a public denunciation of the OWI leadership, criticizing their predilection for fancy "advertising techniques" over solid reporting. Moreover, the writers complained, the OWI censored data that shed an unfavorable light on any aspect of the war effort. They condemned in particular the decision by top officials in the Domestic Branch to edit a report the writers had produced on food production during wartime after Secretary of Agriculture Claude Wickard and James F. Byrnes, the director of Economic Stabilization, grumbled that the report was insufficiently optimistic. The Office of War Information, the writers charged, had become an "Office of War Ballyhoo" that prevented its employees from telling the "full truth."[62]

Most of the writers had worked for MacLeish at the OFF before following him to the OWI, and they undoubtedly shared some of his frustrations with the way the agency had evolved. But the claim that American propagandists had abandoned their onetime commitment to aggressive truth-telling oversimplified the situation. Even MacLeish understood that the "truth" was a highly malleable concept—more of a spectrum than a fixed point. While the writers undoubtedly expressed some pent-up frustration at how much they had been asked to push the boundaries of truth, in reality propagandists always molded the facts to suit an interpretation. The real questions were which interpretation to emphasize and, more to the point, who should decide. As with MacLeish's resignation, the writers' revolt pointed to larger questions over the true purpose of a government information agency within the overall bureaucratic framework.

As the OWI's internal divisions spilled out into the open, some began to worry that skeptics in Congress might see the signs of dissent as an invitation to pounce.[63] In the coming months, a series of embarrassing incidents showed that the writers' controversy was the least of the OWI's problems. Some of these quandaries might have been ameliorated with better management, but most of them exposed deeper fault lines intrinsic to the production of U.S. government propaganda.

By the summer of 1943, complaints began to pour in about the topics covered in some of the OWI's most popular publications. Critics attacked the agency for using taxpayer dollars to produce glossy leaflets extolling the virtues of the President and "New Dealism." Some even accused the OWI of functioning as an unofficial re-election committee for the President's fourth term. They angrily denounced reproductions of Vice President Henry Wallace's "Century of the Common Man" speech at Madison Square Garden and the fulsome booklet detailing "The Life of Franklin Roosevelt." OWI officials tried to defend themselves by pointing out that these pamphlets were produced by the Overseas Branch for distribution abroad in order to advertise American ideologies and the leaders of the American government to foreign audiences, not to stump for FDR. Congressman John Taber (R-NY), the most persistent critic of the OWI, nonetheless claimed that he had received reports of U.S. servicemen reading such material while stationed overseas.[64]

Materials targeting a domestic audience focused on more generic themes, such as unity, prosperity, and democracy, or on the role of individual interest groups in the war effort. Of course, the ostensibly nonpartisan nature of the materials put out by the Domestic Branch provoked just as much, if not more, outrage, most notably with the publication of "Negroes and the War." As the centerpiece of its strategy to reduce tensions through integrating the African-American experience into the national narrative, the Domestic Branch commissioned a lavishly illustrated, seventy-page pamphlet that appeared in early 1943. As an indication of how important the OWI considered the subject of domestic racism, the agency spent more money distributing "Negroes and the War" than any other wartime publication, with the exception of FDR's "personal message." The ostensible purpose was twofold: to show white Americans just how important black Americans were to the nation's past, present, and future, while simultaneously appealing to black Americans to support a fight for the sort of "democracy" that had largely meant subjugation, disfranchisement, and violence for them.[65]

Unsurprisingly, the OWI wound up pleasing no one. Black leaders objected to the patronizing and heavy-handed introduction, in which Chicago journalist Chandler Owen tried to make the case that a victory for Hitler meant a return to slavery for African Americans. They also found a predominantly visual product for African Americans condescending. Yet the criticisms from African Americans can only be characterized as gentle in comparison to the vitriolic reaction of several southern congressmen, who blasted the OWI for preaching "racial equality" and using the exigencies of war to "force upon the South a philosophy that is alien to us."[66]

Against the backdrop of the controversy over "Negroes and the War," the House Appropriations Committee voted in June 1943 to slash all funding for the Domestic Branch. Although the Overseas Branch consumed over three-fourths of the OWI's thirty-five million dollar budget, some legislators worried that they would be accused of harming the war effort if they went after the group that produced some of the propaganda that supported military operations. Ultimately, a less hostile Senate restored just enough funding to keep the Domestic Branch from going under entirely. From 1943 on, though, the OWI limped along, having avoided, as Elmer Davis later recalled, the "odium of having [Congress] put us out of business," even though it declined to authorize "enough to let us accomplish much."[67]

Sadly, the OWI destroyed its credibility with southern congressmen—from the party of Roosevelt, no less—with nothing to show for it. Racial discrimination was a problem that would only be solved through political and legal changes and a full-scale propaganda campaign, not through the distribution of milquetoast government brochures. Moreover, the attempt to rewrite the African-American story as one of participation and progress was far better suited to an overseas audience than to American citizens, who already knew the score. By pointing to the importance of addressing the overwhelmingly negative perceptions of American racism throughout the world the OWI might have defused some of the criticisms directed toward "Negroes and the War" and other such publications. Of course, hard-core segregationists likely would not have appreciated the distribution of these sorts of messages abroad any more than at home. Still, had OWI officials been able to articulate a global mandate for producing such materials on behalf of the United States, they would have been better able to defend themselves.

The third major crisis of 1943 managed to combine an intragovernmental squabble over who spoke for the United States; the question of whether the OWI made policy or simply reported on it; and the domestic political consequences of efforts to "project America" overseas. The problem began in July when the Fascist Party in Italy forced Benito Mussolini from power and the Italian king nominated Pietro Badoglio, a party stalwart and the infamous leader of the conquest of Ethiopia, to replace the deposed dictator. Based on previous policy directives, and with little coordination with State Department officials, Sherwood's chief lieutenants created overseas broadcasts for the Voice of America that treated a potential Badoglio administration with outright hostility. They quoted a *New York Post* columnist who blasted Badoglio as the "moronic little king who has stood behind Mussolini's shoulder for 21 years." Taking the attitude that "fascism is still in power in Italy," the OWI suggested on the air that the Allies would not rest until they eliminated all vestiges of fascism everywhere.[68]

The State Department immediately objected to the OWI directly contradicting official U.S. policy. FDR and Secretary of State Cordell Hull thought Badoglio substantially more likely than Mussolini to pull Italy out of the war and they were furious that a U.S. government agency had exposed their policy for what it was: a marriage of convenience with an antidemocratic leader. The next day, the president personally criticized the broadcast, stating that it did not represent government policy and had not been appropriately cleared with either Hull or Sherwood (although the latter had in fact given his consent). The OWI's enemies immediately pounced, citing the broadcast as yet another example of the agency's incompetence.[69]

This episode would hardly be worth remembering, if not for the critical issues it raised about the role of propaganda in U.S. foreign policy. Although most reports focused on the war of words between the State Department, the OWI, and the President, several contemporary commentators picked up on the larger implications of the conflict. War correspondent William Shirer actually defended the OWI in his weekly column on wartime propaganda. "Our propaganda is failing," Shirer said, "because our foreign policy—if you can call it that—is what it is." In his view, the President had abandoned the idealistic principles of the Atlantic Charter by cutting deals with dictators, and he could not see why U.S. propagandists should be expected to defend such policies.[70]

The *New York Times* columnist Arthur Krock, a frequent critic of FDR, took the opposite position, seizing on the issue as another opportunity to attack the administration's foreign policy as bumbling and confused. The OWI not only "manufactured 'public opinion,'" Krock said, it "recklessly launched its own 'foreign policy.'" On the first accusation, Krock had a point. The controversial broadcast quoted only commentators who were critical of Badoglio, suggesting that the "moronic little king" remark was a "typical unofficial reaction." The only U.S. policymaker cited was Cordell Hull, whose statement was taken out of context in order to suggest that the U.S. position on Italy was more uncompromising than it really was. Even more questionable was the use of a fictional "American political commentator" named "John Durfee" to dismiss the notion that Badoglio represented any improvement over Mussolini. As Krock rightly noted, these tactics raised serious questions about Sherwood's level of commitment to the "strategy of truth." However, Krock's other complaint, about the OWI creating its own "foreign policy," was more complicated than he recognized. He did not address the fact that every single time the OWI spoke for the United States it effectively made "foreign policy." If not *the* "Voice of America," it was certainly *a* "Voice of America." And if it was to function simply as a publicity machine for the State Department, then why not just turn the transmitters over to Cordell Hull?[71]

OWI officials understood this dilemma well. In the spring of 1943, *Public Opinion Quarterly* devoted an entire issue to the various activities of the OWI, with most of the articles written by agency staffers. A piece on the Overseas Branch, penned by one of Sherwood's deputy directors, Joseph Barnes, acknowledged the requirement that OWI messages "stay carefully inside the limit of official United States foreign policy." Barnes then vaguely noted that "to some critics, this has seemed an act of abdication in the field of psychological warfare." The obvious, but unstated, conclusion was that official State Department policy did not always make for good propaganda. This article was published several months before the Badoglio incident, yet the incident happened anyway. Clearly, MacLeish's departure had failed to resolve the question of who really made foreign policy. It also exposed the absurdity of running an overseas propaganda program outside the jurisdiction of the State Department, as though overseas broadcasts were separate from U.S. foreign policy.[72]

During the spring and summer of 1943, the attacks on the OWI in Congress and the media reached a fever pitch. Republicans teamed up with conservative Democrats to accuse the agency of having a staff riddled with "crackpots," "Communists," and "incompetents"; serving as a covert advertising agency for the Roosevelt administration; and advancing a liberal social agenda, especially for reaching out to African Americans in trying to promote domestic unity. Milton Starr had been right about the dangers of approaching the third rail of American politics, although he was wrong about the need, long term, for the federal government to at least pay lip service to civil rights for foreign policy purposes.[73]

While domestic politics surely played a role in the attacks on the OWI, some of the criticism stemmed from a deeper divide over the nature of U.S. foreign relations and the nation's role in the world. Ohio Senator Robert Taft, the noted Republican critic of American internationalism, spoke for many when he declared that "this nation can neither scare its enemies nor further its own war by talk."[74] The dismissive attitude of traditionalists like Taft toward the role of images and ideas in diplomatic and military affairs exposed a deep skepticism about the importance or even the existence of "soft power." Taft also expressed the concerns of isolationists, who correctly saw the OWI as a symbol of the nation's rapidly expanding role in global affairs. After all, why would the government care about the nation's image in the world unless it intended to engage the world?

The hostility toward the OWI also stemmed from a conservative distrust of government propaganda and government more generally. "America needs no Goebbels sitting in Washington to tell the press what to publish," Representative Joe Starnes (D-AL) declared.[75] Of course, people like Starnes were not just leery of the U.S. government having its own "Goebbels"; they were also concerned about who would play that role and what they would say. Representative John Lesinski (D-MI) neatly summed up these fears when he revealingly called for U.S. propagandists to be "American born, American educated, and American indoctrinated."[76]

These sorts of comments help to explain why the OWI generated so much hostility in such a short time. After accounting for traditional

suspicions of propaganda in a democratic society and the role of partisan politics in inflaming the rhetoric, the common thread connecting
all of these crises was a debate over how government propagandists
would portray the nation and its policies. This makes sense, for in order
to "project America" one first had to define "America"—an inherently
political exercise.

"Toward a New American Imperialism":The Final Days of the OWI

As the war wound down, the OWI faced a new series of complicated
questions relating to the future of its overseas propaganda operations.
Everyone understood that the Office of *War* Information would shut
down when the war ended. But would its work continue under new
auspices, or would it expire when the OWI closed up shop? At the
beginning of the war, the State Department made clear that it did not
regard propaganda as a foreign policy matter, but during the course of
the war it fully embraced the mission of shaping overseas perceptions
of the United States. It made sense that much of the OWI's Overseas
Branch would be transferred to the State Department after the war
concluded. During the final year of the war, OWI officials worked
doggedly to ensure that the work they had done would carry on in the
postwar world.

A committee on "Informational and Cultural Activities" set up in
January 1945 brought together representatives from both the OWI and
the State Department to facilitate the transition and to "insure that
any of OWI's experience which may have post-war implications should
not be wasted." The assumption, clearly expressed at the committee's
first meeting, was that "in the fields of cultural relations and public
information the end objective is to have the Department take over and
continue on a peacetime basis certain activities of the OWI."[77] Most
of the activities in question related to the OWI's extensive network of
facilities for mass communication, especially the Voice of America. The
major challenge was finding a way to maintain the communications
model developed by the OWI while tweaking the message to accommodate the transition from war-specific content to material that would
"project America in a broader sense."[78]

Back in 1943, when Robert Sherwood defined the "Projection of America" as the long-term strategic objective of OWI propaganda, the State Department had not yet been willing to embrace such a nakedly self-serving theme, but reservations of this sort rarely surfaced in postwar planning sessions in 1945. Despite a few uncomfortable questions about whether the "Projection of America" amounted to anything more than a crass attempt to "sell America," the vast majority of policymakers accepted, and indeed embraced, the idea that "making other peoples favorably disposed toward us" would "aid in the implementation of our national policies" and serve "our own interest." Put even more explicitly: "We are telling the rest of the world about the United States not because we want liking and admiration as ends in themselves, but because we realize that in order to work effectively and harmoniously with us in the creation of a lasting peace, other nations must understand us better than they have in the past."[79]

In the latter years of the war, the "Projection of America" turned into an explicit strategy to facilitate and mitigate fears of American hegemony. The United States needed, as one memo put it, "to counteract the growing feeling abroad that the U.S. is embarking on a period of commercial imperialism." Other officials unambiguously described the "Projection" campaign as part of the effort to fashion "a new American imperialism," which they contrasted with the more overt domination of the European empires.[80]

The OWI's long-range media strategy in the last year of the war makes clear that even after all the public rebukes, setbacks, and internal turmoil, many of the guiding strategic principles from the early days remained intact. These principles were then transferred to the State Department in 1945, along with a significant number of OWI programs and personnel. The presence of Archibald MacLeish at the State Department only reinforced the connection between the two entities. Much of the credit for facilitating this transition goes to MacLeish and the OWI officials themselves, for emphasizing the long-term as well as the short-term possibilities of their most important initiatives. For years, they had considered not only how a given initiative could help to win the war, but also how it could be extended into the postwar period.

Because of their commitment both to a comprehensive government information program and to American internationalism, broadly speaking, OWI officials were some of the earliest and staunchest advocates for transferring the bulk of their operation to the State Department after the war. "Preliminary discussions" between the two groups began in mid-1944. In September, OWI Director Elmer Davis encouraged the President to remember that the "OWI has built up a unique body of experience" that should not be overlooked in addressing the "question of how the story of America is to be told after the Overseas Branch of OWI retires." The stakes, Davis suggested, could not be higher: the nation's "overall influence for good in world affairs" depended upon its ability to get its "legitimate day-to-day story across to Latin Americans, Europeans, Africans and Asiatics in such a way that these people will continue to look to the United States for leadership and guidance."[81]

With reference to the Voice of America, Davis pointed out that, in general, "private enterprise" would not be able to "provide as many *types* of material, of at least equal *volume* and *quality*, to as many *places*, as are now provided by OWI." While acknowledging that, in theory, it might be preferable to have "these activities...completely free of the suspicion of 'official propaganda,'" Davis ultimately concluded that this was a case where the nation's interests could not be fully met through privatization. In short, "if ability to pay were the primary criterion, whole areas would be left without service of any kind."[82] At one point, Davis had questioned the "propriety of conducting propaganda warfare through the agency of the Government which is responsible for diplomatic relations and negotiations with other Governments." Now everyone seemed to accept that, for better or worse, the State Department was precisely the place for the production and distribution of overseas propaganda and information. The nature of modern U.S. foreign relations, which could not be reduced to "diplomatic relations and negotiations with other Governments," demanded it.[83]

Near the end of World War II, the OWI leadership summarized these arguments in a group memo to President Truman on the future of the federal information programs. As most wartime agencies were preparing to shutter their doors, OWI officials "emphatically" urged Truman to expand the government's "information service...to the rest of the world." "Never again," they declared, "should America as a nation let the telling of its official story be left to chance.... Never again should the nation...be satisfied with an unbalanced picture of America which must result if private telling in many media is left wholly unsupplemented."[84] Two weeks later, the President signed Executive Order 9608, which dissolved the OWI and transferred its functions, along with those of the Office of Inter-American Affairs, to the State Department. At the beginning of World War II, foreign policymakers did not regard overseas propaganda as important enough to their job to incorporate it into the State Department; four years later, the State Department adopted the functions of the Office of War Information even though there was no longer a war.

4

"Foreign Relations, Domestic Affairs"
The Consolidation of U.S. Public Diplomacy

U.S. OFFICIALS RECOGNIZED SOON after the war began that, for better or worse, the world as they knew it had ended. Stanford University historian turned State Department analyst Harley Notter captured this mood among policymakers well in his description of the attitudes expressed at the first meeting of the State Department's Committee on Postwar Foreign Policy, held barely six weeks after Pearl Harbor:

> The fluidity introduced into world affairs, by the revolutionary course of events in [the past two] decades, by the changing character of thought and action everywhere since the war had begun, and by the anticipation that this process of change would continue after the war, made necessary a thorough study of the entire emerging scene. The future of states as separate and sovereign entities and the character of their rights and relationships were unsettled. The position, nature, and number of great powers were in flux. Beliefs and desires of whole peoples and areas were being shaped anew.[1]

While the war obviously did not eliminate the sovereignty of nation states, it did transform the nature of the international system and reconfigure the number and alignment of great powers. Moreover, the resulting instability left U.S. officials searching for ways to shape the "changing character of thought and action everywhere." If "beliefs and desires of whole peoples and areas were being shaped anew," then it behooved the United States to ensure this process occurred in a way that advanced the objectives of U.S. foreign policy. This was the thinking behind President Truman's decision in August 1945 to combine the overseas information programs of the OWI with the State Department's existing programs in public information, cultural diplomacy, and educational exchanges. By unifying under one umbrella all of the government's initiatives for shaping the image of America in the world, U.S. officials formed the matrix of what is now called public diplomacy.[2]

Although the World War II experience convinced most U.S officials that they had to think of the nation's image in the world as a foreign policy issue, the onset of the Cold War significantly amplified concerns about foreign perceptions of the United States. Notwithstanding the relative geopolitical weakness of the Soviet Union, the potential appeal of international communism in the unstable postwar world posed a metaphysical threat to the precepts of the American Century. While the United States possessed, as historian Melvyn Leffler suggests, a "preponderance" of political, economic, and military power, U.S. officials going back to Woodrow Wilson believed that communism feasted on economic dislocation and political instability.[3] In the world of 1945, safeguarding the image of "America" became a political and economic imperative, not just a cultural issue; for the same tools of mass communication that propelled American ideologies into the furthest corners of the globe could be used to attack and undermine the American Century.

As much as the geopolitical threat of the Soviet Union did to expand the U.S. government's interest in information policy and the battle for "hearts and minds," the focus on America's image in the world would have existed with or without the Cold War. Public opinion specialist Ralph Block made this point clearly in 1948 when he said that U.S. public diplomacy "would not reduce its caloric content...to an amiable and comfortable library fireside glow" even if the "present international tension abated." In Block's view, the entire cultural and informational apparatus owed its existence not to the Soviet threat but to the fact that "the United States has a strong vital belief in the foundations of its existence which, even in a period of international equilibrium, it feels bound to propagate."[4] The ideological appeal of communism, in other words, emerged in the postwar period as merely the most potent, not the only, obstacle to the United States' emergence as an empire of ideas.

While the image of "America" helped to determine the environment in which policymakers operated, they only had so much control over that environment. Although some of the perceptions of the United States would come from the attitudes and actions of government officials through their policies and addresses, most would not. The nation's image—as the point of convergence between the domestic and the foreign—grew organically from the perceptions that people abroad formed about the attitudes and actions of people at home. Paradoxically, the nature of the American Century bequeathed extraordinary power to the policymakers who presided over the creation of the national security state, while simultaneously precipitating an astonishing dispersal of authority over foreign relations, more generally. Archibald MacLeish encapsulated this entire line of thinking when he declared at a State Department meeting in 1945 that "modern electric communications" had made "foreign relations domestic affairs."[5] MacLeish meant that mass communications had rendered foreign perceptions of "America" an integral component of the nation's relations with the external world, whether policymakers liked it or not. The Truman administration's decision to consolidate control over the practice of public diplomacy signaled a basic acceptance of this reality. Notably, the new public diplomacy shop at the State Department worked not only on "projecting America" outward, but it also developed an extensive apparatus for interacting with domestic audiences.

During the early years of the Cold War, a contentious running battle over public diplomacy exposed competing visions of the nation and its role in the world. Once again, discussions about "projecting America" led to fierce disagreements about whether to do so, how to do it, and what should be said. Perceived turning points, such as the landmark Smith-Mundt Act of 1948, turned out to matter less than some had hoped. Overall, the coming of the Cold War gave public diplomacy a specific mandate, but it did nothing to resolve the perpetual dilemmas inherent to the enterprise. Archibald MacLeish and Robert Sherwood might have left government service, but the debates they had presided over would continue.

The Wizard of Madison Avenue

To succeed MacLeish as Assistant Secretary of State for Public Affairs, President Truman and his new Secretary of State, James Byrnes, turned to forty-five year old William Benton, a brilliant, hard-driving former Madison Avenue marketer.[6] Benton had grown up in Minneapolis where his mother was a school superintendent and his father a Congregationalist minister and college professor. After graduating from Yale and winning a Rhodes scholarship to attend Oxford, Benton joined Chicago's Lord and Thomas advertising agency in 1927 as a copywriter. He soon built his reputation as an accounts manager rather than a creative genius. Benton made his biggest splash at Lord and Thomas when he convinced one of his clients to purchase "Amos and Andy," a popular radio minstrel routine, as a vehicle for advertising their struggling product. This arrangement proved so successful that it soon became the dominant sponsorship model for the fledgling radio industry. Widely regarded as a rising star in the profession, Benton left Lord and Thomas to start his own advertising firm with Chester Bowles, a future colleague in government service. Their firm, Benton and Bowles, flourished during the Depression by pioneering such techniques as the live studio audience, applause and laughter signs, and slickly produced commercial breaks that rendered obsolete the traditional method of a dryly read advertising monologue. By the time Benton left the industry in 1935, his company had become one of the country's top advertising firms.[7]

Wealthy beyond his wildest dreams and somewhat disillusioned with the corporate life, Benton decided to follow his parents into the educational profession. He had little trouble securing a position as the vice president of the University of Chicago. His work there, as the *New York Times* later described it, amounted to "advertising a university." During these years, Benton also found time to purchase two struggling businesses, the Muzak Corporation and the Encyclopedia Britannica, both of which he built into huge successes that netted him many millions more. He vastly expanded the audience for Muzak and he made the Encyclopedia more attractive to families and schools by adding numerous peripheral materials that increased its effectiveness as a study aid. He even turned over a substantial portion of the profits from the Encyclopedia to the University of Chicago endowment.[8]

Benton embodied everything the State Department hoped to bring together in 1945. He understood the world of education, he understood the power of mass communications for disseminating images and ideas, and he had actually helped to develop the use of radio as an advertising tool. He also had extensive experience with public opinion polls and survey data. Truman and Byrnes obviously hoped that Benton could sell "America" as he had so successfully sold so many other brands. But first he had to sell public diplomacy to a group of hostile legislators.

"A Radical Departure in the Methods of Conducting Our Foreign Relations"

In his initial appearance before Congress in October 1945, Benton gave a remarkable speech endorsing legislation to solidify a permanent place for the State Department's fledgling programs in public diplomacy. He addressed a skeptical crowd, many of whom viewed public diplomacy and its component parts as, at best, a new-fangled waste of time and money and, at worst, evidence of communist thinking. Throwing caution to the wind, he gave a passionate address explaining the importance of these initiatives to U.S. foreign policy in the postwar period. "There was a time," Benton said, "when foreign affairs were ruler-to-ruler relations"; even after "monarchies gave way to representative governments the relations often continued to be secret and private through ambassadors"; but, in the last twenty years, "the relations between nations ha[d] constantly been broadened to include not merely governments but also peoples." Echoing Robert Sherwood and Archibald MacLeish, he argued that policymakers simply could not, or at least should not, ignore the fact that "the peoples of the world are exercising an ever larger influence upon decisions of foreign policy."[9]

Benton's address constituted the opening salvo in a two-year struggle to convince Congress to pass legislation that would make the newly created Office of International Information and Cultural Affairs (OIC) a permanent component of the State Department structure. After the legislative battles over the OIC in the fall of 1945 proved far more intense than most could have imagined, nearly everyone recognized that, without formal congressional approval, the continued existence of the OIC would depend upon surviving the vicissitudes of the yearly appropriations process.[10]

Over the next several months, Benton attempted to drum up support on Capitol Hill for the OIC. He tried everything to convince Congress that "the United States Government—and specifically the State Department—cannot be indifferent to the ways in which our nation is portrayed in other countries." He stressed the "profound changes in the conduct of foreign relations in the Twentieth Century," the "broad base of mutual understanding which makes for world peace," and the possibility to "build a firmer foundation for our commerce." He even appealed to the fiscal responsibility of congressional conservatives, noting that the annual cost of his entire program would not "equal the cost of a battleship." But nothing worked, and the bill died in the Senate at the behest of Ohio's Robert Taft.[11]

Throughout this process, Benton and his colleagues endured the same alarmist rhetoric and demagogic denunciations of their work as their predecessors in the OWI, in many cases from the same people. In addition to the standard array of accusations about employing "radicals," several legislators offered specific critiques of both the theory and the practice of public diplomacy. Mike Mansfield, a young Democratic congressman from Montana, worried that the State Department would present a narrow vision of "America" to the world. As he put it, "you have to show them more than New York and Atlanta." Meanwhile, Republican Representative John Vorys of Ohio worried that exchanges of information would dilute the United States' comparative advantage—technologically, militarily, and economically. Georgia Democrat Eugene Cox, the powerful chair of the House Rules Committee, offered the most damning criticism of all: he accused Benton of trying to recreate the OWI within the State Department.[12]

Cox was not alone in comparing the State Department's new public diplomacy shop to the OWI. Many of the fiercest critics of the

OWI resurfaced to denounce Benton and his operation. They liked government propaganda during the Cold War no better than they had during World War II and simply recycled the same denunciations about the infiltration of foreign ideologies and the political orientation of the propagandists and their message. The congressional opponents of public diplomacy came from many different backgrounds and represented a variety of political factions. There were the unreconstructed southerners, like Cox and Leonard Allen (D-LA), who believed that Roosevelt and Truman had abandoned the authentic principles of the Democratic Party; the budget hawks—most notably Richard Wigglesworth (R-MA) and "Generous" John Taber (R-NY), the "fiscal vigilante," who once proposed reducing government expenditures by firing one million of the 2.2 million employees on the federal payroll; the midwestern provincials, such as Vorys and Karl Stefan (R-NE); and the zealous anticommunists like Senator Styles Bridges (R-MD), the "Gray Eminence of the Republican Party," who blasted Roosevelt and Truman for capitulation at Yalta and (later) in China. A pugnacious group, two of them gained notoriety for getting into fistfights on the floor of Congress. Collectively, they regarded America's corps of public diplomats as a hotbed of "pinks and punks" and "alien-minded radicals."[13]

What was it about public diplomacy that so infuriated them and consistently provoked such vituperation? Some of it, of course, might be explained by partisanship. Although public opinion polls showed strong support for funding government efforts to tell "America's story" to the world, Republicans could nevertheless castigate Truman's State Department for wasting money on a capricious extravagance, just the sort of idealistic project one would expect from the fancy-pants elitists at Foggy Bottom.[14] After World War II, this line of criticism conveniently buttressed Republican accusations that Democrats were "soft" on communism both overseas and within their own administration. Yet the incessant and bipartisan nature of these attacks—and the fact that the association of public diplomacy with "communistic" behavior predated the Cold War—suggests deeper motivations. That deeper hostility stemmed from what the House Appropriations Committee collectively labeled "a radical departure in the methods of conducting our foreign relations."[15]

As originally conceived by Archibald MacLeish, Robert Sherwood, William Benton, and others, the "radical departure" of U.S. public diplomacy was an attempt to respond to several "radical" transformations in the nature of U.S. foreign relations: first, the mobility of ideas and ideologies that posed a fundamental challenge to the authority of the nation state and its leaders in the international arena; second, the blurring of boundaries that made U.S. domestic affairs a tangible component of the nation's foreign relations; and, finally, the potential of international engagements to alter domestic structures.

Implicitly or explicitly, the critics of early public diplomacy invariably rejected these premises, or at least the clear implication of these premises. They did not necessarily dismiss the notion that perceptions of the United States mattered to U.S. foreign policy. While some scoffed at the notion that ideas could turn back the tide of communism, despite the nature of communism as an ideology, others acknowledged that the United States needed some sort of "public diplomacy." Yet all the critics agreed that they did not like either the message or the messengers from Truman's State Department. Beyond a political disagreement over how to advertise "America" to the world, they had a philosophical difference, resisting the conception of image as a mutually constructed, inherently contested, phenomenon.

Benton, following MacLeish, described the "voice of America" as a "voice with ten thousand tongues," but that raised the questions of which tongues, and what they would say. This was never clearer than at an appropriations hearing in March 1947 that became one of Benton's most frustrating moments at the State Department. Benton's critics grilled him from every conceivable angle. They first sparred over the efficacy of propaganda and cultural relations. Karl Stefan brought up the Truman Doctrine to argue that it would take tangible military and economic assistance, not "cultural and informational fanfare," to "halt the march of totalitarianism." Benton responded as an advertiser, pointing out that policies did not "speak for themselves" and that economic loans and gifts could be understood in many different ways.[16]

As so often happened in these hearings, Stefan scoured the list of materials the United States sent abroad and then, in testimony, zeroed in on the most sensational items. Most commonly, these exchanges focused on works by communists or alleged communists. Over time, policymakers got the message and removed any book, work of art, or other cultural artifact with any conceivable connection to a radical political agenda. So Stefan focused, instead, on Edmund Wilson's moderately racy *Memoirs of Hecate County*, which appeared on the list of books to be sent to U.S. libraries overseas. After dramatically asking all women to leave the room, he read several choice passages aloud.[17]

Stefan then flashed up slides of paintings from a well-reviewed, but highly abstract, show of modern art the State Department had put together for an international tour. "Mr. Benton, what is this?" Stefan barked out. "I can't tell you," Benton replied. Stefan continued: "I am putting it just about a foot from your eyes. Do you know what it is?" After Benton repeated that he would not even "hazard a guess of what that picture is," Stefan scolded him: "You paid $700 for it and you can't identify it." Stefan closed his examination of Benton by quoting from a letter he had solicited from one of his constituents, a mural painter from Shelby, Nebraska. The artist from Shelby called the exhibit the "product of a tight little group in New York," neither "sane" nor "American in spirit." When Stefan asked Benton whether the exhibit depicted "America as it is," Benton responded: "that was not the purpose of the art."[18]

Benton's rejoinder entirely missed the most important point. The State Department, playing its role in supplementing private cultural exchanges and conversations, put together an art show to counteract what policymakers perceived as the contemptuous attitude of foreigners toward American culture. In so doing, they emphasized certain aspects of American art (abstract expressionism), while largely ignoring others (folk art and mural painting). Benton and his staff made a calculated, strategic judgment about how best to capitalize on American culture to enhance the nation's image, but this was an inherently political activity, subject to endless debate about who should speak for America and what they should say. In this particular case, Stefan had the last word when the House voted to slash all funds for public diplomacy from the State Department budget.

This battle encapsulated a broader debate about the true purpose of public diplomacy. If America really was a "voice with ten thousand tongues," then there was only so much the government could do to shape the nation's image in the world, and its message had to be credible to be worth anything at all. If, on the other hand, images and ideas were merely weapons of (cold) war, then the point of government propaganda was to say whatever was necessary to defeat the enemy. As Representative Henry Cabot Lodge, Jr., (R-MA) suggested in a congressional hearing in 1947, "since you cannot broadcast all the facts, there is a matter of selection which arises." While conceding the advantage of trying to "make it a little more subtle than propaganda as some of the totalitarians have used it," Lodge saw no reason to try to be objective. Fight fire with fire, he concluded.[19]

These competing approaches to public diplomacy differed less in the importance they assigned to the nation's image in the world and more in the importance they assigned to the public's role in defining that image—a process that might be described as public participation in U.S. foreign relations.[20] Public participation, as interpreted by Benton and his predecessors, included "public opinion," but it was more than that. It referred to the full range of domestic activities that shaped perceptions of the United States abroad—anything with the potential to generate international headlines. The argument from public diplomats such as MacLeish and Benton was not so much that public participation was to be celebrated, although they were somewhat more sanguine about it than some of their colleagues, such as George Kennan, who saw American pluralism as a potential Achilles' heel in the ideological competition with the Soviet Union.[21] Rather, they insisted that public participation was a force to be reckoned with, a powerful constraint upon the way they constructed their message.

The nature of the American Century as an empire of ideas required policymakers to account for any aspect of American culture with the potential to enter global communication networks. In the end, the question was what made the best propaganda? In making such a judgment, public diplomats often found themselves discussing the United States in a way that many Americans found unpalatable. This might be because they chose to emphasize some of the "ten thousand tongues" while minimizing others; or it might simply be a matter of reporting unpopular truths so as to avoid outright lies that could be easily contradicted by readily available information.

The State Department and Public Opinion Studies

Acknowledging the role of public participation in U.S. foreign relations did not mean that public diplomats ignored methods for shaping American attitudes towards the major foreign policy questions of the day. On the contrary, the assumptions that initially drove the creation of public diplomacy—the idea that "the peoples of the world are exercising an ever larger influence upon decisions of foreign policy"—virtually demanded that policymakers take public opinion more seriously than they had in the past. It was within this context that the State Department's Office of Public Opinion Studies emerged.[22]

On August 31, 1945, when President Truman signed Executive Order 9608, which dissolved the OWI but transferred its overseas propaganda operations to the State Department, he made no mention of "domestic affairs." Politically speaking, this was a prudent decision; the President and his administration wanted nothing to do with the radioactive shell of the OWI's Domestic Branch. In explaining the decision to continue wartime propaganda programs during peacetime, Truman focused instead on the changing "nature of present day foreign relations," which "makes it essential for the United States to maintain informational activities abroad as an integral part of the conduct of our foreign affairs." He noted that the U.S. government would not attempt to compete with the private media, but that it must ensure that "other peoples receive a full and fair picture of American life and of the aims and policies of the United States Government."[23]

What Truman, Benton, and Byrnes did not admit was that the State Department had already essentially adopted many of the functions of the Domestic Branch of the OWI. In 1944, under Edward Stettinius, it established an Office of Public Information, which included the Office of Public Opinion Studies. An Office of Public Affairs and a Division of Public Liaison followed soon after. All of these operations then became part of the comprehensive approach to public diplomacy that emerged in early 1945. The chronology here is important: The techniques for surveying public opinion that MacLeish promoted at the OFF and the OWI made their way into the State Department in 1944; they grew in prominence, not surprisingly, when MacLeish joined the department the following year; and they became fully integrated under Benton, the advertising guru who understood public opinion surveys as well as anyone.

While domestic information activities have not typically been considered a component of public diplomacy, since diplomacy generally refers to actions in the international arena, Benton and his successors presided over a large operation for shaping domestic attitudes about foreign policy issues. The creation of this apparatus demonstrated that, from the State Department's perspective, domestic information campaigns were an essential part of public diplomacy. Indeed, in an internal assessment of the execution of Executive Order 9608, policymakers noted that the principles underlying the overseas information programs were basically "parallel with those now guiding the Department's domestic information programs."[24]

From the outset, the driving force behind the Office of Public Opinion Studies was H. Schuyler Foster, Jr., a former professor of political science at Ohio State University. As a scholar, he specialized in studies of the mass media, interest group politics, and propaganda.[25] In 1943, at age thirty-seven, Foster left academia for the State Department. During his twenty-two year tenure, his office authored tens of thousands of surveys (on a daily, weekly, and monthly basis) of American public opinion on every conceivable issue related to U.S. foreign policy and produced endless special reports on discrete topics, such as the United Nations, U.S.–Russian relations, and the Korean War.

Foster and his staff utilized an expansive concept of "public opinion" that went far beyond simply accumulating relevant polling data. Even when using polls, his reports typically compared responses to dozens of questions from several different polling firms before drawing conclusions.[26] More than anything else, Foster tended to rely on editorial opinion from newspapers, magazines, and opinion journals from around the country. As he later explained, "editorial discussions are inherently more capable of considering a foreign policy issue in depth than one or two polling questions," which gave him additional insight into the sources of opinion.[27]

The reports from the Office of Public Opinion Studies also paid considerable attention to domestic interest groups. On countless issues, from the UN Genocide Convention to the "Great Power Veto" in the Security Council, the Office recorded the position of dozens and dozens of organizations—from the American Civil Liberties Union to the American Veterans Committee, from Hadassah to the Polish-American Congress.[28] In other cases, Foster's office devoted entire studies to the attitudes of particular interest groups and to the organizations representing those groups. Various surveys examined the opinions of "patriotic" organizations, farmers' collectives, church groups, and business and manufacturing associations.

In a speech he gave in 1960, Foster explained why he approached public opinion studies in the way he did. Essentially, he channeled Archibald MacLeish:

> Indeed, we all now realize that any action taken by Americans in dealing even with their own local problems—without any foreign person present or directly involved—can be picked up and instantly reported around the world. With present-day means of communication this treatment may be accorded developments in any country; but it is of particular importance in the case of this Nation, which is the acknowledged champion of the people's rights and welfare in the settlement of world problems. Any news item which affects other countries' judgments about the United States may affect the capacity of our Nation to carry out its role of world leadership, to secure the cooperation and collaboration of other countries in carrying out programs designed to promote the peace, the prosperity, and the welfare of peoples throughout the world—including our own country.

Foster then listed all the other ways in which the public contributes to U.S. foreign relations in the broad sense: paying taxes (i.e., supporting foreign aid), military service, consumption and trade, private travel, and exchange programs. For him, all these considerations combined to shape perceptions of the United States; over none of them did the government exert complete, or even substantial, control.[29]

The dispersal of authority that Foster described highlights one of the central dilemmas public diplomats faced in establishing their place in the postwar foreign policy bureaucracy. On the one hand, it was their job to monitor and then manage public opinions—to shape public attitudes at home and abroad. On the other hand, they understood clearly how limited their authority in this realm really was. When people like MacLeish, Benton, and Foster spoke of the public participating in the foreign policy process they did so with an awareness that this only made their jobs harder. In a classic Catch-22 scenario, the role of the public in shaping foreign policy and foreign relations justified the need for public diplomacy while also making its practice immeasurably more difficult.

To Scare, or Not to Scare?

The increasing relevance of public participation to U.S. foreign relations sent a clear message to U.S. officials that the success of the American Century as an economic and an ideological project hinged upon building public support for the administration's strategic priorities at home as well as abroad. Increasingly, U.S. officials turned to the methods of propaganda to get people speaking their language. By 1947, that was the language of the Cold War.

During the first few months of that year, the ideological conflict with the Soviet Union escalated rapidly. In March, an already tense atmosphere at the Moscow Conference of Foreign Ministers turned downright hostile, as President Truman upstaged the meeting by giving a dramatic address to Congress on the future of Greece and Turkey. Since World War I, Britain had treated that region as its sphere of influence, providing substantial aid to the autocratic but friendly ruling parties in each country. With the empire crumbling and the mother country in severe financial straits, Clement Attlee's government informed the United States that it could no longer bear that burden. The Truman administration feared that, without British aid, one or both of the regimes might collapse, opening the door for a communist revolution. In a speech subsequently dubbed the "Truman Doctrine," the president made the case that for communism to prevail in these two places—one the gateway to Europe, the other the gateway to the Middle East—would directly threaten the national security of the United States. Furthermore, his pledge to help "free peoples maintain their free institutions" suggested that this new "doctrine" might have broader applicability. While he never specifically mentioned the Soviet Union, he made his target perfectly clear when he referred to the violation of the Yalta protocols in Eastern Europe.

Truman knew that he might well encounter resistance to the idea of involving the United States in another foreign crisis so soon after the end of the war, to say nothing of identifying as the new enemy a nation that had been valorized as a crucial ally less than two years before. The resounding

Republican victory in the 1946 midterm elections also raised a new obstacle, since both houses of Congress were in the hands of the opposition party. Senator Arthur Vandenberg, the Michigan Republican widely regarded as the leader of his party's "internationalist" wing on foreign affairs, reportedly warned Truman that he would have to "scare hell out of the country" in order to get Congress to pass the Greek/Turkish aid bill. Truman and his State Department decided to do just that.[30]

They had very little time to put something together. The United States found out in mid-February that Britain intended to cut off all aid on March 31. Undersecretary of State Dean Acheson hastily called a planning meeting for February 28, attended by representatives from the relevant geographical desks at the State Department, the legal and economic offices, and the Office of Public Affairs. They had to formulate not only the specifics of the assistance package but also a fully formed public relations strategy to accompany its announcement. Francis Russell, who had run the Office of Public Affairs since its inception three years earlier, took the lead in deciding how to sell the administration's proposal to Congress and the public. Acheson wanted "the matter ... put over forcefully." He noted the dilemma of crafting a statement that would be strong enough to convince the American people but not so strong as to completely torpedo Secretary of State George Marshall's efforts in Moscow. In the end, Acheson made it clear that, if he had to choose, he did not want to "weaken any statement ... to an extent that it would undermine the success of the request to Congress."[31]

Acheson also asked Russell to "prepare a statement about the general situation in the world." It would be the job of the public diplomat to frame the request for aid within the larger context of the emerging Cold War. Plotting strategy with his colleagues from Acheson's committee, Russell wondered how explicit he should be in framing U.S. intervention as a response to the Soviet Union. The representative from the Russian desk pointed out that there were ways of making the "situation perfectly clear without mentioning Russia." So Russell chose, instead, to develop the case that the United States had an obligation to come to the "assistance of free governments everywhere." He decided to push the theme of democracy versus autocracy, arguing that the "Greek situation furnishes us with [the] best possible occasion to tell [the] story that has to be told."[32]

Throughout the process, U.S. officials consciously emphasized the Greek side of the aid package, hoping to tap into a cultural identification with Greece as the birthplace of democracy. Of course, there was a fundamental problem with this line of argument, as everyone more or less acknowledged: it was a real stretch to describe the monarchy that ruled Greece as "democratic." Turkey, which had not held free elections since Ataturk established his nation's independence in the early 1920s, could hardly be characterized as such either. In the meeting to develop a PR strategy, Russell pointed out that many people would question the decision to "support the monarchy." John Jernegan from the Office of Near Eastern Affairs immediately started to outline potential rebuttals to this line of criticism. Greece was a "constitutional" monarchy, he said; the "whole political operation goes on underneath the king"; outside observers determined that the "plebiscite for the king...reflected popular will"; and, while "it is true that the government is corrupt...it is not basically fascist." Ultimately, Russell settled on, "the Greek government, like all governments, is not a perfect institution." There was also the matter of appearing to succeed the British as an imperial power in the region, which U.S. officials expected to become a prominent theme in communist propaganda. The best that Jernegan could recommend was to "avoid mention of the British as much as possible." Over the next two months, Truman and his top officials pushed these themes over and over.[33]

Some objected to the use of such an emotional appeal couched in idealistic principles of unlimited scope. The columnist Walter Lippmann, the most prominent critic on this issue, wrote a series of articles disparaging the administration for launching a "cold war" against the Soviet Union, which went a long way toward popularizing that term. One column, which compared the Truman Doctrine unfavorably with the Monroe Doctrine, sent Russell over the edge. He drafted a scathing three-page letter that accused Lippmann, essentially, of failing to do his homework in raising questions that the administration had already answered before Congress. But when he asked Acheson for permission to send it, he discovered that Acheson had already had a very "vigorous" discussion with Lippmann over his columns and did not want to further inflame the situation. In fact, Acheson and Lippmann had almost come to blows over this issue at a Washington dinner party a few nights before.[34]

Wary that Lippmann's critique might take hold, Russell carefully monitored public opinion toward the Greek-Turkish aid bill. The initial report, ten days after the president's speech, showed opinion roughly divided on the question of whether to extend aid. Over the next several months, people gradually came around to the administration's position. The bill ultimately passed in May 1947, receiving roughly three-fourths of the votes in both houses of Congress. By the end of the debate, a majority of the American people had come to accept the death of the wartime alliance, and they blamed Soviet mendacity for its demise. Precisely what role Russell's propaganda strategy played in that shift cannot be decisively determined, but his involvement represented the first time that the State Department called on the domestic wing of its public diplomacy shop to sell the politics of Cold War.[35]

Selling the Marshall Plan

The techniques that the State Department developed for selling the Truman Doctrine both helped and hindered the subsequent push for the thirteen-billion-dollar European Reconstruction Program (ERP), popularly known as the Marshall Plan. Without question, the President's decision to "scare hell" into the country considerably complicated his efforts to go back to the same well. By mid-1947, the widespread spirit of euphoria that accompanied the war's end had begun to fade. In the United States, partisan bickering about communist infiltration at home and Soviet advances abroad signaled a new political climate; overseas, some sniped about America's imperialist designs, while others, ironically, questioned its ultimate commitment to the rebuilding process. And now there was a genuine emergency on the horizon.

Internal State Department analyses made it clear that the European economy could not afford to wait for a more hospitable political environment in the United States. By mid-1947, after two years and nearly ten billion dollars in U.S. loans and grants, the European economy still remained perilously close to collapse. It was quite simply unable to sustain the level of productivity required either to purchase or to create the basic goods necessary to survival. With the harsh European winter fast approaching, the humanitarian toll upon many war-devastated countries threatened to escalate even further. If the future of the "free world" had not, perhaps, depended on propping up sclerotic anticommunist regimes in Greece and Turkey, the same could not be said for the collapse of the European market.[36]

In the end, the Marshall Plan owed its success to a highly effective domestic propaganda campaign.[37] Utilizing techniques developed in the push for the Truman Doctrine, policymakers worked in tandem with private interests to convince skeptics that, in the words of the plan's primary architect, George Kennan, "the principles on which modern European civilization [had] been founded" were in danger.[38] Without this effort, it is entirely possible that Congress would not have authorized what became the largest foreign aid package in the history of the United States.

The initial rollout for the ERP began with two high-profile speeches given in May and June 1947—the first by Dean Acheson in Cleveland, Mississippi; the second by Secretary of State George Marshall at Harvard University's commencement.[39] Both speeches were intentionally cautious, more in the style of a carefully argued legal brief than a slick public relations campaign. Marshall and Acheson sought to drum up support for another new aid package, this one over fifty times larger, while avoiding the polarizing response to the Truman Doctrine a few months before. Responding to Acheson's speech, Raymond Swing of ABC concluded that "the administration now sees the folly of the emotional selling campaign used to back the Greek-Turkish program."[40] Even within the Truman administration, there was growing skepticism about the tactics used to sell the Truman Doctrine. Robert Lovett, one of the charter members of the so-called "wise men" of the foreign policy establishment, admitted at a Council on Foreign Relations meeting in May 1947 that "the American people...have in some respects been treated as infantile; as though they are not sufficiently mature to warrant their possession of the facts about these obligations."[41]

During the summer of 1947, representatives of seventeen nations met in Paris to hammer out the details of the ERP. An important early decision involved whether or not to include the Soviet Union and its satellite states. Ultimately, U.S. leaders decided to "play it straight," as Kennan put it, and invite the Soviet Union to participate. However, they were counting on Stalin to reject the offer because of provisions relating to the pooling of resources, open accounting, and economic integration. This prediction proved correct: Stalin regarded the entire operation as an aggressive effort to seal off Western Europe from Soviet influence and he declined involvement and pressured Soviet satellites in Eastern Europe to do the same.[42]

With the participants and the terms set, attention returned to the United States, where the administration geared up for a massive information campaign in the fall. The first move was to name the program after George Marshall. Much like the "Monroe" Doctrine, which was actually designed by John Quincy Adams, the "Marshall" Plan largely belonged to George Kennan, but the "Kennan" plan would not have had the advantage of a built-in spokesman who was a genuine war hero. The media quickly and routinely began referring to the European Reconstruction Program as the Marshall Plan the day after Marshall's speech at Harvard.[43]

The branding effort was just the first piece of an elaborate public relations strategy. The tactics in the State Department's PR campaign, although not exclusive to public diplomacy, came straight out of the "public liaison" playbook put together over the past decade by MacLeish, Benton, and others. There were countless public speeches by prominent members of the administration; vast quantities of high-gloss, professional publicity materials; officials dispatched to seek endorsements from well-established national organizations and associations; private contacts with individual legislators and other opinion leaders; careful monitoring of public opinion on countless questions related to European reconstruction; articles commissioned and planted in major newspapers and magazines; and the formation of the Committee for the Marshall Plan, an ostensibly independent public pressure group whose letterhead boasted some of the most prominent names in the foreign policy establishment.[44]

Policymakers from the Office of Public Affairs planned and coordinated this whole operation. In September, they distributed a lengthy secret memo that laid out the contours of the information problem and a proposal for managing it. This report described public opinion on the Marshall Plan as favorable but "un-crystallized"—meaning that people could easily change their minds in response to the public debate. The overall goal was to make sure "the American people accept, however reluctantly, America's continuing involvement in world affairs."[45]

The memo then outlined a series of "information themes" designed to "crystallize" public opinion at home and to rebut foreign critiques. The message was as broad as the Marshall Plan itself: The United States, as an economic "giant," had a moral responsibility to the war-torn nations of Europe. At the same time, "the reconstruction of Europe" was an issue of "self-interest" because, without U.S. intervention, "Europe will probably cease to exist and be replaced by totalitarian states." Simply put, "an economically sound Europe...has always been necessary to our economic prosperity." One concern that often turned up in surveys was a nagging sense that European countries were not doing enough to "help themselves" and that Congress had not exercised enough oversight on how previous aid money was spent. This was a common dilemma with foreign aid. Attach too many strings and risk alienating the recipient; attach too few and invite relentless second-guessing at home over how the money was spent. So information specialists simply insisted that any future money spent on European reconstruction would receive the closest scrutiny both from the White House and Congress. Another theme countered accusations (Soviet and otherwise) that the Marshall Plan was an aggressive move toward American economic imperialism in Europe. This was a "peace offensive," they insisted, and "not militaristic, anti-communistic, or an infringement of national sovereignty." The real trick, of course, would be conveying these views to people at home and abroad.[46]

Throughout the debate, U.S. officials proved quite adept at getting the media to convey the administration's perspective on the European crisis. The media component of the PR campaign amounted to trading access for friendly coverage. In an excellent example of this dynamic in action, two officials from the Office of Public Affairs sought out and met with *Washington Post* publisher Philip Graham in August 1947. They discussed the possibility of devoting a special section of the *Post* to the deterioration of relations between Russia and the United States, "showing the development of the present situation that has led to the Marshall Plan." Graham promised to assign Ferdinand Kuhn, one of the paper's most prominent foreign affairs columnists, to put the section together. Kuhn also happened to be the former deputy director of the Overseas Branch of the OWI, so he could be counted on to make a strong case for the government's position.[47]

Not only did the *Post* publish the sixteen-page "special section" of pure, unadulterated propaganda on November 23, but Graham made Kuhn the paper's chief correspondent on ERP matters. This was a classic example of the revolving door of public-private service, and it illustrated the lasting effects of the World War II propaganda apparatus. Over the next six months, Kuhn, who had written about the Marshall Plan only twice up to that point, authored twenty-nine articles on the European crisis. Almost all of them pushed one of the State Department's talking points, from the desperate need for aid to the Cold War implications of withholding it; from the enthusiastic response in European countries to public promises that Congress and the administration would watch carefully over the expenditures. In a remarkable conflict of interest for a reporter, Kuhn also gave speeches to multiple domestic organizations on the importance of the Marshall Plan.[48]

The Committee for the Marshall Plan also provided a significant boost to the State Department's behind-the-scenes efforts. The Committee enlisted prominent policymakers and pundits to give speeches and pen articles for national publications, which were then printed and reprinted for nationwide distribution.[49] Dean Acheson, who had just stepped down from his first tenure at the State Department, played a particularly important role. Since the State Department and its officials were prohibited by law from formally lobbying for their own initiatives—a law Congress passed in response to the actions of the OWI—Acheson was simply invaluable. He worked tirelessly, giving presentations around the country and on Capitol Hill. As one of the original authors of the legislation, he could speak with greater authority than virtually anyone else.[50]

Alger Hiss, also recently of the State Department, wrote one of the more notable pieces authored by a member of the Committee. At that point still a respected member of the foreign policy community, Hiss produced a wonkish article for the *New York Times Magazine*, opining on the danger of abandoning European reconstruction and criticizing those who attacked the Marshall Plan for aiding "socialist" countries.[51] An even stronger statement came from the chair of the Committee, Henry Stimson, who had served as both a Secretary of State and a Secretary of War. Writing in *Foreign Affairs*, Stimson made a powerful argument against the idea that "the troubles of Europe and Asia are not 'other people's troubles.'" Utilizing the language of public diplomacy, Stimson concluded that "there are no mere 'foreigners,' no merely 'foreign' ideologies, no merely 'foreign' dangers, any more. Foreign affairs are now our most intimate domestic concern. All men, good or bad, are now our neighbors. All ideas dwell among us."[52]

As with the propaganda surrounding the Truman Doctrine, it is difficult to measure the net impact of this highly coordinated campaign. However, the Committee certainly laid one more brick in the wall of "elite" consensus. It did so through creating a public-private interest group—a tried-and-true method "uniquely and typically American," as Dean Acheson said.[53] After hearing impassioned pleas from leaders of countless national organizations, major newspapers, magazines, and radio stations, to say nothing of direct messages from current and former government officials, many Americans must have wondered how they could possibly oppose such an important piece of legislation. By the end of the year, the bill seemed likely to pass. Most of the remaining pockets of resistance evaporated after the communist coup in Czechoslovakia on February 25, 1948, which completed the descent of the Iron Curtain over Eastern Europe. After an overwhelming vote in Congress, President Truman signed the ERP into law on April 3, 1948.[54]

Defining the Enemy

The hard-hitting domestic campaigns for the Truman Doctrine and the Marshall Plan coincided with an increasingly aggressive tone in U.S. overseas propaganda. As early as January of 1947, a strategic guidance paper stated definitively that the Soviet Union had declared "psychological warfare" on the United States. Although the paper discouraged U.S. officials from returning fire, especially if that meant meeting the "Russians on terrain selected by them," calls for restraint clearly would not last for long. The memo predicted that Soviet messages touting the virtues of "socialism" and the benefits of a "planned economy...will carry a considerable appeal" in the war-torn countries of Europe. It also noted that the Soviet critique of "imperialism" would play well in "colonial areas." Overall, U.S. officials concluded that Soviet propaganda "is likely to have a considerable negative effectiveness in a world in which many people are going to be insecure and anxious."[55]

By the summer of 1947, these concerns had intensified. "The nature and scope of the current Soviet propaganda attack," one analyst complained, "must be considered a key factor in the determination of world opinion about the U.S. and its policies." If this was true, propagandists had "no alternative but to take direct and positive action to meet [Soviet criticisms]."[56] After all, if Europeans regarded the recently proposed Marshall Plan as an imperialist plot to take over the continent, as Soviet propaganda claimed, then the U.S. government might as well take thirteen billion dollars and light it on fire in the Capitol rotunda.

At the same time, public diplomats worried that responding to Soviet charges would give the impression that they had no message of their own. There was little evidence that people around the world lacked a clear conception of the United States and its values. But this fear—that the United States was not doing enough to explain what the country was for, rather than what it was against, and that it lacked a crisp, clean sales pitch to rival the appeal of communism—surfaced time and again in discussions of propaganda in the years to come. This was perhaps the product of being deeply committed to propagating American ideas, while also needing, paradoxically, to believe that the other side started the ideological war.

While U.S. officials fretted over the increasing efficacy of the Soviet propaganda message, Soviet Premier Josef Stalin grew more and more concerned about the European accolades for the Marshall Plan. Also troubling to Stalin, several of the Eastern Bloc countries initially showed an interest in participating before Stalin convinced them otherwise. In response, he announced the creation of the Communist Information Bureau (or Cominform) in September. The initial meeting of the Cominform brought together Communist Party leaders throughout Eastern Europe to forge a unified front against the West and to formulate an organized rebuttal to the Marshall Plan.[57]

News of the Cominform set off alarms inside the State Department, where fears of communist propaganda nullifying the enormous expenditures of the Truman Doctrine and the Marshall Plan reached a fever pitch. Policymakers recognized that the accusation that the United States was remaking the European economy in its own image had enough truth to convince enough people. As a result, both Congress and the White House started to take information policy much more seriously after the creation of the Cominform.[58]

In December 1947, the newly formed National Security Council issued NSC-4, which called for "strong, coordinated information measures to counter" the Soviet Union's "intensive propaganda campaign...to undermine the prestige of the US." NSC members focused in particular on the threat that Soviet propaganda posed to U.S. "economic aid to certain foreign countries, particularly in Europe." This was, they concluded, "one of the principal means by which the US has undertaken to defend its vital interests." Yet, the "nature and intent of this aid...is unknown to or misunderstood by large segments of the world's population. Inadequate employment of information measures is impairing the effectiveness of these undertakings."[59] To address these inadequacies, NSC-4 proposed a new interdepartmental committee composed of representatives from the State Department as well as the Army, Navy, Air Force, and the CIA. It awarded control over this group to the Assistant Secretary of State for Public Affairs. Ultimately, this measure failed to achieve its lofty goals, for largely the same reasons other efforts to force the U.S. government to speak with one voice also failed. But its status as one of the NSC's first directives signaled the importance of ideological elements in the emerging Cold War.[60]

By the end of 1947, U.S. policymakers had reached the conclusion that "merely to report the news factually, and to present objectively the policies and practice of the U.S., without reacting or referring to the charges brought to bear against us is no longer enough." Despite this rather startling disavowal of "objectivity," policymakers still insisted, as they had going back to the OWI, that "our strongest asset continues to be truth."[61] Propagandists had long understood that the "policies and practice" of the United States might not be interpreted abroad in the way that the U.S. government intended. Now they also had to worry about Soviet attacks that might exacerbate that problem. For the first time since the end of World War II, U.S. propaganda had a clearly identified external "enemy." Now, it needed a more coherent structure to wage ideological war.

"We Must Not Hide Freedom's Light Under a Bushel"

Against the backdrop of an escalating Cold War, Benton decided to take another shot at securing permanent legislation for the bulk of his programs. The embarrassment of having the funds for his entire operation slashed finally pushed him to seek a legislative patron to help him smooth over conservative objections to his approach. Republican Congressman Karl Mundt of South Dakota answered Benton's call. In May 1947, Mundt, along with his Senate colleague, New Jersey Republican H. Alexander Smith, introduced a bill to create a permanent program in public diplomacy. Karl Mundt was not the likeliest savior, but he was the timeliest. A fierce anticommunist and a staunch critic of the New Deal, Mundt came to the defense, essentially, of a series of initiatives that conservatives had associated with the quasi-communist tilt of Franklin Roosevelt's foreign policy. Mundt differed from many of his political compatriots, however, in that he saw the potential value of mass communications for U.S. foreign policy. A former college teacher, Mundt preached the need to spread democratic values "to bring added happiness to additional people in foreign places." The United States "must not hide freedom's light under a bushel," he said.[62]

Over the next several months, Benton and Mundt lobbied Congress relentlessly. They capitalized upon the emerging Cold War by playing up the mendacity of Soviet propaganda, thus reframing their arguments in the "realist" framework of "national security." The new Secretary of State, George Marshall, threw his weight behind the bill as well. Trading on his considerable reputation, Marshall testified before Congress about his experiences with Nazi propaganda during World War II and persuaded his friend, Dwight Eisenhower, to do so too. For Marshall and Eisenhower, the battlefield experience had convinced them that image was no ephemeral triviality.[63]

As Benton left the State Department in September 1947, the tide finally began to turn after several congressmen journeyed to Europe and the Middle East on a well-publicized fact-finding trip to examine the information programs on the ground. The American visitors described the situation in Europe as worse than they had imagined. In their eyes, misimpressions of the United States abounded, for which they blamed Soviet propaganda. They also now viewed the problem of image through the prism of the billions of dollars the U.S. government had pledged to Europe under the Truman Doctrine and the Marshall Plan. What if Europeans perceived these aid packages as part of an American plot to take control of the European market? After the trip, many of the most skeptical legislators finally accepted Benton's logic on at least one point: Policies did not speak for themselves.[64] In January 1948, two years of theoretical improvisation and institutional chaos came to an end when Congress passed Public Law 402, *The United States Informational and Educational Exchange Act of 1948*—typically known as the Smith-Mundt Act, in honor of its two sponsors.

The task of coordinating and implementing the huge catalog of jobs legislated to the State Department under the Smith-Mundt Act fell to George Venable Allen, who succeeded William Benton as Assistant Secretary for Public Affairs in January 1948. A career foreign service officer who had just returned from a stint as the U.S. ambassador to Iran, Allen differed from his predecessors in approaching foreign policy from the standpoint of a traditional diplomat. "The information program," he said in a speech given shortly after he took the job, "is but one of the implements we employ in our efforts to achieve our great foreign-policy objective. I would by no means claim that it is our most important implement." He also took a much harder line against communism—a stance colored, no doubt, by his participation in the first Cold War standoff during the fall of 1946 over the presence of Soviet troops in northern Iran. He left no doubt that he saw the Cold War as a "struggle between good and evil."[65]

Although Allen's appointment cemented the gradual shift in the strategy and tone of U.S. public diplomacy, even he continued to endorse the "strategy of truth" throughout his tenure. "What we are is more important than what we say we are," he stated definitively in a speech he gave at Mount Holyoke College in June 1948. Later in the same address, he ruminated on the ultimate failure of the Goebbels propaganda machine during World War II: "Why did they not succeed [long-term]" after devoting "more time and effort and money than any other nation to the

work of information?" The answer, Allen thought, was "relatively simple": "The Nazis...failed because they did not tell the truth" and "listeners marked it down as easily recognizable propaganda." From this,
Allen concluded, in an obvious rebuke to the State Department's pesky
critics in Congress, that "in our information activity, we must present
our civilization in its true color if we are to be effective. That color is
gray—not lily-white."[66] In the end, he believed in the basic assumption
behind the "strategy of truth": The better people understood the United
States the more they would like it. Information specialists just had to
make sure that the world received, to use Harry Truman's phrase, a "full
and fair" picture of the United States.

In emphasizing the importance of America's image in the world,
Allen also endorsed the fundamental premise behind public diplomacy,
as defined by MacLeish and Benton. In short, the information and
exchange programs represented "a new technique" for dealing with
profound changes in the global environment over the past decade or
so. "In the past," Allen said at a UNESCO conference in 1949, "two
peoples conducted their relations with each other...through a little
group of selected officials called diplomats." Now, the U.S. government tried "to penetrate into the living-room of every individual" in
every country where the United States had foreign policy interests. If it
was indeed, as Allen said, in the nation's interests to access foreigners'
"living rooms," then public diplomacy had to be viewed as a means of
stepping in "where old and traditional ways fall down."[67]

Getting to "Know North America"

George Allen and his colleagues clearly hoped that the Smith-Mundt
Act, a bill authored by two Republicans, would put an end to the
long-standing use of the information programs as a partisan battle-axe.
They did not get their wish. Almost before the ink dried on President
Truman's signature, yet another scandal broke out over the Voice of
America's overseas broadcasts. It featured all the same themes as similar
uproars in years past: somber calls for investigations, threats of funding
cuts, and defensive responses from beleaguered officials. Once again, the
whole episode stemmed from outrage over the way in which these broadcasts depicted the United States to foreign audiences. The only major

difference was the party responsible for producing the objectionable material in the first place.

The controversy began in March 1948, when a few congressmen got hold of several scripts for the "Know North America" series that NBC created and broadcast to Latin America on behalf of the State Department. Based on *Inside the U.S.A.* by John Gunther, who had collaborated with propagandists going back to the early days of the OWI, the scripts described in detail the culture of various regions in the United States. The goal was for *Latinoamericanos* to get to "know" their neighbor to the north a bit better. In fairness to the critics, many of the characterizations based on Gunther's book were inane and insulting to the United States. If anything, these programs reinforced the kinds of stereotypes that the State Department wanted to undermine.

Wyoming got hit particularly hard. An episode that recounted its wide-open frontier days dwelled upon its reputation as a "center of vice and corruption," in which major public officials were "outlaws." Then, the program cut to two imaginary tourists attending a public exhibition from this period: "Look!" one said to the other, "what magnificent Indian girls." "Feathered and naked!" his friend replied, "I wonder what they're going to do?" Other states did not fare much better. For Nevada: "In Las Vegas people get married, and in Reno, they get divorced." In Utah, Mormons supposedly confiscated 10 percent of the income of every person in the state. If anyone refused to pay, the church sent out "a little army called avenging angels...with convincing arguments...made of rubber or wood." Alabama was the "darkest" of states, the place where the "colored people suffered and struggled" more than anywhere else. Its largest city, Birmingham, was derided as a product of iron and steel and, "like those two metals, hard and poorly made." One throwaway line tarred two different regions with the suggestion that "New England was founded by hypocrisy and Texas...by sin." But the description of Colorado topped them all: Colorado had been hampered in its progress, apparently, because too much of the state's wealth was controlled by women and "the ladies are conservative and they don't wish to let go of what they have...like all women."[68]

Allen, Marshall, and Truman all claimed innocence, noting that the offending material came not from the State Department but from NBC. Although the Voice of America did spot checks of the material sent out by private networks on its behalf, it did not, officials said, have enough people on staff to read every episode word for word. Even so, Truman knew that this looked bad, coming so soon after the Smith-Mundt Act, and he ordered a thorough internal investigation. Not surprisingly, both houses of Congress launched their own inquiries. Congressional supporters of public diplomacy from both parties tried to help out by directing the investigations away from committees staffed with the programs' harshest critics. But with various legislators labeling the broadcasts "putrid" and "trash," and old foes like John Taber re-emerging to call for funding cuts, procedural abracadabra would not be enough.[69]

Collectively, the investigations revealed a story with several interesting aspects. The scripts, it turned out, were written by a fifty-two-year-old Venezuelan man named Rene Borgia, a writer and translator who had visited the United States off and on for over three decades. During the past six years, NBC had often hired him to write scripts for its overseas broadcasts on behalf of the State Department. He defended his work in various ways, first saying that he actually wanted to write "beautiful" scripts, but NBC representatives constantly demanded that he write in a different style. Clearly, the suits at NBC lacked "culture," Borgia told reporters. To satisfy his bosses, he tried to be funny, while also attempting to break down certain negative perceptions of the United States held by people south of the border. He also pointed out that most of the offending passages were direct quotes from Gunther's book, and critics took them out of context by omitting the responses that actually tried to rebut the stereotypes. An independent analysis by Neal Stanford of the *Christian Science Monitor* confirmed Borgia's claims on this point, but this explanation satisfied no one. In a reprise of the charges directed at the OWI, several members of the House blasted NBC for hiring an "alien" to describe the United States to foreign audiences. In fact, the final House report on the controversy included the astonishingly shortsighted demand that overseas broadcasts be prepared exclusively by American citizens.[70]

The administration reached strikingly different conclusions about the whole episode. With a "faint ironical smile," as the *New York Times* described it, President Truman reminded reporters that it was actually Congress that had demanded that the State Department farm out the Voice broadcasts to private companies whenever possible. Conservatives in Congress had long accused government propagandists of impinging upon private enterprise with their information activities. The Smith-Mundt Act made it very clear that the government should only distribute material in cases where private industry either would not or could not.[71] The "Know North America" controversy demonstrated that privatization might help to reduce the threat of government competition with private enterprise, but it offered no guidance on the deeper issue of what should be disseminated overseas on the government's behalf.

In his June postmortem for Truman, George Allen provided the most thoughtful analysis of what had transpired over the past three months. The "outstanding result of the investigations," Allen concluded, "has been that members of Congress now appear clearly to consider the Department fully responsible for close supervision of the private networks for any broadcasts paid for by public funds." This was an odd development—especially coming from the ersatz advocates of privatization—and not one that Allen was entirely comfortable with. What were the broader implications, he wondered? Did Congress really want the administration to censor material created by private companies? If many of the offending passages came directly from Gunther's book, did that mean that copies of *Inside the U.S.A.* should be removed from the State Department's overseas libraries? Or, worse yet, that someone should go through each copy and "excise the offensive passages"? Where did the government's censorship responsibilities end? Were they not headed toward "something very close to the totalitarian theories we oppose with all our energies"?[72]

Also troubling was the entirely predictable decision by NBC and its fellow networks to withdraw completely from overseas broadcasting. They were willing to lease their facilities to the State Department, but they wanted no part of political controversies of this sort. Ironically, Congress had generated the very outcome it originally hoped to prevent: turning overseas broadcasting into a government enterprise. In some ways, this made Allen's job easier, but he did not view it as a positive development overall. Broadcasts from NBC did not seem so much like propaganda, even when they were. With the Voice of America, by contrast, what U.S. officials gained in terms of control over the final product they lost in terms of authenticity. In the end, however, public diplomats found that they could not win for losing since they were responsible for the content no matter who produced it. Although the Smith-Mundt Act established a place for public diplomacy within the foreign policy bureaucracy, it did nothing to reduce the dilemmas inherent in trying to manage even the smallest slice of America's image abroad. Even in the relatively discrete realm of overseas radio broadcasting, the politics of "projecting America" remained as thorny as ever.[73]

"One Which Certainly Does Not Reflect Credit on This Country"

Public diplomats confronted an even trickier set of questions when dealing with Hollywood films. As OWI officials had discovered during World War II, motion pictures were, at once, the most influential medium for shaping perceptions of the United States and the least subject to government influence. Although propagandists had the resources to produce documentary shorts and other bare-bones informational pieces, they could not—and did not want to—compete with the lavish slices of Americana that came out of Hollywood. Nor did they generally control the distribution of those films abroad (although there were exceptions to this rule, such as Western Europe under the Marshall Plan).

To be sure, it was not as though Hollywood artists and executives routinely worked to undermine the Cold War. The infamous inquisition by the House Un-American Activities Committee, and the subsequent blacklisting of uncooperative witnesses, ensured strict adherence to the anticommunist orthodoxy of the political culture at large. Propagandists actually faced a much subtler problem. The Cold War, as an undeclared war with vague and open-ended objectives, offered no easy standard by which to evaluate motion pictures, no equivalent to the World War II standard of "will this picture help us win the war and defeat the Axis"? Beyond making communism look bad, what constituted victory in an ideological war?

In the State Department's examination of Hollywood films, the Cold War figured only tangentially. Most of the films that attracted policymakers' attention had nothing to do with foreign policy, as such. Since their job was to improve the nation's image abroad, policymakers cared primarily about the way that foreign audiences would understand American society through the movies. They fixated in particular on whether a given picture perpetuated or countered negative stereotypes of the United States. As an official in the State Department's Division of Motion Pictures put it, "many of the misconceptions which exist about us abroad, which our information program is trying to correct and eradicate, are caused by Hollywood-made films." Their task was to disrupt that trend as much as possible.[74]

There was no one theme that public diplomats singled out more than any other. During the late 1940s, films that raised red flags at various points included offerings as diverse as *Gentleman's Agreement*, *Grapes of Wrath*, *Fort Apache*, and *State of the Union*. Since each of these films posed a different sort of propaganda problem, a brief examination of how U.S. officials responded to them reveals much about how they approached Hollywood in general. *Gentleman's Agreement*, the memorable exposé of anti-Semitism in American high society, threatened to evoke memories of the Holocaust while drawing attention to the explosive subject of racism in the United States. *State of the Union*, a Frank Capra picture starring Katherine Hepburn and Spencer Tracy, told the story of an industrialist who decides to run for President only to run smack into extraordinary levels of corruption—sort of "Mr. Smith Goes to the White House." The concern was that this "sadly erroneous picture of the United States" would damage the credibility of the American presidency, "particularly in an election year." *Grapes of Wrath*, the John Ford classic based on the John Steinbeck novel, painted a harrowing portrait of the vicissitudes of capitalism through the prism of the Dust Bowl and the Great Depression. Aesthetically, it ranked as one of the greatest films ever made; thematically, it did not exactly offer a ringing endorsement of the American system, and U.S. officials worried that it would send the wrong message to places like Western Europe. *Fort Apache*, another John Ford film starring Henry Fonda, portrayed the U.S. Army in a very poor light. Fonda played a disgruntled Civil War colonel banished to a fort in Arizona, who decides to reclaim his lost glory by launching a mission to hunt down a recalcitrant Apache leader and his tribe and herd them on to a reservation. Toward the end of the film, the Apache leader gives a powerful speech in Spanish blaming the U.S. government for the deaths of Indian men, women, and children. As one official commented in a considerable understatement, "the entire film is one which certainly does not reflect credit on this country."[75]

In each case, officials from the Motion Picture Division at the State Department contacted the export arm of the Motion Picture Association of America (MPAA). Their requests varied. In some cases, they asked that the films not be distributed in certain areas, such as Western Europe for *Grapes of Wrath* and Latin America for *Fort Apache*. In other cases, they asked to have certain scenes or pieces of dialogue edited out, such as the incendiary speech by the Apache chief. They usually found sympathetic ears at the MPAA, but the organization had limited power to coerce studios into making changes. With *State of the Union*, U.S. officials contacted the MPAA about making changes to the script, but Capra flatly refused. Then they asked Loews International, which held the distribution rights to the film, to limit screenings overseas. The president of Loews, who "had worked with the OWI...and has always been willing to cooperate," told them that he wanted to help, but Capra had a stake in foreign earnings and would not countenance such a loss.[76]

Desperate to do something, one official in the Motion Picture Division hatched a novel plan. Why not prepare a script to run as a prologue to films that the State Department feared would "have a detrimental effect on the United States"? This "prologue would point out that complete freedom of expression, speech, etc. exists in the United States and...we in the US are so sure of the benefits of such freedom of expression that we even make no objection to satires on our political affairs."[77] That was what public diplomats had been reduced to: begging the big studios to add a saccharine trailer to certain films distributed overseas—films that contained messages that U.S. officials found problematic. This sort of effort obviously amounted to very little when compared to the awesome power of the images generated by Hollywood. As a result, it tells us more about the nature of the problem than about the efficacy of the solution. Simply put, a broader legislative mandate did not necessarily translate into greater influence over the ideological realm.

*   *   *

The decision at the end of World War II to award the State Department control over the instruments of public diplomacy stemmed from an awareness that the image the United States projected to the world mattered to U.S. foreign policy and U.S. foreign relations. Everything that public diplomats tried during the immediate postwar period—from radio broadcasts to art exhibits to domestic propaganda campaigns to liaisons with motion picture executives—flowed from the assumption best articulated by Archibald MacLeish in early 1945, when he said that mass communications had made foreign relations domestic affairs. Although the desire to promote the United States as an empire of ideas would have existed with or without the subsequent emergence of the Cold War, that development provided public diplomats with a ready-made agenda well suited to their putative areas of expertise. It also intensified the process that MacLeish described, since the ideological nature of the conflict further destabilized the boundary between domestic and foreign at the very moment that managing foreign perceptions of domestic events became more important than ever before.

U.S. officials were not helpless to defend themselves against this uncomfortable reality. The decision to create a massive new domestic information apparatus at the State Department gave the makers of foreign policy a set of tools to try to shape the domestic affairs they now regarded as so important to foreign relations. Yet the bottom line remained the same: There was only so much that public diplomats could do to project the sort of "America" that they thought best, at home or abroad. And even those meager efforts seemed to provoke endless amounts of controversy.

Wedding the practice of public diplomacy to the imperatives of the Cold War offered some measure of insulation from domestic critics of the information programs, but it also carried significant risks. As the veteran propagandist Charles Hulten noted in 1950, public diplomats too often "emphasize[d] the 'cold war' aspects of our work" in explaining it to the public. They would talk about "projecting America," he said, but only the aspects that dealt with "'getting the peaceful intentions of the U.S. and the free world' known in areas where our cold-war adversary doesn't want them known." "'Projecting America' is not in itself an end," Hulten reminded his colleagues. "It is a means. We have confused it with an end." "Projecting America," he implied, was not just about containing communism ideologically but about selling American values.[78]

What Hulten might have pointed out, particularly in light of the communist revolution in China the previous fall, was that the "Cold War" itself was broader than a competition with any one country. By focusing so heavily on efforts to counter Soviet propaganda, U.S. officials implicitly sent the message that combating the Soviet Union was the overarching, if not the only, objective of U.S. foreign policy. With the Cold War moving onto an increasingly globalized terrain, this sort of Eurocentric perspective posed a grave danger to the larger project of promoting the American Century as an economic and ideological alternative to international communism, particularly in decolonizing areas. To a great extent, the ability of the United States to respond to the challenge of revolutionary nationalism in Asia and beyond depended upon the image that the nation projected in these areas. This posed the next great challenge for the evolving practice of public diplomacy.

5

"The Flat White Light"
Revolutionary Nationalism in Asia and Beyond

THE PERIOD FROM EARLY 1948 to mid-1949 might be described as the golden age of the Truman administration's Cold War policymaking. The president and his advisors basked in the glow of successful initiatives such as the Marshall Plan, the Berlin Airlift, and the formation of the North Atlantic Treaty Organization (NATO). As much as people fretted about the growing tensions with the Soviet Union, the United States seemed for a time to have the upper hand in what was often portrayed as a zero-sum game. The public had also moved beyond any initial reservations to embrace the logic and the language of containment, thanks in part to the gonzo rhetoric of the Truman Doctrine and George Kennan's celebrity turn as the mysterious "Mr. X," the author of a much discussed article on the "Sources of Soviet Conduct" in the magazine *Foreign Affairs*. The president's surprise re-election in 1948, after two years of relentless attacks from what Truman dubbed the "do-nothing" Congress, represented the high point of his tenure in the White House.

That all changed in the summer of 1949, when the State Department publicly acknowledged that Mao Zedong's Chinese Communist Party (CCP) had prevailed in its thirty-year struggle with Chiang Kai Shek's Kuomintong (KMT) for control of China. United States officials had known for several months that, despite substantial American military aid, the KMT had lost all credibility as the governing party in China. A total takeover by the CCP was just a matter of time. Suddenly, Asia went from the periphery to a central front in an increasingly globalized Cold War.

For U.S. public diplomacy, the Chinese Revolution represented an information problem of the highest order of magnitude, both at home and abroad. Domestically, the Office of Public Affairs took the lead on "interpreting" the significance of events in China to the American public. In practice, this mostly meant defending the Truman administration from increasingly aggressive attacks on its foreign policies. Long before Mao officially declared the existence of the People's Republic of China on October 1, there were clear indications that the fragile bipartisan foreign policy consensus of the early years of the Cold War had dissolved. On August 5, the State Department released a thousand-page analysis of the Chinese Revolution known as the "China White Paper." Secretary of State Dean Acheson argued in a cover letter that "nothing the United States did or could have done within the reasonable limits of its capabilities could have changed the results," which led one Republican senator to label this tome the China "Whitewash."[1]

Undeterred, the Office of Public Affairs worked to disseminate the ideas of the White Paper to as wide an audience as possible. Hoping for a multiplier effect, the State Department printed 6,500 copies of the mammoth document and distributed them to members of Congress, the press, leaders of prominent national organizations, and other writers, educators, and business leaders. Meanwhile, the Office of Public Affairs condensed the major premises of the White Paper into a set of talking points for prominent officials. Francis Russell, its director, drafted the substance of the information Acheson presented to Congress, in other public addresses, and in the cover letter he attached to the White Paper. Among the highlights of Russell's efforts at damage control: The Chinese Revolution evolved out of a long internal struggle that came to a head during World War II. Therefore, "it is not a case of having chosen a wrong policy which resulted in failure. It is, rather, a case of having made the strongest possible bid to accomplish something that was worth every effort even though there was never any great hope of success—and of having failed in that effort." In fact, if the United States had really wanted to, it "probably" could have "driven the communist armies out of China." But doing so would have "left four hundred million Chinese convinced that the United States was engaged in imposing upon them by force a regime in which they had lost all confidence and which they were sure was operating not in the interests of the Chinese people as a whole."[2]

Conservatives were thoroughly unimpressed by these mostly accurate, albeit self-serving, arguments. They angrily demanded answers to the unintentionally revealing question of "Who lost China?"—as though the United States once possessed the largest nation on earth and then misplaced it. Despite the absurdity of this formulation, U.S. officials did have to look at themselves in the mirror and wonder whether their relentless focus on Europe had led them to underestimate such dynamic and rapid changes in Asia.

The implications of the Chinese Revolution were huge. On a practical level, the Truman administration's major postwar objective in Asia—rebuilding the Japanese economy along liberal capitalist lines— depended heavily on unfettered access to the Chinese market. On a symbolic level, Mao's victory was even worse. In addition to moving the world's most populous nation to the other side of the Cold War ledger, it closed the very door that had inspired John Hay to call for an "open door" for trade half a century earlier. The Chinese Revolution also sent a powerful message about the limits of American power, economic and otherwise. If anything, Chiang's close connection to the United States had weakened his standing with a population that harbored a deep hostility toward the repeated intrusions of Western powers into its affairs over the past century. What if this was the beginning of a pattern? What if anti-Western sentiments could increase the appeal of communism in other places? With the massive postwar wave of decolonization already under way, the Soviet domination of Eastern Europe suddenly looked like a much smaller problem than it had just three years earlier.

For public diplomats, the Chinese Revolution prompted an equally troubling set of questions about the overall direction of U.S. information policy. In 1942, when U.S. officials decided to expand the cultural relations programs beyond the Western Hemisphere, China was the first place they looked. Seven years later that effort came to a crashing halt, along with everything else the U.S. government thought that it was doing in Asia. To what extent, if any, did Mao's triumph reflect a failure of efforts to "project America"? Had the U.S. government done too little to sell the Chinese on an alternative to communism; or, for that matter, had it done too much? Public diplomats had hardly begun to address these questions when the Korean War broke out nine months later, shaking the foundations of U.S. foreign policy for the second time in less than a year.

Together, the crises in China and Korea precipitated a complete overhaul of U.S. information policy. In April 1950, between these two landmark events, the top-secret directive NSC-68 called for intensifying the Cold War and escalating spending on every conceivable method for waging it, including psychological warfare. Shortly thereafter, the President himself called for U.S. propaganda to adopt a more aggressive tone in launching "a campaign of truth." Despite these developments, old dilemmas re-emerged as U.S. officials continued to battle over who really spoke for the United States, and what the message would be. The Korean conflict, in particular, provoked another round of questions about the place of public diplomacy within the foreign policy process. Once again, reorganization promised to solve these sorts of conflicts— this time through the creation of a new agency, the Psychological Strategy Board; once again, it failed.

In a larger sense, the explosion of revolutionary nationalism in Asia posed a fundamental challenge to the content, if not the form, of U.S. public diplomacy. It forced officials to engage that which they had long ignored: the toll that years of Europe-first policies had exacted on America's image in the non-Western world. How could the United States explain away all that European aid that strengthened colonialism around the world? This was a serious information problem not likely to go away anytime soon. Nor was this complicated dynamic restricted to the quickly evaporating formal boundaries of the colonial world. It applied, as well, to areas such as China and Latin America that had been subjected to various forms of Western dominance through less formal methods of imperialism. It was no accident, after all, that these were the two places where the Roosevelt administration first tested out the practice of cultural diplomacy—a technique designed to replace the sort of big-stick imperialism of the past with a less coercive empire of ideas. In many ways, the rise of what would become known as the

"Third World" was nothing new for public diplomats. The officially appointed custodians of America's image in the world had long confronted the terrible challenge of threading the needle between supporting allies in Europe and maintaining credibility in the developing world. The dilemma that U.S. foreign policymakers now faced in full force would have sounded hauntingly familiar to the OWI officials who struggled to justify the alliance with Great Britain in broadcasts to India. The same could be said for the cultural diplomats who, in 1942, listened to Henry Wallace warn that the United States had arrived at the height of its power at a time "when the so-called backward or inferior races...are coming into their own."[3]

Public diplomats did not necessarily approach the "Third World" with a greater degree of nuance and sensitivity than did their colleagues in the State Department and elsewhere in the U.S. government. It was not as though they had routinely criticized their colleagues for devoting too much attention to Europe, or too little to the rest of the world. They were not that clairvoyant—or, perhaps, not that gutsy. It would be more accurate to say that, because of the nature of their work, they encountered these kinds of issues a bit earlier, and in a more acute form.

The U.S. propagandists who concluded in January 1947 that the Soviet Union had declared "psychological warfare" on the United States also predicted that the communist appeal would play well in "colonial areas." Over the next several years, these kinds of assessments grew more pronounced. In July 1948, the State Department issued a confidential directive to U.S. diplomatic and consular officers regarding U.S. information policy toward "anti-American propaganda." Focusing on the need to "influence opinion in third countries," it noted that often people in those countries "do not react with shock, anger or indignation to the charges made in anti-American propaganda as do some Americans." It also acknowledged the "anti-American attitudes [that] often exist within strongly nationalist but non-communist groups in third countries." Although no one seemed to make the connection, one clue as to why actually appeared in a different section of the report. The authors complained about certain "false or distorted stereotypes" of the United States, noting that many "people of third countries"—populated largely by people of color—believed that "American democratic principles are loudly proclaimed as a cloak for undemocratic practices and for the purpose of concealing wide-spread racial and economic discriminations."[4] In 1948, these kinds of sentiments mostly seemed like an annoyance, an information problem to be overcome. By 1950, the objective of reaching out to people of "third countries" had grown into a matter of pressing public policy.

The "Haves" and the "Have-nots": The China Syndrome and Public Diplomacy

Five days after Mao Zedong declared the existence of the PRC, Francis Russell convened the first meeting of a top-secret State Department working group on the China situation. The group brought together some of the country's top China experts from both inside and outside the government. It also included a number of officials, such as George Kennan, who were responsible for contextualizing developments in China within the broad sweep of U.S. foreign policy. Russell began by instructing the attendees that the press had not been briefed on the existence of this group, and if any reporters questioned them about it they should downplay its significance. No need to further the already prevalent impression of a department in crisis, desperately searching for answers.[5]

After some preliminary remarks, Kennan opened with a long statement about the importance of what might be called the China syndrome. He made clear that his primary concern about the Chinese Revolution was not that it constituted a Soviet "victory," per se; for various reasons, he regarded the prospect of a Sino-Soviet bloc as extremely unlikely. He cared far more about the reverberations it might send throughout Asia and beyond. "It very often seems to me," Kennan complained, "that 2/3 of our problems with respect to the rest of the world today is to determine what is really the desirable and advisable stance of a 'have' nation to 'have-not' nations, because a very large part of the world is composed of 'have-nots,' not just in Asia but elsewhere, and that is a very, very bitter problem." Kennan assigned China a "place of peculiar importance" in dealing with that "problem," since "it can be regarded as the most 'have-not' of all the 'have-not' countries."[6]

The unapologetically Eurocentric diplomat waded into this discussion with obvious ambivalence. On the one hand, he found the situation a highly irritating distraction from his priorities. "I think it is easier," he opined, "for a camel to pass through the eye of a needle than for a country like our own to find [the] language and approach to people who have very little and [a] chance of little more." On the other hand, "if we can find the answer with regard to China I am sure we have found 3/4 of the answer with respect to any other areas of the world."[7] Whether this was true or not—and it could only be true if the United States faced exactly the same issues in most of the world's countries—Kennan's remarks demonstrate just how much the Chinese Revolution shook even the most hard-boiled realists. In its response to the Chinese Revolution, Truman's foreign policy team, so steeped in the traditions of European balance-of-power politics, clearly began to feel what NAACP Executive Secretary Walter White described in 1945 as the "rising wind" of people of color throughout the world.[8] In conflating the particular concerns of the Chinese people with those of all the world's "have-nots," Kennan danced around the subject of race without offering any definitive conclusions.

The following month, another State Department roundtable chaired by Francis Russell delved much deeper into that sensitive subject. Here Dean Rusk played the role of the traditionalist trying to steady himself on shaky global terrain. Rusk, unlike Kennan, had extensive experience dealing with Asian policy matters. He served in the China-Burma-India Theater during the war and then joined the State Department in early 1945, where he worked on United Nations affairs. He also helped to resolve (at least temporarily) U.S.-Soviet tensions over the peace agreement in the Pacific with his role in the ill-fated decision to divide Korea in half at the 38th parallel.

Rusk was a complicated, but cautious, man who struggled throughout his career to accommodate occasional progressive impulses within his essentially conservative temperament and worldview. This could not have been clearer during his awkward attempt to explain to Russell's distinguished panel just what the United States faced in dealing with decolonization. In a group that included Hamilton Fish Armstrong of the Council on Foreign Relations, Wilsonian internationalists Clark Eichelberger and Leo Pasvolsky, and renowned intellectuals Robert Hutchins, Grayson Kirk, and Reinhold Niebuhr, Rusk stood out for his extended disquisition on the "problems created by the emergence of new states into the world communities":

Those new states...are coming out of the Far East, the Middle East, Africa. They are going to be states that do not have the political, economic, or the same, shall we say, moral backgrounds, same religious systems, as the rest of the countries. They are not Anglo-Saxon in tradition; they are not necessarily democratically inclined; they may be sensitive in their relations with us because of racial issues and long memories of unpleasant relations with the white in the western world.[9]

Despite the arresting racism and paternalism of his remarks, Rusk was not totally hostile to the profound world-historical changes spawned by decolonization. Nor was he totally oblivious to the contradictions of describing "Anglo-Saxons" as "democratically inclined." When one of his colleagues suggested that the United States should divide the world into democracies and non-democracies and then align itself with nations it regarded as "democratic," Rusk responded that things were not that simple:

I think it would be difficult to get a great majority of the rest of the world to concede that we are enough of a democracy to be entitled to draw particular lines on that sort of a concept...I am worried about the fact that these autocracies that you are talking about also exist in my native state of Georgia, and they exist with respect to 50 percent of the population of the people of Mississippi. I think that creates a problem for us.[10]

Cold War or no, the subject of decolonization inevitably raised uncomfortable questions about America's own record on race and democracy—what Ambassador Henry Cabot Lodge, Jr., and others would call "our Achilles' heel before the world."[11]

The image problem that Rusk identified did not begin in 1949. The Russians, along with the Germans and Japanese before them, had been blasting the United States for years about the hypocrisy of American professions of democracy, but the Chinese Revolution introduced a new dynamic. Just as the Roosevelt administration could not fully deflect Japanese charges of racism by calling the Japanese "imperialists," the Truman administration could not really dismiss similar attacks from the Chinese by labeling the Chinese "communists." To make matters worse, the Chinese critique of the United States seemed far more exportable than the Japanese model of pan-Asian solidarity via military conquest.

For public diplomats, an image problem of this magnitude could not be ignored. Starting in December 1949, acting Assistant Secretary of State for Public Affairs Howland Sargeant gave several public addresses pushing a new global emphasis in U.S. public diplomacy. In a speech to the Public Relations Society of America, Sargeant opened with the rather blunt admission that the United States had failed as a country in its public relations with much of the world: "Our security must be based on understanding, and not solely on military or economic strength. We know that we are peaceful. We know that we want to help other nations as good neighbors, and not to exploit or dominate them. The trouble is that a lot of foreign people just aren't convinced."[12]

One could certainly quarrel with Sargeant's benign characterization of U.S. motives. Nevertheless, his explanation of the origins and the implications of America's image problem across large swathes of the globe warrants further attention. "The economic gulf," he pointed out, "that separates us from most of the rest of the world creates fear, envy and resentment." Moreover, "the blossoming nationalism of former colonial peoples results in acute national pride and sensitivity. The abrasive rubbing of East and West in the cold war showers sparks of fear and confusion everywhere."[13] In other words, the overemphasis on Cold War tensions created the impression in much of the rest of the world that the United States cared only about Europe.

Here was a perfect illustration of the perils of what George Allen had described as trying "to penetrate into the living-rooms of every individual": Preaching to others could not help but invite intense scrutiny of just how well one lived up to one's own sermons, especially when they came from officials associated with a military and economic engine of almost unimaginable might. Allen was right: "What we are is more important than what we say we are." Where Allen and his colleagues miscalculated was in assuming that "what we are" would play equally well everywhere, and that everyone, if accurately informed, would see America the way that U.S. policymakers did.

From NSC-68 to Korea

During the first half of 1950, policymakers struggled to balance devoting greater attention to the global dimensions of U.S. foreign policy with an increasingly hostile ideological battle with the Soviet Union. In April, the National Security Council produced the long-awaited top-secret report, NSC-68, that would become the proverbial blueprint for U.S. Cold War policy. It cast the Cold War as a clash between "slavery and freedom" on a "worldwide" scale, while focusing almost exclusively on "the Kremlin" as the source of evil in the world. Its recommendations at once affirmed the containment principles of the past, while calling for a massive military buildup so that the United States could "negotiate" from a stronger position and, if necessary, go to war. The authors, led by über-hawk Paul Nitze, consistently struck a tone of aggressive confrontation. They called for supplementing the current policy of promoting "the steady development of the moral and material strength of the free world" with a "projection into the Soviet world in such a way as to bring about an internal change in the Soviet system."[14] The "containment" doctrine now apparently included, or had been replaced by, "rollback"—that is, the elimination of communism from areas where it had already taken hold.[15]

For public diplomacy as an enterprise, the implications of NSC-68 were ambiguous. It talked extensively about the psychological aspects of the "struggle for men's minds," yet said nothing about promoting mutual understanding, intellectual exchange, scientific and technical assistance, or anything else of a cooperative nature. It spoke only to those who saw propaganda as a weapon of ideological war. This was consistent with the general approach of the National Security Council, which tended to emphasize military rather than diplomatic aspects of "security."

That same month, President Truman addressed the American Society of Newspaper Editors and asked the press to help the government launch a "campaign of truth" to expose Soviet "lies" about the United States. This speech is remembered mostly because public diplomats soon adopted the "campaign of truth" as their new slogan, replacing the prior mantra of presenting a "full and fair picture." Historians have treated this substitution as evidence that public diplomats abandoned the more even-handed approach of the immediate postwar period in favor of harsh Cold War rhetoric that demonized the Soviet Union. This conclusion is not entirely unwarranted, especially since Truman's speech did coincide with the undeniably aggressive tone of NSC-68. However, it ignores the parallels between Truman's demand for a "campaign of truth" and Archibald MacLeish's invocation of the "strategy of truth" before the very same group eight years earlier. Truman, like MacLeish, complained that newspapers too often failed to call a spade a spade; they too often failed to sort out the "facts" from the "deceit, distortion, and lies" of America's enemies. Truman particularly deplored the emphasis on trivialities at the expense of giving people the information they needed "to make up their own minds." He lamented, with obvious bitterness, the "nonsense about striped trousers in foreign affairs," noting that "far more influence is exerted by the baggy pants of the managing editor." To report the news in this way, he claimed, was a violation of the "mutual trust" between citizens and a free press in a democracy. MacLeish would have endorsed every single one of these points.[16]

Before public diplomats could even work through the implications of Truman's call for a "campaign of truth," the stakes escalated considerably. A little over two months later, on June 25, 1950, roughly 75,000 North Korean troops stormed across the 38th parallel in a brazen attempt to conquer South Korea and unify the Korean peninsula under one government. The Truman administration responded by going to the United Nations to request authorization for U.N. forces to undertake a "police action" to repel the North Korean invasion and restore the 38th parallel as the international boundary between two independent nations.

The Korean War cemented the perception, already reflected in NSC-68, of the Cold War as a fight to the death that required an all-out mobilization for total war. It also allowed policymakers to implement the shift in policy from "containment" to "rollback." After U.N. forces led by General Douglas MacArthur repelled the initial North Korean invasion and restored the South Korean government, the Truman administration went back to the United Nations for an authorization to cross the 38th parallel and wipe North Korea from the map. Dean Acheson famously summed up this entire situation by noting that U.S. policymakers had put themselves out on a very thin limb with the massive increases in defense spending that they proposed in NSC-68—and then "Korea came along and saved us." Korea also reinforced the primary lesson of the Chinese Revolution: A new theater of the Cold War had opened in Asia and it would almost certainly not be the last.[17]

Today Korea may be the "forgotten war," but at the time it could hardly have mattered more. The Korean War did not create new dilemmas so much as it intensified older ones: Containment, atomic weaponry, military preparedness, ideological war, international organizations, economic reconstruction, European alliances, and America's burgeoning credibility gap in the non-European world all remained consequential, yet a new sense of urgency infused U.S. policymakers' approach to each of these subjects. Their attitude was not unlike what Archibald MacLeish described to Van Wyck Brooks on the eve of World War II: "The terrible changes and menace of our time make things true again the way the flat white light before a storm shows all the shapes and contours of the earth."[18] That description could readily be applied to everything that had happened in Asia going back to the Chinese Revolution.

For the most part, the problems policymakers faced were not born of neglect. To paraphrase John Kennedy, the United States had not slept through the late 1940s and the kinds of issues it faced could not be resolved simply through working harder, or with a greater sense of urgency. People could differ over whether or not the North Korean invasion was a plot hatched in Beijing and/or Moscow, but once the Truman administration committed the United States to defending South Korea with military force, the possibility of a hot war involving both China and the nuclear-armed Soviet Union had to be acknowledged. The simple fact of U.S. intervention meant that the conflict could quite conceivably turn into World War III. As a result, basic policy decisions became matters of life and death—not just for other people, but for Americans as well. At the same time, the nature of the Korean conflict as an undeclared war—a "police action," in the antiseptic parlance of the time—left officials confused about how far to go in placing the U.S. government on a war footing.[19] All of this created the odd mixture of intensity and ambiguity that characterized much of the foreign policymaking of Truman's final years in office. When combined with the sharp plunge in the president's popularity and the harsh backlash against the New Deal order at home and abroad, few decisions came easily.[20]

Like everyone else, public diplomats had to consider what more they could have done. In July 1950, their old colleague William Benton, now a senator from Connecticut, accused the U.S. government of having been "criminally negligent" in failing to counteract the Soviet Union's "insidious propaganda" in North Korea. The perpetual battles over public diplomacy, he said, had reduced the Voice of America to a "hoarse whisper." Benton's argument seemed to be that if only propagandists had done more, the North Korean people would not have gone along with the allegedly Kremlin-directed invasion. The dubiousness of this analysis aside, the Korean War did force public diplomats to reconceive their mission once again. Greater attention to the non-Western world would be paired with an increasingly rigid Cold War framework, posing even tougher choices.[21]

The unpredictability within the larger political landscape exacerbated many familiar quandaries of public diplomacy, as policymakers struggled to respond to the Cold War turning "hot"—but only to a limited extent. Policymakers had to consider, for example, whether to recalibrate their entire operation to fight a total war like World War II, or whether to keep doing what they were doing, which was already close to all-out psychological warfare. And what about their messages? Existing NSC directives awarded military commanders control over ideological warfare in their theater of operations. But how big was that "theater"? Did it include all of Asia, or even beyond? After all, the United States entered the Korean conflict in the name of containing a communist offensive that, according to the official rationale, originated in Moscow via Beijing. So how much did a police action on a narrow peninsula in Asia really transform the global war of ideas, and how much say would the State Department have vis-à-vis the Pentagon in answering that question?

The Strange Career of the Psychological Strategy Board

On August 17, 1950, General Douglas MacArthur was in Tokyo, plotting the famous amphibious landing at Inchon that commenced the U.S. military operation in the Korean War. Back in Washington on that same day, President Truman announced the formation of a "Psychological Strategy Board" to coordinate the U.S. government's approach to the war of ideas.[22] There was no question that some sort of intervention was needed. Psychological operations began within twenty-four hours of the North Korean invasion. Within a week, U.S. planes dropped some twenty-four million copies of nine different leaflets throughout the country. Meanwhile, U.S. transmitters in Japan worked overtime to broadcast newly designed radio programs across the Sea of Japan. Yet early reports out of Korea detailed significant conflict between the military and the diplomatic approaches to the war of ideas.[23]

State Department officials on the scene described the situation as a "real mess." At the end of the first month of the war, the State Department's information post was still the only outfit capable of conducting psychological warfare in any meaningful way. But instead of running the show, public diplomats found themselves detailed to one of MacArthur's civilian aides, if not frozen out entirely. They complained not just about the restrictions on their autonomy, but also about severe limitations on the operation itself. Instead of preparing numerous messages targeting distinct population groups throughout the north and south—what might be called tactical psychological warfare—the vast majority of the leaflets focused only on boosting morale among South Korean troops with generic professions of American benevolence and paeans to MacArthur's greatness.[24]

The Psychological Strategy Board (PSB) was supposed to resolve this sort of organizational muddle. While it failed to do that, it did result in one of the more revealing episodes in the history of public diplomacy. First under the control of the State Department, and then under an external director who reported to the president, the PSB brought together representatives from State, the CIA, and the various branches of the armed services. Ideologically, its stated goal—to help the U.S. government "speak the only kind of language the Kremlin understands"—effectively conveyed the temper of the times.[25] As with all previous efforts to align these institutions, the PSB suffered from a lack of operational authority. Ultimately, it functioned as little more than an advisory board, despite a presidential directive that awarded it control over the planning and coordination of psychological strategy. Yet its failures cannot be chalked up solely to its limited reach. On a

more basic level, the PSB once again exposed many of the theoretical conflicts that had plagued American approaches to "psychological
strategy" from the very beginning: civilian vs. military; white vs. gray
vs. black propaganda; image as spin vs. image as reality.

The ambiguous obligations of fighting a limited war for the future
of the "free world" only exacerbated these troubles. Public diplomats
at the State Department wondered: "Is there a real or fundamental difference between the present situation and a wartime situation? Is the
same kind of organization required for both situations?"[26] Particularly
in the early stages, it was unclear how Korea fit into the larger picture.
Ideally, the PSB would have addressed this situation, but it suffered
from the same symptoms. Although clearly a reaction to the military
imperatives of the Korean War, the composition and the mission of
the PSB gave any informed observer a strong sense of déjà vu. A board
to coordinate the many different aspects of psychological warfare—
military and diplomatic, covert and overt—had not only been the goal
of numerous NSC directives over the past several years, but had also
consumed most of the attention of the OWI's Overseas Branch in the
latter years of World War II. Little appeared to have changed, as the
Korean War prompted another round of what psychoanalysts refer to
as the "return of the repressed."

To bring everything full circle, the president appointed Edward
Barrett to run the PSB. There was perhaps no one better prepared
than Barrett to implement the idea of the PSB. He had spent his entire
life in and around the information business. The son of a newspaper-
man from Birmingham, Alabama, he attended Princeton University,
where he served as the "chairman" of the famed *Daily Princetonian*.
He started his career as an editor at *Newsweek* magazine, a position he
held for almost a decade until he went to work as a propagandist for
Wild Bill Donovan's COI in the early days of the war. After Donovan
left to run the OSS, Barrett became the chief of the Allied armies'
Psychological Warfare Branch in Europe and then the director of the
Overseas Branch of the OWI. When the OWI folded, he returned to
Newsweek as an executive editor for a few years before beginning his
second stint as a government propagandist when he replaced George
Allen as Assistant Secretary of State for Public Affairs in early 1950. If
anyone could make the PSB work, surely he was the one.[27]

Commentators applauded Barrett's appointment and the general concept of the PSB, although several also expressed frustration that it had taken so long to come together. Few people noticed that this was not the first effort of its kind. Neal Stanford, the generally perceptive foreign policy analyst for the *Christian Science Monitor*, opened his article on the creation of the PSB with the caustic remark that the "United States is finally getting around to taking the psychological war offensive against international communism." Most accounts characterized it as a long-overdue defensive response to what one reporter referred to as worldwide "Kremlinism." Another common refrain claimed that the Korean War finally pushed the State Department to abandon its "hesitancy about the use of the word 'propaganda' to describe" its own activities. Conventional wisdom held that the Truman administration had, at long last, shown a willingness to get its hands dirty in "waging its side of the war that is now going on in men's minds." Looking back a year later, a reporter for the *New York Times* described Korea as the "Pearl Harbor stroke" for psychological warfare."[28]

The idea that U.S. propaganda, prior to the Korean War, suffered from excessive reticence did not even remotely correspond to reality. However, the war had prompted the State Department to turn up the volume, so to speak, on the VOA's transmitters. The PSB set out to make that message not only louder, but also more effective and more consistent with the voices coming from other parts of the government. In theory, it made sense; in practice, Barrett fared no better than anyone else who had attempted this over the past decade. For one thing, his status as an insider proved more of a liability than an asset since he so clearly held a considerable interest in deciding who should ultimately call the shots. Representatives from the Pentagon immediately grumbled about setting up the PSB as a State Department operation rather than an "independent agency."[29]

Overlapping mandates accounted for only a fraction of the PSB's difficulties. Another issue cut much deeper: The hope behind the PSB was that greater communication would help to bridge the divides between the various government entities engaged in psychological warfare. These debates could not be resolved through talking, however, since they reflected contradictory and often mutually exclusive visions about the role of ideas in U.S. foreign policy and foreign relations. As a product of the MacLeish tradition at the OWI, Barrett continued to emphasize the strategy of truth, even as he adopted an increasingly hard-line posture on the Cold War during his second tenure in government service. The author of a book entitled *Truth Is Our Weapon*, he took the position that the best medicine for an ailing image was just "acting right and letting people know about it." In an interview conducted many years later, he argued that for the most part his office "tried to stick to the truth and to tell nothing but the truth," even if "we didn't always tell the whole truth." Regardless of whether Barrett and company could have squared the "strategy of truth" with the various forms of "sykewar" and disinformation produced by the Pentagon and the CIA, the fact is that they did not.[30]

This disconnect affected both the kinds of operations the PSB pursued, as well as the sorts of ideas they sought to convey. A little over a month after the war began, Barrett's team at the State Department prepared a comprehensive assessment of "information policy objectives" to account for the impact of Korea. They framed their analysis in broad terms, focusing on how their messages about the war could improve the image of U.S. foreign policy generally. They recommended that U.S. propaganda explain the Korean War as part of a global struggle against communism, as an operation conducted under the legal sanction of the United Nations, and as an altruistic endeavor to come to the aid of an ally victimized by unprovoked aggression. They thought it equally important to emphasize that the operation in Korea would not detract from U.S. commitments to NATO countries and elsewhere in the world. In fact, it showed just how far the United States would go to support all nations "sharing a common devotion to peace, freedom and justice."[31]

The Pentagon and the CIA, by contrast, tended to define "information policy objectives" on a short-term, mission-to-mission basis. It was not that one group was right and the others were wrong. Rather, different institutions operated from different assumptions and in pursuit of different objectives. Just as public diplomats knew their credibility could not survive being associated with distributing disinformation, a military commander such as Douglas MacArthur had little interest in the global impact of a psychological warfare campaign in Korea. The presence of the CIA, which utilized everything from disinformation to paramilitary covert action, added yet another layer of complexity to this whole equation. These were the sorts of complications and contra-dictions that Franklin Roosevelt had tried to neutralize by establishing the Office of War Information as an independent propaganda agency, separate from the State Department, the Office of Strategic Services, and the War Department. Now Barrett tried, without any real author-ity, to bring them all together again, while attempting to serve as a neutral mediator on policy debates in which he held an obvious profes-sional stake.

In six months under Barrett's leadership, the PSB met a few times with little progress to show for the effort. In fact, Barrett and his staff spent much of their time responding to the flanking maneuvers of the CIA and the Pentagon, both of which tried to wrest control of the PSB away from the State Department in favor of an independent agency with no one entity in charge. Yet, as State Department officials pointed out, even an "independent agency" would not really resolve the larger questions of authority: "It is difficult to see how the Board or the Chairman [of an independent PSB] could act independently. We would like to ask whether Defense and JCS envisages binding decisions by the Chairman in the absence of agreement within the Board." On that point, they were right. It did not really matter who ran the PSB so long as each department retained operational control over its own psychological programs. The PSB could only go as far as the level of cooperation between its members allowed.[32]

*   *   *

By early 1951, some of Truman's top foreign policy advisers began to complain privately about the lack of direction in psychological strategy. In January, the National Security Council devoted a session to critiquing what its members perceived as the weakness of the U.S. propaganda mes-sage compared to that of the Soviet Union. This concern was not new, but it took on new meaning in the context of reinvigorated debates about how the U.S. government should approach the war of ideas. Specifically, U.S. policymakers worried that the "dynamic appeal" of communism, which "inspires a spirit of altruistic and militant rebellion reminiscent of early Christianity," trumped anything the United States could offer. For them, the most alarming part about communist ideology was its transnational, cross-class, cross-racial appeal. "Unlike the Nazi's propaganda," which depended upon selling certain "nationalistic or cultural claims," the "idea of 'revolution'" promised to "solve all prevalent economic and social problems" regardless of situation or circumstance. More revealing, though, than the NSC's assessment of the Soviet appeal was its characterization of the problems with the U.S. counter-message. It criticized U.S. policymakers for producing "a relatively orthodox 'advertising campaign.'" In an obvious slap at the State Department's public diplomacy shop, the NSC report concluded that "it does no good...to 'sell' our brand of democracy as if it were a soft drink or an efficient detergent." Doing so left potential target audiences with a choice between "a passive freedom from the bottom up and a dynamic authority from the top down." The NSC left no doubt about which path it expected people in troubled circumstances to embrace.[33]

It is hard to decide which part of this assessment stands out the most: the slightly jealous enthusiasm of the power of communist ideology; the scathing indictment of the "advertising" model of propaganda; or maybe the palpable fear that the United States could not win the war of ideas just through telling the American story. It was one thing to complain that the United States had not told its story well enough, often enough, or loudly enough. It was another thing entirely to describe the basic idea of "projecting America" as flawed. Even so, the NSC report did not truly signal an outright rejection of the dominant approach to U.S. propaganda over the past decade, so much as it pointed to the level of frustration with the current situation.

In March 1951, the press caught wind of rumors that Truman was also unhappy with the lack of progress and was considering another shakeup in the chain of command for political warfare. A few weeks later, on April 4, the president announced major changes to the Psychological Strategy Board. Essentially, the Pentagon and the CIA got their way: Barrett was out, to be replaced by an independent administrator who would report to the National Security Council rather than to the Secretary of State. It was not an auspicious start for the PSB. If Barrett could not pull this off, then who could?[34]

In June, the president turned to Gordon Gray, president of the University of North Carolina, to head up the reconstituted PSB. Born into wealth and privilege, the son of the president of the R. J. Reynolds

Tobacco Company, Gray had already distinguished himself in several different professions. After graduating from college, he moved to New York to practice law, before moving back to his native North Carolina, where he served two terms as a state senator. Like Barrett, he had considerable experience in the news business, having owned a newspaper and a radio station in Winston-Salem. But he differed from Barrett in having accumulated a remarkable service record in the military. After Pearl Harbor, Gray actually declined a commission as an officer to enlist as a private. Less than seven years later, he became the Secretary of the Army. In the spring of 1950, he left that position to take the job at UNC, but barely a year later Truman summoned him back to government service. In terms of Gray's potential impact upon the PSB, two things about his biography stood out: the first was his obvious managerial skill; the second was his military background, which suggested that he would side with the Defense Department in disputes with the State Department over psychological strategy.[35]

By the end of the year, Gray had the reconstituted PSB up and running. In one early accomplishment—no mean feat given the government boom in postwar Washington—Gray secured separate offices for the PSB on Pennsylvania Avenue, diagonally across from Truman's temporary quarters in Blair House. The proximity to the president signaled Gray's personal connection; the location, away from the "home turf" of any particular department, symbolized the hopes for autonomy. Although the official "Board" consisted only of Gray and one representative each from the State Department, the Defense Department, the CIA, and the Joint Chiefs, there were four "offices," supported by a staff of around fifty people, to implement the recommendations of the Board. Since the PSB held no authority over actual "operations," the staff did what it could to improve the consistency and effectiveness of existing projects. Much of its work focused on making sure the government's left hand knew what its right hand was doing. In addition to policy planning, PSB officials gave the quest for better coordination a bit of a personal touch through following up with other government departments and agencies to make sure they understood the Board's directives. The PSB staff also tried to put together a systematic process for evaluating psychological warfare activities, from Voice of America broadcasts to the Korean War leaflet bombs. Social scientists, such as "sykewar" theorist Daniel Lerner and public-opinion guru Hadley Cantril came aboard to offer methodological advice in formulating the evaluations.[36]

With the new setup in place, Gray told Truman that he wanted to return to the presidency of UNC, a position he never formally relinquished. Once again, the administration would have to find a new person to take the reins. Another college president, Raymond Allen of the University of Washington, soon emerged as the leading candidate. A philosophy professor and a medical doctor, Allen's primary qualification for running the PSB seemed to be his work for the much-publicized commission on government reorganization headed by former president Herbert Hoover. His reputation as a fierce anti-communist, who made headlines for firing three professors accused of having ties to the communist party, probably did not hurt either. The strangest thing about Allen's appointment was that almost immediately after the announcement he accepted a position as the chancellor at UCLA and declared that he, too, would only stay about six months. Given that Truman had only a year left in office, the odds that the PSB could change the landscape of psychological strategy within that timeframe were low. Admiral Alan Kirk, former ambassador to Russia, ultimately replaced Allen. By this time it was the musical-chairs atmosphere—not who sat in those chairs—that really mattered. The *New York Times* not unfairly blasted the Truman administration for giving psychological strategy such "casual treatment."[37]

By the end of 1952, the Board had taken on forty some projects while convening dozens of interdepartmental advisory panels to examine some of the most pressing issues in the global war of ideas. Not surprisingly, given all the obstacles that the PSB faced, the quality of outcome and impact varied greatly among these projects, and there was so little time left. As president, Dwight Eisenhower took psychological warfare (as well as public diplomacy) in a new direction, creating his own organizational structures and bringing in his own people. His decision to close down the PSB a few months after taking office surprised no one.[38]

As with the Office of War Information before it, the lasting legacy of the Psychological Strategy Board can be found more in what it attempted than what it accomplished. Its struggles, however disappointing from a policymaking perspective, epitomized the continual challenges of defining the role of propaganda and public diplomacy under conditions of "total war." In this case, the job of synchronizing the many "voices" of the U.S. government was just the beginning. The real quandaries came in trying to decide which psychological strategies to deploy and what effect they would have upon America's image in different parts of the world.

Collateral Psychological Damage

Although the war of ideas was often misunderstood as a zero-sum game—the American Century versus international communism—it rarely produced clear-cut winners and losers. Measures that helped the nation's image in one area might simultaneously do great damage elsewhere. For example, as much as the Marshall Plan did for America's image in Europe, in the colonial world it was generally viewed as a project for strengthening colonialism. The PSB repeatedly butted up against these kinds of uncomfortable contradictions because of its broad mandate that stretched around the globe and across the government. Its records demonstrate a thorough preoccupation with the ideological dynamics of an increasingly globalized Cold War, as U.S. officials grappled with what might be called the collateral psychological damage of adopting the interests of Western Europe as their own in the postwar period.

The resulting crisis, as the PSB found out, could not be addressed solely through greater sensitivity to local cultures or regional differences. Instead, it required policymakers to question their own assumptions and to confront the prospect that Cold War imperatives had led them, whether through indifference or naïveté, to perpetuate the tyranny of colonialism. This was not, of course, an easy pill to swallow, and even public diplomats, whose job it was to make these sorts of evaluations, rarely put it this bluntly. In this case, an effort undertaken in a sincere (albeit self-serving) attempt to promote peace and prosperity in Europe had undermined U.S. credibility in large parts of the world. Maybe there had been no choice. After all, policymakers did believe that the Europe-first strategy of the immediate postwar period was the only way to prevent a return to the economic and political catastrophes of the 1930s. At the same time, there was no Marshall Plan for Africa or the Middle East, and even in Asia, aid flowed very selectively, more often than not targeting places and projects that advanced the interests of Westerners. There was simply no good way to spin these facts.[39]

For propagandists, there was a profound irony in this entire predicament: The initial attraction to the techniques of public diplomacy—in particular, the impulse toward treating the nation's image as a foreign policy issue—stemmed in part from the belief that, with traditional imperial structures starting to crumble, the United States would have the opportunity as well as the need to reach out to millions of newly autonomous peoples. Public diplomats had not failed to anticipate the nature of this problem; rather they had failed to convince their colleagues in other areas that it mattered enough to make it a fundamental consideration in the formulation of policy. As Gordon Gray complained to President Truman, too many people regarded "psychological strategy" as nothing more than "word warfare"—that is, putting the "best possible interpretation" on decisions made by others. Much like Archibald MacLeish, Gray took the position that "virtually no major decision or action of the government in the foreign field is without the deepest psychological considerations."[40]

This notion—that no foreign policy decision, from dropping a bomb to providing foreign aid, should be made without first considering its psychological ramifications—represented a remarkable shift in thinking from the pre-World War II era. But, for that idea to work, the officials in charge of dropping the bombs and authorizing the foreign aid would have to consult with psychological strategists before making their decisions. Typically, they did not. ("We'll make the policy and then you can put it on your damn radios," Paul Nitze memorably barked at Gray.)[41] Ultimately, despite the hope that the PSB would raise the profile of the psychological strategy, it found itself handcuffed by the same limitations as had each of its predecessors. Maybe this was inevitable, maybe image would always take a backseat to other considerations in foreign policymaking, but that did not make it wise.

*   *   *

Although the PSB's inability to implement its own recommendations rendered the results of its numerous strategy sessions largely moot, its many analyses provide a wealth of information on the growing alarm within the Truman administration about America's image outside of Europe. Some of this anxiety might be chalked up to the shock of the Korean War, but much of it dealt with matters far away, at least geographically speaking, from East Asia.

One particularly poignant episode from 1952 serves as an excellent introduction to a discussion of the PSB's concerns about America's image in the Third World. On March 29, over 600 self-styled intellectuals gathered at the Waldorf-Astoria in New York City for a meeting of the American chapter of the Committee for Cultural Freedom. Although remembered today primarily for its connections to the CIA, the Committee for Cultural Freedom generated a great deal of attention in its own time for its blockbuster gatherings of high-profile anti-Stalinist liberals and for the combustible atmosphere that typically ensued. This session was no exception, as a fight nearly broke out when the old Progressive Era journalist Max Eastman offered up an enthusiastic defense of McCarthyism and lambasted the use of the term "witch hunt" as a communist "smear tactic."[42]

Perhaps hoping to observe some fireworks, perhaps wanting to check in on the government's investment, the PSB sent staff member A. P. Toner to report on the meeting. Strangely, his account offered only a brief mention of the fight over Eastman's remarks and entirely ignored the keynote address given by the State Department's Howland Sargeant. Toner dismissed the performances of most of the speakers as "uneven in quality and unproductive of new ideas." Instead, he devoted his entire report to analyzing a handful of more obscure presentations, particularly one by renowned Yale University philosopher F. S. C. Northrop, author of *The Meeting of East and West*.[43]

Toner used Northrop's ideas, which were saturated in the Orientalist essentialism of the era, to develop his own conclusions about U.S. Cold War policy. Toner began with Northrop's observation that, typically, "Western conquerors have gone to the East under two pretexts: (1) to protect them, and (2) to bring them a superior culture." As long as the Soviet Union managed to link the United States to this tradition, Toner pointed out, no amount of American economic aid could possibly counteract this perception. As he put it, "joint trust is necessary if our economic aid and other programs are to be effective." Toner then complained about the way that communists had managed to appeal to "indigenous cultural traditions," despite the fact that, in his view, "communism is antithetical to native culture." However, he also noted Northrop's conclusion that direct attacks on communism would not work and neither would simply "selling [American] values." Instead, the United States should work to revitalize and strengthen local cultures, apparently out of a belief that people confident in their own culture would naturally reject communism and choose the American way. Although neither Northrop nor Toner offered any specifics on how the United States should pursue this agenda, their position amounted to the cultural equivalent of John Hay's second Open Door note, which argued back in 1900 that U.S. interests would best be served by strengthening Chinese territorial integrity.[44]

Toner's report squared with other information pouring into the PSB on the state of the ideological competition with communism beyond the borders of Europe. Several PSB memos focused on the question of how to improve perceptions of the United States in the Middle East, Africa, and Asia. U.S. officials were particularly concerned about the Soviet "lie" that "America's main objective is not peace, but world domination." This line seemed likely to strike a chord among people with a long history of various forms of oppression. How to rebut these charges, though? Aggressive attacks on the Soviet Union risked perpetuating the notion that these areas were just "pawns" in a Cold War game, while loudly trumpeting American values might actually confirm fears that the United States sought world domination.[45]

The most interesting and revealing parts of these assessments dealt with the distinctive challenges that psychological strategists expected to confront from region to region. In the Middle East, U.S. officials worried about religious differences and "lingering resentment" caused by aid to Israel. The concerns about East Asia all stemmed from the ramifications of the Chinese Revolution. By establishing a huge ideological base for communism in the region, it made decisions about the allocation of resources "in the face of other demands...especially Western Europe" that much more difficult. Would massive infusions of time, effort, and money even make a difference? The presence of a communist-controlled China also shaped the dynamics in Southeast Asia, "which has only recently emerged into American consciousness." Regarding South Asia, the report expressed approval for the "emergence of responsible non-communist governments," but also concern about Indian "non-alignment" and Pakistani "dissatisfaction with U.S. policy and aid." The remarks on Latin America exhibited the already standard Cold War characterization of the Western Hemisphere: Communists exploited "political, economic, and social instability," "rising nationalist feeling," and "almost universal dislike of the United States." However, U.S. officials did at least acknowledge that the emphasis on rebuilding Western Europe had "disrupted normal trade relations" in the Western Hemisphere, and that "many people in Latin America are suffering economically."[46]

A particularly noteworthy aspect of one estimate addressed perceptions of the United States in Africa. Nearly a decade before the massive postwar wave of decolonization arrived in full, members of the PSB had already set their sights on Africa's "human and economic resources," its raw materials, and its "strategic location." The authors acknowledged that it "may not claim a top priority in our planning scale," yet insisted "we cannot afford to ignore the growing impact of the area." Anticolonial sentiment in French North Africa, the Anglo-Egyptian dispute over the Sudan, and the "bitter internal wranglings" of apartheid South Africa raised the most immediate concerns. However, the bulk of the analysis pointed to the future, noting that Africa contained "three-quarters of the world's dependent peoples, who are pressing in various relentless ways toward independence."[47]

*   *   *

In the early 1950s, whenever U.S. policymakers contemplated the prospect of people pressing in "relentless ways toward independence," they thought first of India. As late as 1942, the British still clung to the hope that a crackdown on Indian nationalism would buy enough time for them to get that country under control. Yet this move, which involved imprisoning Gandhi, Nehru, and a host of other prominent advocates of independence, only inflamed the situation. In 1947, Clement Attlee's government finally faced reality and turned India loose.[48]

India soon became the model for other aspiring nationalist movements around the world, for European powers keenly interested in the future of decolonization, and for the United States as an early test of how to win hearts and minds among newly independent peoples. U.S. policymakers regarded India as a critical barometer for measuring the success of their effort in responding to decolonization. The participants at an NSC meeting in January 1952 put it bluntly: "if we lose India we lose Asia." Yet, in the estimation of Paul Hoffman, who knew something about social and economic instability from his time running the Marshall Plan in Europe, "India in 1952 stands where China stood in 1946."[49]

In an indication of India's importance within the grand scheme of things, President Truman appointed Chester Bowles as the U.S. ambassador for the final two years of his administration. Bright and capable, Bowles had earned a sterling reputation as a tireless public servant, not to mention a loyal Democrat. As William Benton's old business partner on Madison Avenue, he also understood the importance of image as well as anyone. James Byrnes had initially approached Bowles about replacing Archibald MacLeish as Assistant Secretary for Public Affairs in 1945, but Bowles turned down the job and recommended Benton instead. Throughout his long post-advertising career, Bowles oscillated between local, national, and international politics, holding an astonishing array of government posts that included White House economic policy advisor, Governor of Connecticut, delegate to UNESCO, U.S. Congressman, Undersecretary of State, and Ambassador to India, a position he occupied not only under Truman but again under Kennedy and Johnson.[50]

Members of the Psychological Strategy Board regularly consulted Bowles about India, asking for his evaluation of the political dynamics there, as well as his recommendations for improving America's image in the region. His views, although complicated, may be characterized as generally optimistic, with considerable reservations about certain aspects of U.S. policy. Bowles consistently voiced several concerns about Indian perceptions of the United States: first, that U.S. policy focused too much on projecting a "tough, military-minded" attitude; second, that the United States needed to do more in the area of economic aid to counteract the idea that it had nothing to offer but militarism; and, finally, that it needed to work harder at distancing itself from the legacies of Western colonialism.

In July 1952, Bowles wrote PSB Director Raymond Allen about a recent trip he took to the movies, in which the theater showed two newsreels about the United States. Both pictures focused almost entirely on America's military prowess—in the rigorous training of its troops and in producing fearsome weapons of almost unimaginable power. For Bowles, this experience raised broader questions about the overall direction of U.S. policy. He noted bitterly that he just happened to see these two films on the same day that the U.S. Congress drastically reduced economic aid to India under the Point IV program, the Truman administration's ambitious initiative to promote economic modernization in the developing world. How, he wondered, could the United States construct a policy that "can maintain the support...of the American people," while also remaining "keyed to the difficult revolutionary period in which we are living"?[51]

Bowles also reached the troubling conclusion that "in effect, we have taken over the traditional foreign policy which the British have maintained." He referred here not just to India, but to the whole project of Western global hegemony, which, in his view, the United States had "underwritten" since 1917. Although he did not explain the reference to 1917, it was both the year that the United States finally entered World War I on Britain's side and the year of the communist revolution in Russia. What worried Bowles was not the emphasis on the communist challenge, as such, but the fact that U.S. policy had "been developed in such European terms" that it could not effectively respond to "the world situation as it exists today." The United States needed a truly "global policy" that recognized "that the balance of power in Europe can be upset not only by what happens in Europe, but by developments in Asia."[52]

Allen's reply indicated that he either disagreed with or, more likely, failed to understand Bowles's point. In a striking illustration of the ethnocentrism and cultural solipsism that marred so much of U.S. propaganda, Allen argued that the problem was not America's image as a "tough military-minded nation," but Soviet efforts to smear the United States with the "label of war-monger and imperialist." The U.S. government did not need to cut its defense spending in favor of more economic aid, but rather to make clear that its military "provided a shield of strength to shelter not only the United States but all the free world." If only propagandists could neutralize the communist message, Allen argued, they could commit their full energies to exporting the principles of the Constitution and the Declaration of Independence.

He described these ideals as "the heritage of men everywhere...the same for the farmer in Kansas as for the farmer in Punjab."[53]

*   *   *

Allen's protests to the contrary, the problems that Bowles outlined had broad implications well beyond India. The final year of the Truman administration also witnessed important developments in the early stages of America's Longest War in Vietnam. The French attempt to re-occupy Vietnam—an effort heavily funded by the United States— had largely failed. Ho Chi Minh's Viet Minh forces controlled significant portions of the country. Leo Hochstetter, who spent time in Vietnam during the early 1950s as a publicist for the Mutual Security Agency, spoke for many when he concluded in 1952 that if "a plebiscite were held today...a decisive majority would vote for the Communist Viet Minh regime." Quite simply, the French and U.S. efforts to install the Vietnamese Emperor Bao Dai as the head of a "French puppet government" had not succeeded, since the majority of the Vietnamese people regarded "Ho Chi Minh as standing for the freedom of Indochina."[54]

This situation created tremendous difficulties for U.S. policymakers, particularly those responsible for monitoring America's image in Southeast Asia. The remarkable part of their analysis is not that they identified a problem—it was fairly hard to miss, less than two years before the French withdrawal after the disaster at Dien Bien Phu—but that they understood the precise nature of the dilemma the United States confronted in Southeast Asia. They just failed to find a solution that would allow the United States to balance its support for the French with its desire to win the allegiance of the Vietnamese people. As the *Pentagon Papers* would later demonstrate, psychological strategists were not the only ones during this period who expressed doubts about the long-term trajectory of U.S. policy in Southeast Asia. But their focus on image did give them a keen sense of the broader problems the United States faced in the region.

Hochstetter, for example, immediately diagnosed the contradiction at the heart of U.S. policy in Vietnam. Echoing Bowles, he observed that efforts to supply economic aid to the Vietnamese people, particularly under the Point IV program, had done little to improve perceptions of the United States. Unsurprisingly, locals tended to focus instead on the billions of dollars in military aid to their colonial overlords. As Hochstetter summed it up, "too much importance was attached to the tanks that we were giving and not enough to the tractors." Or, more graphically: "the village homes destroyed by American napalm bombs made more of an impression...than the trachoma sufferers who had been cured by American medical care." However, Hochstetter was less insightful when addressing what to do about this predicament. Maybe a better message would do the trick, he suggested. If only "our propaganda" could "bring home to the natives the connection between our military aid and their welfare." This was, in a nutshell, the problem an entire generation of policymakers tried and failed to solve, as U.S. officials, including psychological strategists, too often focused on improving the message even as their own analyses pointed toward more fundamental problems with the policy itself.[55]

There were, to be sure, plenty of warnings about the dangers of ignoring the long-term consequences of U.S. actions in Indochina. In an analysis based on contemporaneous CIA intelligence estimates, one PSB staffer encouraged Raymond Allen to adopt the sort of recommendation that Hochstetter and others could not quite bring themselves to endorse:

> The only means by which we can truly marshal the strength and support of the colonial areas is by vigorously and consistently championing an historically American concept—anti-colonialism. The time has come to re-examine the premises upon which our present policy of backing the British and the French to the detriment of the colonial areas has been based.[56]

Although the problems caused by such a policy obviously extended well beyond Indochina, the shortcomings of U.S. policy in that area provided perhaps the clearest distillation of the broader issue:

> The war against the Viet-Minh is costing a billion a year, but offers no hope of achieving a military decision. At the same time, sympathies within Vietnam lie with the Viet-Minh, which is looked upon

as a nationalistic movement of liberation. The U.S., thanks to its military aid program is equated with the French colonialists.[57]

Given the situation, this analyst suggested, the United States must pressure France to guarantee withdrawal in the near future, then supply U.S. aid in the meantime to help build a non-communist Vietnamese army to hold the country after the French left. Or the United States could continue down the same path, hoping that the French would not leave and put the United States in the position of training such a force on its own. The U.S. government chose the latter option. In a vacuum, of course, each policy had its merits. Maintaining French support for U.S. policies in Western Europe was not a trivial matter. Yet there was no doubt which option would look better in most parts of the world. Under the first scenario, the United States could claim that it played a major role in ending colonialism in Indochina; under the second, it would be propping up the existing system. The real question was how much considerations of America's image would factor into the decision-making process. The answer turned out to be very little.

* * *

The ramifications of the U.S. decision to perpetuate the European colonial order in Southeast Asia became clear in relatively short order. In the Middle East, the same dynamic took much longer to develop, although it has reverberated for a considerably longer period of time. When decolonization began in the late 1940s, Cold War considerations led the U.S. government to adopt a set of policies that largely reinforced existing patterns, rather than undermining them. As the PSB's records make clear, U.S. policymakers actually recognized most of the potential pitfalls for America's image in the Middle East long before the United States ever established itself as a hegemonic power in the region. However, they failed to develop any coherent response to the tensions they identified. A perceptive take on the shortcomings of British and French policies was often juxtaposed with a confusing, at times almost delusional, analysis of what the United States could do differently, denouncing Orientalist ideas in one paragraph only to then deploy them in the next.

During the early 1950s, psychological strategists frequently commented on the immense hostility toward the European presence in the Middle East, as well as the threat to the United States if it became identified with that tradition. At various points, U.S. officials complained about the Europeans' general ignorance of, and indifference to, local cultures and religion; about their preference for stability through tyranny as an antidote to anti-Western nationalism; and about prioritizing access to oil and to markets above all else, especially an authentic commitment to social, political, and economic development.

The French, in particular, faced an extremely fragile situation in the region then known as the "Near East." They had already lost formal control over their long-standing mandates in Lebanon and Syria, although they still exercised considerable political and economic influence in each country. Meanwhile, their colonies in North Africa had also begun to slip away, eventually culminating in the bloody and brutal Algerian War that started in 1954. Recognizing a growing synergy between the various resistance movements, France tried to strike a delicate balance between swinging the iron fist in North Africa and offering a velvet glove to potential allies in its former territories in the Middle East. Whether this strategy made sense from the French perspective or not, U.S. officials found it extremely problematic.[58]

Several Arabists from the State Department's Research Division blasted the "innate French hostility to the nationalist aspirations of the Arab Moslem majority in the Near East." They understood that the French preferred to deal with "minority elements in the Arab world" out of a fear that any outbreak of Arab nationalism anywhere would energize the opposition in North Africa. However, when the French colonial office in Beirut complained about Point IV aid to Lebanon at virtually the same time that its counterpart in Damascus rejected several economic development proposals from U.S. firms, U.S. officials openly questioned whether "the methods used by the French in maintaining and strengthening their ascendancy" were "compatible" with American objectives. They complained that the French seemed to have no interest whatsoever in "strengthening the local social, political, and economic fabric to eliminate those weaknesses which have been exploited by the Soviets and communism" and reached the incendiary conclusion that the French cared more about turning back indigenous resistance and potential "UK and US encroachment" than "losing out to Soviet and communist control."[59]

In evaluating the policies and the attitudes of the major European powers in the Middle East, U.S. officials groused far more often about the French than the British, heavily criticizing French imperial strategy. Yet these sorts of distinctions ultimately mattered little to people fighting for their autonomy and independence. The real threat to America's interests in the region, or at least to its image, came from associating itself too closely with Western power broadly speaking. This situation differed somewhat from Southeast Asia since the level of U.S. commitment paled in comparison, but the same basic dynamic came into play. Since World War II, one PSB staffer wrote, the United States had "come to be increasingly identified . . . with Western European interests" throughout "great portions" of the Middle East. "In view of the current French and British positions," another writer argued, "we can not continue to ignore the Arab world as we have appeared to. We must improve our position in Arab eyes." He was also "struck uncomfortably by similarities to China"—about as damning an indictment as one could offer in the early 1950s.[60]

Discussions of how to improve perceptions of the United States generated a wide range of proposals. Some of these ideas, such as training more specialists in Arab languages and cultures, made good sense (although knowledge does not necessarily equal wisdom).[61] Others trafficked in lazy clichés about "democratic institutions and processes" being the "true revolutionary forces in the world today," since no nation had "ever espoused Communism of its own free will." One analyst, quoting Dean Rusk, suggested that U.S. propaganda should emphasize the dubious proposition that the history of the United States had always "been marked by a genuine support for broad nationalist aspirations."[62]

The most interesting and revealing suggestions typically started from a solid premise but wound up invoking the same sorts of ethnocentric tropes that had damaged America's image in the first place. One lengthy PSB memo focused on developing a "positive approach" to the "peoples" of the Middle East. It began by calling for an "honest appreciation of the psychology of the peoples of each country . . . and an understanding of what they hope to achieve as citizens of newly independent and sovereign nations." As a comment on the virtues of listening before speaking, this statement had much to recommend it, but it also opened the door to generalizations about "these people" and "their" motivations. In the end, the authors of this memo managed to crystallize the essence of American Orientalism into a few brief sentences:

> Memory of foreign domination and the rancors generated by it deeply color the thinking and attitudes of [Middle Eastern] peoples. They believe the West regards them as second-class citizens, as inferior in color, status and ability. Consequently, they tend to imagine a patronizing or condescending attitude on the part of Westerners even when this is not so.

The contradictions here were remarkable: distinguishing the actions of the United States from those of other "Westerners" while still buying in to the East-West binary of "we" and "they"; recognizing that previous experiences with "foreign domination" might color perceptions of the United States, only to dismiss the "patronizing or condescending attitude on the part of Westerners" as largely imaginary.[63]

One could easily look at these assessments—so perceptive in some ways, so blinkered in others—and draw simplistic conclusions about the dangerous consequences of cultural parochialism or, for that matter, good intentions. Yet recognizing a harbinger is not the same thing as identifying a missed opportunity. To be sure, the evaluations of U.S. psychological strategy in the Middle East during the early 1950s foreshadowed the difficult place in which the United States would find itself in future regional flashpoints, such as the Algerian War and the Suez crisis. Public diplomats had recognized for years that the U.S. government would face vexing choices between maintaining America's image in Western Europe and maintaining it in the rest of the world. Of course, it was not always a simple matter of "the West" versus everyone else; every country and every region had its own dynamics and its own history in dealing with the United States. In Latin America, for example, the long, tortured history of U.S. intervention damaged the nation's image far more than, say, the Marshall Plan did. Yet, even in Latin America, the generalized perception that the United States stood for colonialism abroad—that it stood with the British against the Egyptians in Suez, with the French against the Vietnamese in Southeast Asia—posed an obvious risk of conjuring up unhappy memories of the "colossus of the north."

The farther the Cold War expanded beyond Europe, the more that accounting for "Cold War considerations" might dictate several different, mutually exclusive, courses of action. Moreover, in some ways the public diplomacy battles for hearts and minds around the globe actually helped to forge a common identity among "Third World" peoples, increasing the likelihood that an antinationalist posture in one place would reverberate negatively around the world.[64] These were the vicissitudes of building an empire of ideas in an age of mass communications. Simply put, the power and mobility of ideas worked both for and against the United States in the founding of the American Century.

*   *   *

By the time Harry Truman left office in January 1953, the chain of events unleashed by the Chinese Revolution in the fall of 1949 had overwhelmed his presidency. Overseas, the Korean War had been stalemated for more than two years. At home, conservative voices dominated the political discourse more than at any point in the previous generation. The administration's seeming inability to respond to the challenge of revolutionary nationalism in Asia fueled the rise of a new brand of intense criticism, exemplified by Wisconsin Senator Joseph McCarthy's accusations of widespread disloyalty throughout the U.S. government. Truman's personal popularity had plummeted from even the modest levels that had been enough to re-elect him four years earlier.

All of these issues combined to shape the trajectory of U.S. public diplomacy during these years. By itself, the Cold War turning hot imbued the battle of ideas with a new level of urgency; the fact that it simultaneously moved beyond Europe reframed the discussion of which ideas to emphasize. Public diplomats had to reconsider not only the intensity of their message and the means for delivering it, but the nature of the message itself. The same old questions all resurfaced—about who spoke for the U.S. government, what they would say, and to whom they would say it—with the stakes for finding suitable answers higher than ever.

All of these discussions took place against the backdrop of the relentless criticism directed at Truman's foreign policy team. McCarthy and the phenomenon he represented created an extraordinary information problem at home and abroad. Public diplomats found themselves responding to a barrage of accusations that required an explanation suitable for both foreign and domestic audiences. Never had the connection between foreign relations and domestic affairs seemed more poignant—and more devastating. In the end, McCarthyism delivered the final blow to the first phase of U.S. public diplomacy, but not before provoking another fierce battle over the projection of "America."

6

"An Unfavorable Projection of American Unity"
McCarthyism and Public Diplomacy

AS MUCH AS THE explosion of revolutionary nationalism in Asia transformed the content and conduct of public diplomacy abroad, it played an equally significant role in changing the political calculus for public diplomats at home. The twin events of the Chinese Revolution and the Korean War essentially destroyed the bipartisan foreign policy consensus of the early Cold War. In its place emerged a new, hyperpartisan atmosphere, in which Republican criticism of American Cold War strategy became strikingly common. For the majority of Truman's second term, it became "open season" on the State Department, as Eric Sevareid of CBS put it.[1]

From this combustible environment emerged Joseph McCarthy, who was fully prepared to do everything he could to ignite further controversy. On February 9, 1950, he gave a speech to the Republican Women's Club of Wheeling, West Virginia. In that address, McCarthy held up a piece of paper that he claimed listed the names of 205 members of Truman's State Department known to the Secretary of State as members of the Communist Party. This went well beyond the standard Republican attack line that, at various points in the past, the Roosevelt and Truman administrations had not worked diligently enough to root out Soviet sympathizers or spies. In this case, McCarthy accused

Truman and his top officials of continuing to countenance—at that very moment—the presence of communists and, by implication, spies. Thus began the Wisconsin senator's relentless carpet-bombing of Truman and his State Department.[2]

For public diplomats, the emergence of McCarthy as a national figure created all sorts of headaches. While he did not initially target them personally, they had to deal with the McCarthy phenomenon in numerous other ways. Schuyler Foster's Office of Public Opinion Studies produced daily reports on the press coverage of the senator's charges. Francis Russell's Office of Public Affairs produced the talking points that guided the State Department's public response to these charges. And various officials at multiple levels wrestled with how best to address the impact of these extraordinary—and extraordinarily divisive—accusations on the image of the United States around the world. One thing was certain: nothing good could come from the publicity that McCarthy soon started to generate. If McCarthy was wrong, it looked bad; if he was right, it looked worse. Either way, the hunt for communists in the U.S. government damaged America's image abroad, and public diplomats had to grapple with that problem.

From February 9, 1950 through the end of the Truman administration, the impact of McCarthyism on the State Department waxed and waned, depending on his targets any given week and the prominence of his platform for hurling accusations. Friends in the conservative media ensured that McCarthy and his charges never wandered too far from the limelight. As the Washington bureau chief for the *Chicago Tribune* later recalled, "McCarthy was a dream story.... I wasn't off page one for four years."[3] However, with the Democratic Party controlling the White House and both houses of Congress during these years, the most the senator could do was to demand hearings and further investigation into his allegations. When he got his way, coverage ramped up; at other times it dwindled to a slow burn. But the threat of new accusations was always there, and given the recklessness of the accuser, everyone responsible for the public image of the State Department had to be on guard.

Not until 1953, after the Republicans captured Congress and the White House, did McCarthy fully set his sights on what certainly seemed an easy and logical target for his accusations: the public diplomacy shop itself. Less than a month after Dwight Eisenhower's inauguration, McCarthy announced that he would be launching an investigation into "mismanagement and subversion" at the Voice of America. The Wisconsin senator's thoroughly predictable decision to join the long list of right-wing critics of the diplomacy of ideas was surprising only in the sense that it took him so long. Although unoriginal, his attacks did prove incredibly consequential. By the end of the year, the incoming Secretary of State John Foster Dulles decided to wash his hands of the entire matter by transferring authority over nearly all aspects of public diplomacy to the newly created United States Information Agency (USIA), where it would remain for almost half a century.[4]

"Trying to Discredit His Government Before the World"

McCarthy's initial accusations against the Truman State Department could not have been more perfectly timed. Just two weeks earlier, the long-running saga of Alger Hiss had finally come to an end when a federal judge sentenced the former State Department official to five years in prison for perjuring himself before a federal grand jury. Most members of the Truman administration had distanced themselves from Hiss as evidence that he spied for the Soviet Union mounted against him, but Secretary of State Dean Acheson took this opportunity to announce that he would continue to "vouch" for his former colleague. Without commenting on the merits of the sentence itself, Acheson cited Jesus Christ's Sermon on the Mount to explain why he could never "turn [his] back" on a friend.[5]

Predictably, these comments provoked an uproar, with the secretary and his boss running for cover as members of both parties called for a new probe into the continuing influence of Hiss in the State Department. Longtime State Department critic Senator Styles Bridges (R-NH) blasted Acheson's support for Hiss as another indication of the Democrats' "bad judgment" in dealing with communists. As evidence, Bridges cited other Republican bugaboos, such as Yalta, the Chinese Revolution, and the alleged abandonment of Chiang Kai-shek and Formosa. Soon, conservative Democrats, including the State Department's old foes Eugene Cox and John Rankin, joined the chorus. By the end of the week, even state legislatures in places such as Mississippi and Texas had passed resolutions calling for Acheson's ouster. At the same time, the conservative press joined the fray, with the *Chicago Tribune* leading the way. The *Tribune* not so subtly connected Hiss's rumored homosexuality to Acheson's supposed effeminacy with the blaring, two-inch headline: "Won't Quit Hiss—Acheson." The State Department's Office of Public Opinion Studies was closely monitoring the growing criticism of the secretary, even before McCarthy's accusations.[6]

Up to that point, the junior senator from Wisconsin was little more than an obscure backbencher who rode a severely inflated wartime service record to victory in the Republican tidal wave of 1946. In the intervening years, he had not shown the discipline to pass important legislation or the obsequiousness to secure large political donations. Up for re-election in 1952, he started to realize that he had little on which to campaign and even less money to do it.[7] What McCarthy did have was a finely tuned political antenna and an extraordinary talent for political demagoguery. In Wheeling, the senator found exactly the sort of campaign issue that could vault him onto the national stage.[8]

Over the next several days, McCarthy repeated his charges in other places, including in a much-publicized telegram to the president himself. "In a Lincoln Day speech Thursday night," McCarthy began (as though the president might have missed the news), "I stated that the State Department harbors a nest of communists and communist sympathizers who are helping to shape our foreign policy." Curiously, though, the alleged number of reds shrank from 205 to 57. On February 20th, he took to the floor of the Senate and spoke for nearly seven hours, off and on, sometimes referring to 57 communists, sometimes to 81 "loyalty risks," a broader category that included the former number plus some "cases of lesser importance." He never explained why he abandoned his initial figure of 205 and later denied under oath that he had ever used that number. However, McCarthy's numbers were not completely made up. Rather, the senator took his figures from several outdated lists compiled by various people over the past several years. The actual problem with McCarthy's accusations was not the lack of a "list," per se, but the fact that his "lists" were outdated, unoriginal, misrepresented, and taken out of context.[9]

The Truman administration and its supporters did not simply lie down in the face of this barrage, but they vacillated back and forth between angry denunciations and ignoring the charges entirely. Two days after the Wheeling speech Truman composed an incendiary personal telegram that accused McCarthy of "trying to discredit his government before the world"—adding, for effect, that "I am very sure that the people of Wisconsin are very sorry that they are represented by a person who has as little sense of responsibility as you have." But the president reconsidered and nixed the telegram before it went out. Two weeks later, following McCarthy's speech before the Senate, Truman changed course again and publicly lambasted his new foe as "the greatest asset that the Kremlin has."[10]

In Congress, some of McCarthy's colleagues (including some Republicans) criticized his demagoguery and his attempt to portray recycled information as original detective work. However, many conservatives either defended his accusations, or suggested that he had raised important questions that needed to be addressed, regardless of the accuracy of the specific charges. The casting of aspersions was aided by McCarthy's loyal allies in the conservative media, who asked few questions and required little evidence before reprinting his charges. Even less credulous reporters who wrote for purportedly liberal papers conveyed McCarthy's accusations, noting the lack of substantiation and the angry rebuttals that came from his targets. However, the conventions of journalism did not really allow them to call him a liar. Moreover, given the recent string of high-profile espionage cases like that of Alger Hiss, many may have assumed that where there was smoke there was fire.[11] The editorial page of the *Philadelphia Inquirer* captured this sentiment succinctly in its conclusion that "as long as these charges persist and are not proved or disproved by a thorough, impartial investigation, public confidence in the State Department will be lessened." In other words, the State Department could not credibly conduct its business so long as McCarthy continued to find an audience for his charges. As a result, public consensus eventually emerged around the calls for further investigation.[12] Then, in June, the Korean War arrived, seemingly confirming everything McCarthy had been saying about how and why the Truman administration had "lost" Asia. Following so closely on the heels of the Chinese Revolution, who could deny that the communists were on the march, and that Secretary of State Dean Acheson and his "crimson crowd" of "striped pants" diplomats bore at least some of the blame?[13]

To Report or Not to Report?

Over the years, McCarthy insinuated off and on that he did not care for anyone or anything associated with the State Department's public diplomacy shop. His initial round of accusations referred to an unnamed "top official" in the information programs who allegedly constituted one of the three "biggest" security threats presently employed at the State Department. The senator never elaborated, though, and his focus soon turned to Owen Lattimore, the renowned Asianist and former OWI official, whom McCarthy described as "the top Russian espionage agent in the United States."[14] Shortly thereafter, McCarthy accused Haldore Hanson, an administrator for Point IV and a former official in the cultural programs, of being an active member of the Communist Party.[15] For the most part, though, public diplomats escaped unscathed in the first round of accusations.

That started to change in mid-1951, when McCarthy questioned the loyalty of William Stone, who worked on international broadcasting in Edward Barrett's office. During World War II, Stone had served, along with State Department "China Hands" Owen Lattimore and John Service, on the editorial board of *Amerasia*, the infamous journal of Far Eastern affairs.[16] For many, just mentioning the name *Amerasia*, which McCarthy often did, evoked thoughts of scandal, espionage, and communist conspiracies. Back in 1945, after an OSS staffer recognized one of his reports reprinted in the pages of the journal, OSS security agents raided *Amerasia*'s New York offices and discovered thousands of pages of classified documents. Ultimately, the FBI arrested its editor and five of his staffers for unlawful possession of classified government documents. There was no charge for espionage because the government could not prove that these documents had been delivered to a foreign power. The Justice Department eventually dismissed most of the charges because of illegal conduct by both the OSS and the FBI. William Stone had not been arrested, but his connection to the journal put him on a list of easy targets, and McCarthy took full advantage. Stone resigned the following year.[17]

These specific cases aside, McCarthyism's biggest impact on Truman-era public diplomats probably came in the form of an increased workload. Since their job required them to monitor and engage domestic public opinion, particularly as it related to the conduct of foreign policy, they spent a great deal of time cataloguing and responding to McCarthy's charges. As usual, they prepared the talking points that top officials like Acheson used when speaking publicly about these matters. At the same time, they monitored foreign reactions to news about McCarthyism. They first had to decide, in an excellent illustration of the remarkable circularity of the whole process, whether to report on McCarthy's investigations via outlets such as the VOA. To address the story potentially spread it even more widely, to say nothing of the risk of stoking the senator's ire if the broadcast did not convey the details in the manner that he wished. On the other hand, to ignore huge news because it reflected badly on the U.S. government threatened the credibility of the entire enterprise. It was the same old saw, as domestic affairs turned into foreign relations and vice versa, with information specialists caught in the middle.

In the end, the VOA chose not to report on McCarthy's initial accusations in his Wheeling speech, reasoning that it was "primarily of domestic interest," presented an "unfavorable projection of American unity," and, most importantly, "was not picked up by the foreign press." Later, when the Senate appointed a subcommittee to investigate McCarthy's charges, the worldwide media latched onto the story, forcing the State Department to engage it.[18] This rationale, although sound from the perspective of public diplomacy, did not please the department's critics. Congressman John Taber (R-NY), a staunch opponent of U.S. propaganda dating back to the days of the OWI, blasted the VOA for broadcasting the story: "Who could possibly think that portraying to foreign countries the fact that it was necessary to have an investigation of the State Department...would do anything towards making the people abroad feel that we were united against Communism?" He was probably right about the way that McCarthyism made the United States look in foreign eyes. The problem was the conclusion he drew from that assessment: "Advertising that the loyalty of the State Department had been questioned would appear to me to be very poor psychology." This was wrong. Whatever harm McCarthy's crusade had caused to America's image came from international coverage of his actions, not from the VOA's acknowledgment of that coverage.[19]

"Come Now, Joe—Let's Be Reasonable!"

As Harry Truman left office in January 1953, the fate of U.S. public diplomacy still hung in the balance. The strange career of the Psychological Strategy Board reminded everyone why a previous generation of policymakers had decided to separate white from black propaganda, military from civilian operations, in fighting the "war" of ideas. That said, did the failed experiment in synchronizing the messages of public diplomacy with the objectives of all-out psychological warfare signal a return to previous arrangements, or another new beginning? For years, various policymakers and pundits had called for removing public diplomacy from the State Department and placing it an independent agency that would administer propaganda, cultural and educational exchanges, and perhaps even economic development programs, such as Point IV. The State Department had already moved in that direction when it created the semiautonomous International Information Administration to run the propaganda programs after Edward Barrett resigned in late 1951. Maybe the change in administration would provide the final push.

The recent presidential election, in which Republican Dwight Eisenhower crushed Democrat Adlai Stevenson by eleven points in the popular vote, offered few clues in this regard. The widely admired Eisenhower, boasting a nearly unassailable reputation as a war hero, saw little reason to provide specifics about much of anything. He famously pledged simply to "go to Korea" and that seemed to be enough. Meanwhile, Stevenson, the erudite governor from Illinois, found himself in the awkward position of running on a New Deal platform that had been weighed down by the sitting president's massively unpopular war in Korea. With Eisenhower talking in generalities, and Stevenson trying to avoid any mention of Truman or his policies, no one articulated any clear plan for what would happen to the Voice of America, the educational exchange programs, the overseas libraries, and any of their other wildly controversial cousins.

Eisenhower's victory clarified the situation only slightly. During the campaign, he hammered Truman for not being aggressive enough in waging the war of ideas in Eastern Europe and in Korea. But how much of this reflected an authentic interest in beefing up psychological warfare, as opposed to simply bolstering his general attacks on the containment strategy? The standard Republican critique of the Democrats' foreign policy held that because of a misguided allegiance to the idea of "containment," the Truman administration had simply acquiesced to Soviet domination of Eastern Europe and stalemate in Korea. Using this logic, Richard Nixon unforgettably described Stevenson as a "man with a Ph.D. from Dean Acheson's cowardly college of communist containment."[20] Furthermore, even if Eisenhower expanded the government's psychological operations, what would that mean? Would he, as a military man, emphasize the sort of "black ops" preferred by Wild Bill Donovan and his successors at the CIA? Or would he also support the expansion of a MacLeish-style public diplomacy program that so many of his fellow Republicans dismissed as nothing more than "cultural and informational fanfare"? Eisenhower had appeared before Congress several times over the years in support of the State Department's embattled information programs, but that was before he declared a party affiliation and ran for president. Where did he stand now?[21]

Within days of his inauguration, Eisenhower convened a "Committee on International Information Activities" headed by New York investment banker William H. Jackson to examine these matters. Although mostly comprised of businessmen and bureaucrats, two members of the committee had considerable experience in information policy: Gordon Gray, the former PSB director, and C. D. Jackson, who soon took on the role of propaganda czar in the Eisenhower administration. Jackson was a veteran of Henry Luce's *Time-Life* empire where he had held several top-level managerial positions, both before and after the war. In between, he worked for the OWI, as well as in the political warfare division of the Allied Expeditionary Forces in Europe, commanded by General Eisenhower. Both Jackson and Nelson Rockefeller, who headed a related committee on government organization for the Eisenhower transition team, favored moving public diplomacy into an independent agency within the State Department orbit. So did John

Foster Dulles, the newly appointed Secretary of State, although Dulles really just wanted to rid himself of the responsibility for running those types of programs.[22] Before these two committees even had a chance to offer formal recommendations, an unpredictable new factor entered the equation. On February 13, 1953, Joseph McCarthy declared that he would be launching an investigation into "mismanagement and subversion" at the Voice of America.

For several years prior to Eisenhower's election, observers had quietly wondered what would happen to McCarthy's relentless crusade to expose "subversives" in the U.S. government if his own party took over the federal government. With McCarthy's decision to investigate the Voice of America, they had their answer. The widely syndicated illustrator Reg Manning perfectly captured this perverse dynamic in an unforgettable cartoon that depicted John Foster Dulles sitting at his desk and opening the top drawer, only to find McCarthy's head poking out. "Come now, Joe—let's be reasonable!" Dulles pleaded.

Part of the problem stemmed from a serious miscalculation by the leadership of the Republican Party after it regained control of the Senate in the 1952 elections. McCarthy, confident of his own re-election in Wisconsin, campaigned vigorously in support of his closest Republican allies and against his bitterest Democratic enemies. Although a fine-grained electoral analysis shows that his participation generally made little difference in the outcome of these races—and in some cases even backfired—the defeat of three of his staunchest critics in the opposition party fostered an exaggerated impression of his influence. (One of the foes McCarthy vanquished in the 1952 election was former Assistant Secretary of State William Benton, who lost his Connecticut Senate seat after introducing a resolution to expel McCarthy from Congress the previous year.) Republicans faced a difficult choice going into the 1953 legislative session: the public perception of McCarthy's role in their collective victory created an expectation that he would receive a leadership position of some sort, but they understandably worried about what he would do with real power.[23]

Hoping to placate the senator and his supporters, party leaders rewarded him with the Chairmanship of the Committee on Government Operations rather than a lesser position on the powerful Internal Security Subcommittee that would have been the most obvious choice given his interests. Republican leaders hoped that by exiling him to a sort of legislative Siberia they had limited the damage he might do, but the Committee on Government Operations contained a seldom-used Investigative Subcommittee that allowed McCarthy to hold hearings, with subpoena power, on any aspect of "government operations." Rather than hurling accusations in the press and pressuring reluctant Democrats to investigate, he could personally haul in witness after witness to testify on any government-related matter.[24]

John Foster Dulles grew nervous when he heard that McCarthy had selected the Voice of America as his first target. Dulles well knew just how radioactive public diplomacy could be, and he did not want to get blamed for personnel, policies, and programs implemented by the previous administration. Looking for assurances that he and his staff would not get swept up into the investigation before they even had a chance to begin their work, he reached out to one of McCarthy's allies in the press. The senator was not interested in the current regime, Dulles was told. Much relieved, he agreed to cooperate fully, ordering his staffers to turn over anything and everything McCarthy requested. Dulles never cared much for public diplomacy, anyway. He certainly was not going to let it get in the way of the things he really wanted to do.[25]

The Loyal Underground and the Voice of America

The *New York Times* reported that McCarthy's investigation into subversion at the VOA would examine the "type of programs put on and whether the contents of these programs have been in keeping with the best interests of the United States."[26] Given the sheer volume of the material pumped out over government airwaves, anyone determined to find something objectionable could easily do so if they spent enough time reading scripts. That had been proven time and again during the various inquisitions into overseas propaganda through the years. Then there were the authors of these scripts. The VOA employed an unusually large number of foreigners because of their language skills. This, above all, was what made it so easy to paint the VOA as a haven for communists or other people of "alien" and "radical" points of view. For some critics, just the fact that they were born outside the United States raised a red flag. And in that climate it only took a few examples to tar the entire operation.

Roy Cohn and David Schine, the senator's faithful assistants—their enemies preferred "hatchet men"—set up shop in both New York and Washington to prepare for the hearings. Their New York headquarters, Schine's plush pad in the Waldorf Towers, was just a short walk from the offices of the Voice of America, giving them easy access to several of their sources, a group of disgruntled VOA employees known as the Loyal Underground. Each of these men and women was eager to testify to what they regarded as serious mistakes and woeful mismanagement by their bosses; they also proved more than willing to speculate about the motives behind those alleged transgressions. Their testimony catered perfectly to a committee hoping to insinuate, without any hard evidence, that there was a conspiracy within the Voice to sabotage U.S. propaganda. The *Chicago Tribune*, McCarthy's go-to paper, also helped by vastly exaggerating the size of the Loyal Underground. Even though only four people had testi-fied to that point, the *Tribune* reported, citing "Senate investigators," that as many as 1,500 disgruntled employees had banded together "in a secret revolt against red influences among top officials." After one day of testi-mony, the conservative daily flatly declared that McCarthy had revealed the existence of "pro-Soviet policies in the Voice of America."[27]

To make their case, McCarthy, Cohn, and Schine immediately zeroed in on several familiar lines of attack. In addition to combing through scripts, they got hold of a recent information policy directive that authorized the use of work by writers with leftist and communist sympathies if doing so served the larger propaganda objective, which it often did, particularly if these sources could be quoted saying compli-mentary things about the United States. Public diplomats had gone back and forth on this issue for years, weighing in effect their professional judgment against their professional reputations. Broadly worded, this directive applied to broadcasters, copywriters, reporters, and anyone else who might produce text for propaganda purposes. Theoretically, it also applied to overseas libraries, although the vast majority of books by controversial authors had been removed years before in response to prior investigations. The goal was to allow propagandists maximum flexibility in selecting the material that best served the interests of U.S. foreign policy. Relying on the professional judgment of U.S. officials may have made sense from the perspective of creating a successful program, but it left a lot to chance.

McCarthy, of course, exploited this directive for all it was worth. He observed that, for some reason, it specifically recommended the novelist Howard Fast as a "Soviet-endorsed author" whose work might give "added credibility" to broadcasts directed toward certain European audiences. Some of Fast's books also appeared in a few overseas libraries. This was trouble. Fast, who once worked as a writer for the OWI, had joined the Communist Party in 1944. Later, when he refused to answer questions before the House Un-American Activities Committee, he was jailed for contempt of Congress (at which point he began his most famous book, *Spartacus*, about a rebellion among Roman slaves). As part of his investigation, McCarthy subpoenaed Fast. There was no compelling reason to interview him except to watch him "take the fifth" and embarrass the VOA. Obviously, he had nothing to do with the decision to deploy his work for propaganda purposes.[28]

The committee also used the Fast case to harp on the State Department for promoting the dissemination of communist information. Strictly speaking, this might have been true, except that McCarthy omitted the fact that top officials rescinded the directive just a few days after it was issued, several days before the hearings began. Apparently, they too saw the possibilities for exploitation. Just to be sure—and to make his own position clear—John Foster Dulles ordered another new policy guidance stating that "no repeat no materials by any communists, fellow travelers, etc., will be used under any circumstances." Several propagandists bitterly observed that this kind of knee-jerk reaction prevented them from even quoting Stalin or *Pravda* for reporting purposes. One top VOA official, Alfred Morton, protested the absurdity of this provision to his superiors. In a confidential memo, he told them that he would continue to quote from Lenin, Stalin, and other communist sources if it helped to further the message of anticommunism. Publicly, State Department officials denied that the order prevented U.S. propagandists from quoting Soviet officials. But when they learned that someone had leaked Morton's memo to McCarthy, the State Department immediately suspended Morton and released the story to the press to demonstrate their vigilance.[29]

Before the hearings even made it into their second week, Dulles accepted the "resignation" of Dr. Wilson Compton, the director of the International Information Administration, the agency responsible for the VOA. As a Truman administration holdover, Compton's departure was not totally unexpected, but it contributed to the perception of an entire operation under siege. The news analysis in the *New York Times* concluded, "McCarthy poses an administration problem." The same day, the *Washington Post* predicted "showdown with McCarthy near." The authors of these stories were not wrong in sensing tension between McCarthy and the administration. What they failed to understand was that, in this case, the senator was actually doing Dulles a favor. The more incompetent the entire operation looked, the easier it would be for him to exile it from the State Department.[30]

Throughout the hearings, McCarthy and company resurrected time-tested critiques about "waste" and the prevalence of "subversive" employees, while exhibiting unprecedented levels of imagination. A disgruntled former VOA engineer testified to "mistakes" and "waste" of such monumental proportions that, in his opinion, they could only have sprung from intent rather than mere stupidity. To be fair, McCarthy baited him into reaching this conclusion by posing leading question after leading question. But the engineer never complained. In one of the more memorable episodes of the entire hearings, his accusations allowed McCarthy to turn a disagreement over the best location to build new VOA transmitters into a massive conspiracy to prevent U.S. broadcasts from reaching the Soviet Union. What essentially amounted to a dispute over astronomy quickly became a "deliberate" effort to construct transmitters more susceptible to Soviet jamming. A jittery State Department validated these accusations when it immediately suspended construction on the two transmitters. The controversy also produced results of a more tragic nature when Robert Kaplan, one of the engineers responsible for selecting the locations of the transmitters, killed himself. "Once the dogs are set on you," Kaplan said in his suicide note, "everything you have done since the beginning of time is suspect."[31]

The VOA fared no better in the second week of hearings. The focus shifted from policies to personalities. Dr. Nancy Lenkeith, a former scriptwriter on the French desk, claimed she was fired for, among other things, defending Abraham Lincoln, praising Whittaker Chambers on the air, and refusing to live on a commune with her supervisor. The last charge obviously raised the most eyebrows and, when it came to that portion of her testimony, McCarthy ostentatiously interrupted her and told the television cameras to stop filming because "children may be listening." As Lenkeith continued, the story grew even stranger. She reported that her boss, the head of the French section, asked her to join him when he left the VOA to live on a Marxist collective, where children would be raised communally. Lenkeith told him that she did not even have a husband, much less any children. He supposedly replied: "that can be worked out."[32]

Things only got worse from there. In early March, another member of the Loyal Underground accused Roger Lyons, the Director of Religious Programming, of being—of all things—an atheist. Wanting to milk this sort of blockbuster revelation for all it was worth, McCarthy asked the witness how he knew this. When he said that he had heard it third-hand from another staff member named Kretzmann, McCarthy called Kretzmann to the stand, which backfired. Kretzmann flatly denied everything, denied that Lyons was an atheist and denied that he had ever said so. Apparently, he had once rebuffed what he considered an inappropriate question about Lyons's religious beliefs with the comment that it was none of anyone's business and Lyons could be an "atheist for all he knew." In fact, Kretzmann knew that Lyons was not an atheist, but he thought it inappropriate to discuss the matter with someone else. Dissatisfied, McCarthy called yet another Voice staffer, who testified that Lyons had not believed in God between 1944 and 1946, when she was "going with him." One of the Democrats on the committee, finally realizing what she had said, interjected to ask whether she might hold a grudge against an ex-boyfriend. She denied it, of course, but realizing where this was headed, McCarthy abruptly terminated the questioning. He never mentioned Roger Lyons again.[33]

The committee turned next to Reed Harris, the highest-ranking public diplomat to appear. Once again, a member of the Loyal Underground provided the base accusation, a complaint that Harris tried to cut back VOA broadcasts to Israel at the very moment that a wave of anti-Semitic violence in several communist countries would have made that propaganda most effective. Harris prepared to defend himself by explaining that his recommendation, which his supervisor vetoed anyway, was a cost-cutting measure. But McCarthy showed little interest in discussing this policy and instead quizzed him about a book he had published as an undergraduate twenty years earlier. *King Football*, which Harris wrote in a fit of pique after Columbia University suspended him for a semester, examined the growing business of college football through an in-depth look at Columbia's program. Harris lambasted Columbia along with the entire college sport as a "semi-professional racket" that only existed so the university could rake in ticket sales and please hard-drinking alumni. McCarthy sniffed a critique of capitalism in this narrative. Even Harris admitted that he would not hire someone who held the beliefs that he held when he wrote the book, and he claimed that he had abandoned these views almost two decades ago. Harris soon realized that the committee intended to focus solely on his background rather than on the specific charges leveled against him. He denounced the entire process as "dirty pool" and accused McCarthy of trying to wring his "public neck." Harris then accused the committee of a "deliberate pattern to destroy and nullify" the Voice of America. Back and forth they went on national television for several hours.[34] This continued for another week, and then, in mid-March, McCarthy announced that he had finished with the Voice of America. Next up: the State Department's overseas libraries.

Book Burning

There was nothing original about this target, either, but McCarthy correctly sensed that his tactics would work even better on the libraries. All he needed was a list of books and periodicals stocked by the nearly 200 overseas libraries and he could start issuing subpoenas. The methodology was incredibly simple: (1.) Identify an author with questionable political associations whose works appeared in overseas libraries. (2.) Find someone—usually an ex-communist—willing to link this author to someone or something subversive. (3.) Call the author to testify. These cases did not require an endless back and forth on the virtues of one policy choice over another, or on unsubstantiated speculation about the motives and mindsets of various employees. McCarthy did not even need the testimony of unreliable (and in some cases unstable) disgruntled employees. He did not have to uncover evidence of communist-sympathizers working in the State Department. Instead, he could simply put the authors on trial, much as he did with Howard Fast at the beginning of the VOA hearings, and then tar the information programs as guilty by association. By March 1953, the State Department's overseas libraries had accumulated approximately two million volumes worldwide. McCarthy estimated some 30,000 of those volumes, by 250 different authors, qualified as "pro-Communist" in one sense or another. He eventually called thirty-three authors to testify during hearings that stretched over four months. These numbers did not really add up, but that did nothing to diminish the fireworks he produced.[35]

As the subcommittee began preparations for the public portion of the hearings, Roy Cohn and David Schine took off on a much-ballyhooed two-week tour of the State Department libraries in Europe. The trip earned the two young investigators no end of grief from the European media. As public diplomats knew, McCarthyism did not play well abroad. Cohn and Schine expected to spend their time exposing waste and inefficiency in the library program while calling attention to the presence of communist authors on the shelves. Instead, they mostly bounced from one awkward situation to the next. In Germany, Cohn staged an embarrassing public reprimand of a U.S. public affairs officer. After announcing that this official had been recalled to Washington to testify before the committee, Cohn proceeded to detail his alleged transgressions, most of which dealt with his beliefs and associations during the 1930s. When the pair got to England near the end of their trip, they found the notoriously aggressive British press waiting to pounce. Everywhere they went, reporters quizzed them about McCarthy's tactics, about where they got their authority, whether they intended to question British citizens, even their ages. (Cohn was twenty-six, Schine a year younger.) After their grilling in England, the American press started to take note. McCarthy's opponents blasted them for shaming the United States abroad. The *Chicago Tribune* defended them against the "smears" of the "European and eastern internationalist press," but this did nothing to repair the damage done to European perceptions of the United States. All in all, the whole junket was a disaster.[36]

Back in the United States, McCarthy geared up for phase two of his investigation of the information programs. He opened with as big a splash as possible, dragging in Earl Browder, the former head of the Communist Party USA, to testify. Browder had written dozens of books, some of which did in fact appear in State Department libraries around the world. At first blush, this made no sense—books by a Communist Party official in a U.S. government library? But Browder was one of those complicated cases where, depending upon the audience, his story might actually help the United States. In 1946, he had been expelled from the Communist Party for trying to distance the U.S. wing of the party from its Russian overlords. To certain audiences, he might appear as something of an American Tito, but McCarthy had no interest in finding out why U.S. officials selected Browder's books for their shelves, and Browder had no interest in helping him speculate. He angrily accused the senator of being "out to get [him]" and refused to respond to the most basic queries, including even the standard opening salvo, "are you now or have you ever been a communist?" If ever there was someone unlikely to be hurt by answering that question it was Browder, but he seemed determined to make the committee's job as difficult as possible. No matter, McCarthy still got his headline: "Browder Jeers at Red Probe."[37]

The committee conducted similar examinations off and on over the next four months. Every time it seemed to be losing momentum, McCarthy issued a new round of subpoenas. The list of literary luminaries to appear included Langston Hughes, Dashiell Hammett, Herbert Aptheker, Lillian Hellman, Dorothy Parker, and Paul Robeson's wife, Eslanda. Some cooperated, some "took the fifth." Some were actually communists, some ex-communists. All had had their books pulled from the shelves of U.S. libraries at one time or another. None of them had any idea why those books were there in the first place. That was not why they were called to testify.[38]

In June, the *New York Times* broke the story of a purge of dozens of authors from U.S. libraries in Germany. It soon became clear that the State Department had blacklisted those books worldwide, not just in Germany. Some authors who appeared on this list, like Dashiell Hammett and Langston Hughes, had recently testified before McCarthy's committee. Others had no direct connection to McCarthy or to communism. They simply wrote about controversial matters in a way that might displease someone looking to be displeased. For example, the libraries rid their shelves of numerous books critical of Chiang Kai-shek and his Kuomintang government out of a fear that some people might confuse "anti-Chiang" with "pro-Mao."[39]

McCarthy's critics, noting that the story began in Germany of all places, blasted the senator for advocating "book-burning." They also blamed Dulles and the State Department for capitulating. The whole controversy reached a depressing nadir five days in, when the *Times* revealed that a few of the overseas librarians, unsure of what to do with the banned books, actually lit them on fire. Dulles hastily issued an order that books should not literally be burned. Recognizing how bad this entire episode looked, Eisenhower used a commencement address at Dartmouth University to denounce "book-burners," although he carefully avoided mentioning McCarthy's name. Even this was too much for the senator and his allies. The President soon "clarified" his original position, explaining that he did not oppose the removal of "communist propaganda" from U.S. libraries, but that skirted the issue. Very little of the material just blacklisted could be described, even loosely, as "communist propaganda."[40]

*   *   *

The short-term damage to the information programs was catastrophic, both at home and abroad. Obviously, being linked to book burning, literally or figuratively, did not advance the image of the United States as a beacon of freedom and democracy. In July, after eleven separate directives related to McCarthy's examination of the overseas libraries, the State Department finally decided that it would not ban "controversial" books after all, only books that proposed the destruction of the United States or constitutional government.[41] By this point, Dulles and Eisenhower had already announced that the entire apparatus of public diplomacy would soon be moved into the United States Information Agency. It had been clear for some time that things were headed in this direction. Nearly everyone in a position of authority seemed to favor putting an independent agency in charge of public diplomacy.[42] In early June, Eisenhower made it official when he proposed a massive government reorganization plan. In some ways, McCarthy simply provided the final shove. But, in the process, he managed to do serious harm to the always-tenuous practice of public diplomacy. He picked its most obvious vulnerabilities, its perpetual weaknesses, and exploited them to maximum effect.

The profound irony of the whole situation was that McCarthyism and its political antecedents actually sprang from the same source as public diplomacy: the heightened mobility of ideas and the permeability of boundaries between domestic and foreign. Looked at one way, this sort of fluidity required the United States to pay much more attention to the image it projected to the world; looked at another way, it meant that the nation had to be permanently on guard against the "invasion" of foreign ideologies. Some people worried about both possibilities equally. But, generally speaking, staunch advocates of public diplomacy worried more about the former; staunch critics, more about the latter. In a kind of metaphysical symmetry, an initiative created as the government's rearguard action against the migration of ideas and ideologies served as a convenient scapegoat for people hostile to that process itself. Critics might not be able to stop this migration from occurring, but they could at least try to prevent the government from facilitating and participating in it. While one might fault Joseph McCarthy and his ideological compatriots for their tactics and their motivations, they rightly sensed that the exchange of ideas raised fundamental questions about what ideas would be exchanged. They also correctly assumed that the State Department's priorities in the selection of those ideas differed profoundly from their own. In other words, McCarthy and his fellow critics of public diplomacy over the years knew who their enemies were, even if they did not always know why.[43]

EPILOGUE

The Creation of the USIA and the Fate of U.S. Public Diplomacy

THE CREATION OF THE USIA marked the end of the beginning. Just as it brought a sense of closure to the story that began back in 1936 at the Buenos Aires Conference, it also opened a new chapter in a narrative that continues to this day. The Eisenhower administration's "solution," suggested by many over the years, promised to reduce organizational confusion and to limit the State Department's exposure to the explosive practice of public diplomacy. However, these objectives, while understandable, failed to address the larger questions about America's image and the role it played in shaping the environment in which U.S. foreign policymakers operated. The decision also seemed to reject one of the most fundamental "lessons" of the OWI experience during World War II: disseminating images and ideas about the United States was, by definition, foreign policy. As Dean Acheson put it in one of his famous "Princeton Seminars," a series of retrospective roundtables he hosted right after leaving the State Department in 1953, "we've seen an independent agency in the OWI days.... we're going back to an almost independent agency and each time people assume we should solve all the problems by putting it in a little different place in the Government hierarchy."[1]

In 1954, shortly after the USIA took over public diplomacy, administrators commissioned a study of "USIA Operating Assumptions."

The product, a five-volume study totaling more than a thousand pages, surveyed the thinking of 142 USIA employees in order to describe the philosophy driving U.S. public diplomacy at that pivotal moment. Analysts were particularly interested in documenting disagreements among policymakers in order to identify the parameters within which subsequent debates would occur. And they found, not surprisingly, a wide variety of ideas about how to conduct overseas propaganda and cultural exchange. As the authors argued:

> Many of the controversies within the Information Agency stem from basic and long-standing differences in outlook which are not likely to be resolved easily as a result of executive or policy decisions. In part they reflect the profound moral issues of ends and means which face democracy in its struggle with a ruthless enemy. These issues are likely to remain alive regardless of the future course of events, and regardless of the philosophy of the incumbent Agency administration, although the position of minority and majority might shift.[2]

In other words, different approaches to public diplomacy originated in different philosophies of foreign policy and foreign relations. The interminable struggle to align ends with means would continue as long as public diplomacy continued; it would not simply melt away through changes in leadership or legislation or, for that matter, the creation of an entirely new agency.

Appropriately, the report concluded not with any actual conclusions, but rather with a series of more than one hundred questions that public diplomats would continue to confront as they moved forward. Among those conclusion/questions were:

> 29. At what point does distortion or slanting in news lead to a loss of credibility?
> 31. Should unfavorable news (or descriptions of unpleasant features in American life) be reported in output or should they be ignored?
> 32. When information harmful to the US is reported must it always be mitigated by favorable information or explanations in the same context, or is it better to avoid any appearance of justification?

45. Should the program accurately reflect all aspects of life in the US, or should it selectively emphasize the favorable aspects?

46. Should material critical of the US be included in output if it is *not* being disseminated by other (unofficial or foreign) media? Should material critical of the US be included in output if it *is* being disseminated by other media?[3]

Over the past fifteen years, U.S. officials in the State Department, the Office of War Information, and in Congress, had debated these very issues—exhaustively, in many cases. That they were no closer, after all that time, to reaching definitive answers did not signify failure so much as it spoke to the intractable nature of the dilemmas that public diplomats had confronted and would continue to confront. The common thread that connected all these questions was the principle identified by Archibald MacLeish when he observed that mass communications had made foreign relations domestic affairs. As much as critics might have wanted to wish or legislate away the convergence of domestic and foreign, the professionals working in the trenches recognized that they enjoyed no such option.

The emergence of U.S. public diplomacy coincided with, and in fact stemmed from, a profound transformation in the nature of U.S. foreign policy and foreign relations. The arrival of U.S. global hegemony in an age of proliferating access to mass communications combined with the decline of European territorial colonialism to place an unprecedented emphasis on the image the nation projected to the world. The quest to build a vibrant program in public diplomacy must be understood first and foremost as the government's attempt to participate in the process of defining the image of "America" to the world. Yet this was a process over which U.S. officials ultimately exercised very little control. This lack of control, although fundamental to the style of empire the U.S. government sought to promote, raised profound concerns. The principal challenges to the American empire came from closed societies—Germany, Japan, or the Soviet Union—whose governments wielded powerful propaganda machines with near-total control over the information channels in their respective countries. How could the U.S. government possibly hope to compete?

In this anxious question lies the explanation for the political and ideological battles that afflicted the entire enterprise of public diplomacy throughout the period covered in this book. Both inside and outside the U.S. government, there were those who worried about the very existence of government propaganda in an open society, those on the other end of the spectrum who wanted U.S. propaganda to more closely resemble the model of its totalitarian counterparts, and those who argued that U.S. propaganda never could compete so there was no point in trying. Public diplomats faced the unenviable task of navigating these concerns to develop an approach to the image question that was both viable and palatable. In the end, they failed more often than they succeeded—sometimes because of their own missteps, but more often because of the difficulty of the task they confronted. Trying to shape the image the nation projected abroad was simultaneously an unyielding and an ideologically charged problem. Yet if image represented a tangible component of U.S. foreign policy and U.S. foreign relations, then someone needed to monitor perceptions of the United States around the world; someone needed to consider the impact of various policies on the ability of the United States to generate more friends than enemies; and someone in an official capacity needed to engage the global conversation on the nature of American power. This was the consequence of the style of empire that U.S. officials had worked so hard to promote for so many years, the undeniable by-product of their determination to spread the American dream.

NOTES

Introduction

1. Elizabeth Becker, "In the War on Terrorism, a Battle to Shape Public Opinion," *New York Times*, November 11, 2001.

2. On the decline of public diplomacy in the post–Cold War period, see the Epilogue of Cull, *Cold War and the United States Information Agency*; and, especially, Cull, *The Decline and Fall of the United States Information Agency*.

3. Harry S. Truman, "Statement by the President Upon Signing Order Concerning Government Information Programs," August 31, 1945, the American Presidency Project, http://www.presidency.ucsb.edu/ws/index.php?pid=12367&st=&st1=#axzz1Y2KeSjb9 [accessed August 8, 2012].

4. Wilson quoted in Foglesong, *America's Secret War*, 1.

5. Important surveys that cover a broad time span include Arndt, *First Resort of Kings*; Brewer, *Why America Fights*; and Cull, *Cold War and the United States Information Agency*. Other works that have defined this field while dealing with a more discrete period or set of issues include Belmonte, *Selling the American Way*; Osgood, *Total Cold War*; McKenzie, *Remaking France*; Krenn, *Fallout Shelter for the Human Spirit*; von Eschen, *Satchmo Blows Up the World*; Krugler, *Voice of America*; Gienow-Hecht, *Transmission Impossible*; Lucas, *Freedom's War*; Bernhard, *U.S. Television News and Cold War Propaganda*; Shulman, *Voice of America*; and Hixson, *Parting the Curtain*. The pioneering works in this genre are Winkler, *Politics of Propaganda*; and Ninkovich, *Diplomacy of Ideas*.

6. This argument is similar to the one that Robert Beisner made many years ago in *From the Old Diplomacy to the New*, where he identifies a shift in conceptions of U.S. foreign policy around the turn of the 20th century.

7. With the exception of Ninkovich's *Diplomacy of Ideas*, nearly all of the work on public diplomacy during the Cold War begins the story in 1945. Yet, in the National Archives' massive collection of records on the history of public diplomacy at the State Department (i.e., before the creation of the USIA) located in Entry 1559 of RG 59, the "Records Relating to International Information Activities" span the period from 1938–1953. The State Department, according to its own filing system, did not think the story began in 1945.

8. There is much more on the domestic section of the CPI than on the foreign section, which foreshadowed the public diplomacy programs of later years. Vaughn, *Holding Fast the Inner Lines*, is the best general history of the CPI, but it focuses exclusively on the domestic section. On the foreign section, see Axelrod, *Selling the Great War*; Mock and Larson, *Words that Won the War*; and Creel, *How We Advertised America*.

9. Creel, *How We Advertised America*, 401 (emphasis in the original).

10. Since the end of the Cold War, and particularly since the beginning of the Iraq War in 2003, scholars have returned to the old debate over whether the United States in the post-1945 period should be described as an "empire." For an important analysis of the place of the United States within the history of empires, see Maier, *Among Empires*. De Grazia, *Irresistible Empire*, emphasizes the role of consumption. The literature on "post-imperialism" is especially useful for thinking about these questions. See Becker and Sklar, eds., *Postimperialism and World Politics*; Bruce Cumings, "The American Ascendancy: Imposing a New World Order," *The Nation*, May 8, 2000, 13–20; and the issue of *Radical History Review*, 57 (1993), devoted to the theme of "Imperialism: A Useful Category of Analysis?" This entire discussion is deeply indebted to the seminal work of William Appleman Williams, particularly *The Tragedy of American Diplomacy*. An excellent examination of various approaches to the study of imperialism (including that of Williams and his many students) can be found in Carl P. Parrini, "Theories of Imperialism," in Gardner, ed., *Redefining the Past*. Two classic works essential for thinking through the role of the United States in the transformation of the global economy in the mid-20th century are Schumpeter, *Capitalism, Socialism, and Democracy*; and Bell, *Coming of Post-Industrial Society*.

11. Some scholars question the sincerity of the Roosevelt administration's commitment to anticolonialism, especially given the president's constant compromises with imperialist allies in Europe. I regard U.S.

policymakers' commitment to decolonization during World War II as genuine, if paternalistic and self-serving, because they saw it as being in their nation's long-term interest—except to the extent that advancing the cause would have shattered the wartime alliance. As Warren Kimball argues in *The Juggler* (p. 132), Roosevelt "believed that decolonization and independence were the directions in which the world was going. Better that the West lead than follow in the wake of revolution. Better to be part of the process than to lose all influence." At the same time, as Wm. Roger Louis points out in *Imperialism at Bay* (p. 10), even American officials were surprised at how rapidly decolonization progressed in the postwar period. On the United States and the British Empire, Thorne, *Allies of a Kind*, and Parker, *Brother's Keeper*, are also excellent.

12. The dilemma that U.S. policymakers confronted, and their decision to seek a solution in the realm of ideology, stemmed from what is typically described as the "dispersal of power" from the state to civil society throughout the 20th century—a concept most closely associated with the work of the Italian Marxist Antonio Gramsci. For Gramsci's explication of the "dispersal of power," see *Selections from the Prison Notebooks*, 104–114, 206–276, and especially 243. Hall, "Gramsci's Relevance," and Livingston, *Pragmatism, Feminism, and Democracy*, are both useful for thinking about how to apply Gramsci's ideas to U.S. history.

13. Cumings, "The American Century and the Third World," 357. This essay was included in the important two-part symposium on the idea of the "American Century" published in the Spring and Summer issues of *Diplomatic History* in 1999. It later appeared in book form as Hogan, ed., *The Ambiguous Legacy*. Although all the other contributors to this symposium use Luce's periodization of the 20th century as the American Century, Cumings sees Luce's article symbolizing—indeed, pleading for—the fundamentally new role the United States would play in the world after 1941.

14. Robert Sherwood, "Long-Range Directive," January 15, 1943, Box 4, Entry 6B, RG 208, NARA.

15. Minutes, Information Service Committee, January 4, 1945, Box 94, Entry 401–403, RG 353, NARA.

16. During the 1940s, Hans J. Morgenthau, the University of Chicago political scientist often credited with founding the "realist" school of International Relations, was chief among those who emphasized the primacy of power politics. See, in particular, his classic text *Politics among Nations*, which devotes very little attention (particularly in its early editions) to ideological forces. George Kennan is probably the best example of someone who believed in the importance of propaganda but viewed it primarily as a means for promoting the decisions of policymakers, not as a tool for responding to greater public participation in the foreign policy process.

17. Over the past two or three decades, concepts of "national security" or "grand strategy" have frequently been used as the primary lens for interpreting U.S. foreign policy during the early Cold War. The most important staples in this genre include Gaddis, *Strategies of Containment*; Leffler, *Preponderance of Power*; Hogan, *A Cross of Iron*; and Trachtenberg, *A Constructed Peace*. By focusing on the creation of the national security state and the formulation of high-level foreign policy "strategy," each of these works, despite their many disagreements, treats policymakers as wielding near total authority in shaping U.S. foreign relations. Although U.S. officials did have a profound ability to affect the course of contemporary events, not to mention the lives and deaths of millions of people, they did not operate in a vacuum. Moreover, to paraphrase Marx, they did not necessarily make policy under circumstances of their own choosing, especially in the cultural and ideological realm.

18. The text of the program, "Your Foreign Policy!" can be found in Francis Russell to George Allen, March 4, 1949, Box 11, Entry 1530, RG 59, NARA.

19. "Legislative History, International Information and Educational Activities," August 21, 1950, Box 65, George M. Elsey Papers, HSTL.

Chapter 1

1. Two years earlier, in July 1934, FDR's informal stop in Colombia en route to Hawaii marked the first visit by a sitting U.S. President to South America. For coverage of the conference, see "Cheering Throngs Welcome Roosevelt to Buenos Aires," *New York Times*, December 1, 1936; "Roosevelt Will Sail Tomorrow for the Buenos Aires Peace Parley," *New York Times*, November 17, 1936; "Buenos Aires Hails Roosevelt Today in Great Pageant," *New York Times*, November 30, 1936.

2. "Cheering Throngs Welcome Roosevelt to Buenos Aires," *New York Times*, December 1, 1936; "Roosevelt Urges America to Unite," *New York Times*, December 2, 1936. In a strange and unexplained coincidence, the heckler was later identified as the thirty-year-old son of Argentinean President Augustin Justo. See "President Justo's Son Seized as the Heckler of Roosevelt," *New York Times*, December 2, 1936.

3. FDR to the Presidents of All Other American Republics, January 30, 1936, in *Report of the Delegation . . . for the Maintenance of Peace*; and Hull, *Memoirs*, I, 493.

4. This follows the periodization of Lloyd C. Gardner in *Economic Aspects of New Deal Diplomacy*. On p. viii, Gardner argues that the Roosevelt administration—"primarily concerned with domestic troubles"—looked inward during its first year. However, it "rejoined the mainstream [i.e. the

Open Door tradition] in 1934 with the adoption of the Reciprocal Trade Agreements Act." The text of Roosevelt's speech is available in *Report of the Delegation...for the Maintenance of Peace*; or available online at "The American Presidency Project," http://www.presidency.ucsb.edu/ws/index. php?pid=15238&st=&st1 (accessed August 8, 2012).

5. "Roosevelt's Speech Heard Clearly Here," *New York Times*, December 2, 1936; and "Argentines Cheer Roosevelt in Rain as He Starts Home," *New York Times*, December 3, 1936. Roosevelt made the belated quip to Samuel Guy Inman, who reported it in his *Inter-American Conferences*, 167.

6. As Cordell Hull made clear in his address as the head of the U.S. Delegation at Buenos Aires, "it is now as plain as mathematical truth that each nation in any part of the world is concerned in peace in every part of the world." Hull, *Opening Address to the Inter-American Conference for the Maintenance of Peace*.

7. Or, as the renowned Latin Americanist Hubert Herring put it, Latin America was "the proving ground for new models in international accord." See Herring, "Zone of Sanity in a Mad World," *New York Times*, November 29, 1936.

8. On various Latin American writers labeling the United States the "Colossus of the North" ("El Coloso del Norte"), see Hubert Herring, "Zone of Sanity in a Mad World," *New York Times*, November 29, 1936.

9. FDR quoted in Gardner, *Economic Aspects*, 109.

10. Wood, *Making of the Good Neighbor Policy*, 296–297. Some critics of the Good Neighbor Policy argue that it was nothing new and that Herbert Hoover proposed most of the same things, but with less PR. For this argument, see Mecham, *United States and Inter-American Security*; and Schoultz, *Beneath the United States*. The most effective repudiations of this view are Gellman, *Good Neighbor Diplomacy*; and Wood, *Making of the Good Neighbor Policy*. For the argument that the Good Neighbor Policy, whatever its origins, represented a transition from military to economic domination of Latin America, see LaFeber, *Inevitable Revolutions*; Green, *Containment of Latin America*; and Koppes, "The Good Neighbor Policy and the Nationalization of Mexican Oil," in which the author describes the Good Neighbor Policy as "hemispheric hegemony by other means" (p. 81). Cobbs, *Rich Neighbor Policy*, suggests that Roosevelt took Hoover's ideas and gave them meaning in a way that Hoover never could, partly through better publicity. My own view is similar to that of Wood: The ultimate significance of FDR's Good Neighbor Policy lies in its public articulation of an ideology of non-intervention and economic development, setting a standard that threatened to expose FDR to charges of egregious hypocrisy if he fell short of his officially stated goals.

11. Hull, *Memoirs*, I, 3–9.

12. On Reciprocal Trade as a return to the Open Door tradition of U.S. foreign policy, see the discussion of Gardner, *Economic Aspects*, above. At the same time, Robert Dallek argues in *Franklin D. Roosevelt and American Foreign Policy* (p. 93) that "whatever Roosevelt's or Hull's intentions, the reciprocal trade program chiefly served American rather than world economic interests." On the other hand, Schlesinger, *Coming of the New Deal*, and Leuchtenberg, *Franklin D. Roosevelt and the New Deal*, both conclude that FDR's trade policy was more liberal than that of other nations in an especially restrictive era.

13. Nye and the "Merchants of Death" hearings are covered in Cole, *Senator Gerald P. Nye*; and Wiltz, *In Search of Peace*. On the Neutrality Acts and "isolationism," more generally, see Cole, *Roosevelt & the Isolationists*; Guinsburg, *Pursuit of Isolationism*; Steele, *Propaganda in an Open Society*; Kuehl, "Midwestern Newspapers and Isolationist Sentiment"; Jonas, *Isolationism in America*; and Wiltz, *From Isolation to War*. Numerous additional citations may be found in Doenecke, *Anti-Intervention*.

14. I use "unilateralist" rather than "isolationist" to describe the political position of legislators such as Robert Taft and Gerald Nye because I have found little to indicate that those typically dubbed "isolationist" had any qualms about repeated U.S. involvement in the affairs of other nations within the Western Hemisphere. What they did object to were multilateral agreements, such as the Reciprocal Trade Act and the Export-Import Bank, and other policies that threatened to drag the United States into foreign entanglements where it could not dictate its own terms.

15. Kimball, *Juggler*, 107–126. Additionally, see Grandin, *Empire's Workshop*, on the place of Latin America within U.S. conceptions of empire during the 20th century. Bemis, *Latin American Policy of the United States*, is also revealing, especially for something written during World War II. On p. 391, Bemis argues that the "practice of the Good Neighbor Policy by the United States in Latin America served as a proving ground for the application of those principles to the Pacific area, Europe and everywhere else, and for a future world order."

16. Both failed. For a detailed explanation, see "Americas Now Aim at Economic Peace," *New York Times*, December 21, 1936; and "Argentina Rejects Hull Trade Policy," *New York Times*, February 16, 1939.

17. Hull, *Memoirs*, I, 495–496.

18. Inman, *Inter-American Conferences*, 76–78; and *Report of the Delegation...for the Maintenance of Peace*, 15, 32–40.

19. For Roosevelt's speech, see *Report of the Delegation...for the Maintenance of Peace*.

20. Veteran Foreign Service officers put together a proposal in early 1938 suggesting that the cultural conventions agreed upon at Buenos Aires should be run out of the Office of Education, which was at that point not

even a cabinet-level department. For a full recounting of the bureaucratic battles over the origins of cultural diplomacy, see Espinosa, *Inter-American Beginnings of U.S. Cultural Diplomacy,* Ch. 5.

21. The phrase "global strategist" comes from the subtitle of Benjamin Welles, *Sumner Welles.* This book includes information on Welles's involvement in Latin American affairs in chapters 6, 14–18. Other good sources on Welles include Rofe, *Franklin Roosevelt's Foreign Policy;* and Gellman, *Secret Affairs.* In general, though, there is not enough good scholarship on one of the most innovative and influential New Dealers.

22. Ninkovich, *Diplomacy of Ideas,* 8–24; for other information on the Carnegie Endowment for International Peace, see Chambers, *Eagle and the Dove;* DeBenedetti, *Peace Reform in American History;* and Patterson, *Toward a Warless World.* On the Institute of International Education, see Duggan, *Professor at Large;* and the *News Bulletin of the Institute of International Education,* which began printing in 1925. Notably, Stephen Duggan also had some expertise in Latin American affairs, having authored *The Two Americas,* a good neighborly survey of U.S.–Latin American relations.

23. Ninkovich, *Diplomacy of Ideas,* 8.

24. Duggan to Messersmith and Welles, February 8, 1938, Box 2, Entry 14, RG 353, NARA; and Espinosa, *Inter-American Beginnings,* 89–91.

25. Ibid.

26. Ibid. On the proximity of the offices, see Espinosa, *Inter-American Beginnings,* 114–115.

27. "Cultural Ties that Bind," *Christian Science Monitor,* January 25, 1939.

28. "Transcript of Remarks and Discussion at the Meeting on Inter-American Cultural Cooperation Held Under the Auspices of the Department of State," May 23, 1938, Folder 1, Box 225, MC 468, UAR. Other information on the public-private nexus can be found in [J. Manuel Espinosa], "The Cultural Relations Program of the Department of State, 1938–1978," July 27, 1978, Folder 4, Box 2, MC 468, UAR; Department of State, "Progress Report of the Division of Cultural Relations," June 1940, Folder 5, Box 2, MC 468, UAR; and Hanson, *Cultural Cooperation Program.*

29. Ibid.

30. Ibid.

31. Duggan to Messersmith and Welles, Feb. 8, 1938, Box 2, Entry 14, RG 353, NARA.

32. "Transcript of Remarks and Discussion at the Meeting on Inter-American Cultural Cooperation Held Under the Auspices of the Department of State," May 23, 1938, Folder 1, Box 225, MC 468, UAR.

33. Edward G. Lowry, "Trade Follows the Film," *Saturday Evening Post,* November 7, 1925: 12–13; excerpted in Merrill and Paterson, eds., *Major Problems in American Foreign Relations,* Vol. 2, 5th ed.

34. "Conference on Inter-American Relations in the Field of Education," November 10, 1939, unpublished State Department pamphlet, copy located in Government Documents, call no. US S1.26/1, Alexander Library, Rutgers University, New Brunswick, NJ.
35. On the origins of the CCAR, see Thomson, *Cultural Relations*, 36.
36. This level of diversity can be seen even at the first meeting for which I found minutes: Minutes of Meeting, Committee of Executive Departments and Independent Agencies to Consider the Question of Cooperation with the American Republics, August 8, 1938, Box 29, Entries 20–22, RG 353, NARA.
37. Minutes of Meeting, Committee of Executive Departments and Independent Agencies to Consider the Question of Cooperation with the American Republics, August 2, 1939, Box 29, Entries 20–22, RG 353, NARA.
38. Briggs to Duggan, July 15, 1939; and "Loan of United States Technical Experts to the Governments of the American Republics," July 15, 1939; both in Box 2, Entry 14, RG 353, NARA. See also the discussion of getting leave time for an official at the Library of Congress in Minutes of Meeting, Committee of Executive Departments and Independent Agencies to Consider the Question of Cooperation with the American Republics, April 26, 1939, Box 29, Entries 20–22, NARA.
39. Minutes of Meeting, Interdepartmental Committee on Cooperation with the American Republics, May 28, 1941, Box 29, Entries 20–22, NARA.
40. Ibid.
41. Espinosa, *Inter-American Beginnings*, 121, 132.
42. For the directive that gave the Cultural Division control of the CCAR, see Sumner Welles, Departmental Order 1047, April 15, 1942, Box 54, Entry 718, RG 59, NARA; and Espinosa, *Inter-American Beginnings*, 161. On the overlap in personnel, see Thomson, *Overseas Information*, 160.
43. For details on how the European war influenced Roosevelt's thinking on Latin America, see [Rowland], *History*, 3–4; and Rivas, *Missionary Capitalist*, 38.
44. Roosevelt's well-documented preference for creating confusing layers of bureaucracy served both to create a moving target for his critics and to ensure that no single official gained too much power—an intentional dispersal of authority over policymaking.
45. The best source on the origins of the Rockefeller memo—establishing definitively, in my opinion, that Rockefeller himself authored the memo—is Rivas, *Missionary Capitalist*, 38–44, and 234, n.13. See [Rowland], *History*, 5–6, for the biographical information on Rockefeller.
46. The text of the memo is reprinted in [Rowland], *History*, 279–280.
47. Rivas, *Missionary Capitalist*, 40–44; and [Rowland], *History*, 6–7.
48. Rockefeller was originally appointed to head the Office for the Coordination of Commercial and Cultural Relations Between the American Republics [OCCCRAR]—a title that was shortened to the somewhat less onerous Office for the Coordinator of Inter-American Affairs [OCIAA] in 1941, and to just the Office of Inter-American Affairs [OIAA] in 1944. OCIAA is used

here, because the majority of its work occurred under that designation and so it is the one most common to histories of the agency.

49. The point about FDR specifically including cultural matters comes from [Rowland], *History*, 7, n.15; Thomson's recollection is from his *Cultural Relations*, 49.

50. Nelson A. Rockefeller, "Report to the President," n. d., Box 455, Entry 1, Central Files, Administration, Reports, RG 229, NARA.

51. The breadth of the economic program is clear from reading the minutes of the early meetings of the Inter-Departmental Committee on Inter-American Affairs. See, for example, the minutes for meetings on August 27, 1940, October 1, 1940, October 8, 1940, and October 22, 1940; all in Box 543, Entry 10, Records of the Immediate Office of the Coordinator, RG 229, NARA. To give a sense of the OCIAA's priorities and their overlap with the State Department: Over the course of its existence, the OCIAA spent approximately 143 million dollars. Nine million went towards "education" (mostly spent on sponsoring educational exchanges), 41 million went towards "information" programs that utilized radio, and motion pictures and publications, and 13 million went towards "economic development and transportation." See [Rowland], *History*, 263–269.

52. Nelson A. Rockefeller, "Report to the President," n. d., Box 455, Entry 1, Central Files, Administration, Reports, RG 229, NARA.

53. Ibid.

54. Ibid.

55. All the quotes in this paragraph come from a speech given by Rockefeller before the Pan American Union, as cited in "Americas Warned on Post-War Role," *New York Times*, March 2, 1941. Additional information on the educational initiatives comes from "Minutes of Meeting of Policy Committee of Cultural Relations Division of Coordinator's Office," November 12, 1940, Box 543, Entry 10, Records of the Immediate Office of the Coordinator, RG 229, NARA.

56. "Rockefeller Board Proves Value in Uniting Americas," *New York Times*, September 2, 1941.

57. Ibid.

58. "Advertising News and Notes," *New York Times*, October 29, 1943.

59. "Minutes of Meeting of Policy Committee of Cultural Relations Division of Coordinator's Office," November 12, 1940, December 9, 1940, and December 30, 1940; all in Box 543, Entry 10, Records of the Immediate Office of the Coordinator, RG 229, NARA; "Program of the Office for Coordination of Commercial and Cultural Relations Between the American Republics and the Inter-American Development Commission," n. d., Box 455, Entry 1, Central Files, Administration, Reports, RG 229, NARA; "U.S. May Subsidize News to Americas," *New York Times*, October 8, 1941; and "Radio Sets Sought for Latin America," *New York Times*, January 24, 1942.

60. "John Hay Whitney (1905–1982)," *Philadelphia Inquirer*, February 9, 1982.
61. Minutes of Meeting of Policy Committee of Cultural Relations Division of Coordinator's Office, December 30, 1940, Box 543, Entry 10, Records of the Immediate Office of the Coordinator, RG 229, NARA; and "Rockefeller Will Aid South-of-Border Films," *Los Angeles Times*, February 11, 1943.
62. Ibid.
63. Minutes of Meeting of Policy Committee of Cultural Relations Division of Coordinator's Office," November 12, 1940, December 9, 1940, and December 30, 1940; all in Box 543, Entry 10, Records of the Immediate Office of the Coordinator, RG 229, NARA; and Roland Hall Sharp, "The Lamp of New World Learning," *Christian Science Monitor*, March 13, 1943.
64. "Portrait of an American Composer," *New York Times*, August 24, 1941; an extensive list of Rockefeller's recruits can be found in [Rowland], *History*, 148; Rivas, *Missionary Capitalist*, 45, has another list; other names come from their appearance in OCIAA documents.
65. Ibid.
66. Minutes of Meeting of Policy Committee of Cultural Relations Division of Coordinator's Office, September 27, 1940, RG 229, Entry 10, Records of the Immediate Office of the Coordinator, Box 543, NARA.
67. Ibid.
68. Roland Hall Sharp, "The Lamp of New World Learning," *Christian Science Monitor*, March 13, 1943.
69. James Reston, "U.S. May Subsidize News to Americas," *New York Times*, October 8, 1941.
70. "Minutes of Meeting of the Executive Committee of the Coordinator's Office," October 13, 1940, Box 543, Entry 10, Records of the Immediate Office of the Coordinator, RG 229, NARA; "Project to enable the Department of State to collaborate with the Office of the Coordinator of Commercial and Cultural Relations between the American Republics in the development of the Coordinator's Program," November 25, 1940, Box 51, Entry 718, RG 59, NARA; Duggan to Bonsal, *et al.*, December 21, 1940, File 20, Box 233, MC 468, UAR; Notter to Bonsal and Duggan, April 1, 1941, Box 51, Entry 718, RG 59, NARA.
71. FDR to Rockefeller, April 22, 1941, RG 59, Entry 718, Box 51, NARA. This copy has a cover letter to FDR requesting the President's approval for the letter to Rockefeller to be sent out over the President's signature. Although the author of the cover letter (and, therefore, the letter to Rockefeller) did not sign this particular copy, handwritten notes by J. Manuel Espinosa identify the author as Sumner Welles. Espinosa's notes also indicate that Welles composed the letter to Rockefeller based on a conversation he had with the President on April 17, 1941. On the clarification of the relationship, see also Espinosa, *Inter-American Beginnings*, 160; and Thomson, *Cultural Relations*, 48–51.

Chapter 2

1. Unsigned memo from the Division of Cultural Relations, September 7, 1939, Box 53, Entry 718, RG 59, NARA.

2. The predominant domestic attitude toward foreign policy during the 1930s—whether characterized as isolationism, unilateralism, or non-interventionism—may be aptly symbolized in political terms by the Neutrality Acts, in economic terms by the Smoot-Hawley tariff, and in cultural terms by the antiwar cynicism of the great Lewis Milestone film, *All Quiet on the Western Front*. On the persistence of support for Smoot-Hawley, even after the Reciprocal Trade Agreements Act mitigated its most egregious effects, see Irwin and Kroszner, "Interests, Institutions, and Ideology." It should also be noted that the Reciprocal Trade Act generated serious opposition until the 1940s. On *All Quiet on the Western Front* as the quintessential cultural expression of antiwar sentiment during the 1930s, see two essays by John Whiteclay Chambers, "All Quiet" and "The Movies and the Antiwar Debate."

3. On *Sergeant York* as the ultimate expression of Hollywood interventionism, as well as a key symbolic moment in the transformation of public attitudes, see Koppes and Black, *Hollywood Goes to War*, 37–39; and Doherty, *Projections of War*, 100–103.

4. Moser, "Gigantic Engines."

5. These polls have generally been overlooked, as historians of the period have tended to focus instead on polls showing that, all the way up to December 6, a majority of Americans opposed a declaration of war. As a result, a far more consequential change in attitudes toward foreign policy has gone largely unnoticed. The conclusion to Cole, *America First*, is a classic statement of the standard position.

6. Public Attitudes on Foreign Policy, Special Report, No. 61, "U.S. Opinion on the Dumbarton Oaks Proposals," May 11, 1945, Box 1, Entry 568J, RG 59, NARA.

7. Henry Luce, "The American Century," *Life*, February 17, 1941, 61–65.

8. Ibid.

9. My conclusions about the influence of the "American Century" concept, and the extent to which it was associated with Luce, are based upon running a series of searches of the *New York Times* database for references to, first, "Luce and 'American Century'" and, second, "American Century" by itself. From 1941–1949 there are 8 references to the former and 36 to the latter; from 1950–1959, 0 and 16; from 1960–1969, 3 and 32; from 1970–1979, 5 and 47; from 1980–1989, 9 and 137; and from 1990–1999, 30 and 405. These numbers suggest that after Luce introduced the "American Century" concept in 1941, it fairly quickly took on a life of its own, as relatively few articles connected him directly to the concept. Then, it virtually disappeared from popular discourse in the United States during the 1950s and early 1960s—the point at which the largely

unchallenged assumptions behind American globalism essentially obviated the need to discuss its contours or to debate its merits. In the wake of Vietnam, however, the widespread attempt to put the American empire into some sort of historical context led to a rediscovery of the notion of an "American Century." This trend accelerated during the 1980s and 1990s, as indicated by the explosion of references to the idea and to the man who popularized the term. All of this culminated at the turn of the millennium in countless attempts to assess the role of the United States in world affairs over the course of the 20th century.

10. Adams made this comment in a letter he penned in February 1818, as he looked back on the revolution later in life.

11. Espinosa, *Inter-American Beginnings*, 164–167.

12. The seldom examined, though remarkably important, records of the State Department Advisory Committee on Cultural Relations are held in three separate collections, none of which is complete. Some portion of the records are available in Box 2, MC 468, CU Historical Collection, UAR; in Box 29, Entries 20–22, RG 353, at NARA; and in the microfiche collection of Harley A. Notter's materials, *Post World War II Foreign Policy Planning*. The Notter Files are also available as a subset of RG 59 at NARA. Notter's files contain the minutes of two meetings in 1944 not available in the other two collections, though his files seem to be missing the records of a key meeting in September 1941, which can be found in the other collections.

13. On the various labels attached to Wallace over the course of his career, see Cabell Phillips, "At 75, Henry Wallace Cultivates His Garden," *New York Times*, October 6, 1963.

14. Wallace's appeal to cooperative internationalism in his "Century of the Common Man" speech in 1942 was partly a rejoinder to what he regarded as the unilateralist arrogance of the "American Century." Later, during his run for president as the candidate of the Progressive Party in 1948, Wallace attacked Luce and the "American Century" idea as "imperialist" and "neo-fascist." (See "Wallace to Tell '48 Plans Monday," *New York Times*, December 25, 1947.) However, from the perspective of someone like Robert Taft—the legendary Republican legislator from Ohio, who was one of the last holdouts against the emerging bipartisan consensus on American internationalism—the contrast between the two men was a distinction without a difference. In 1943, Taft attacked both Luce's "American Century" and Wallace's "Century of the Common Man" as "not what we went to war for." (See "Four Freedoms Aim of War Hit by Taft," *New York Times*, May 26, 1943.)

15. For a sample of contemporary documents that point to Wallace's statements as key to broadening ideas of cultural diplomacy, see "Compilation of Policy Statements of the Cultural Relations Program Approved by the General Advisory Committee," June 15, 1944, Box B94, Papers of the American Council of Learned Societies, Manuscripts

Division, LC. See also two works of scholarship, both written by veterans of the cultural programs, that make the same point: Thomson, *Cultural Relations*, 38–40; and Fairbank, *America's Cultural Experiment*, 7.

16. Minutes of Meeting, General Advisory Committee of the Division of Cultural Relations of the Department of State, February 2, 1941, Box 29, Entries 20–22, RG 353, NARA.

17. Minutes of Meeting, General Advisory Committee of the Division of Cultural Relations of the Department of State, September 17–18, 1941, Box 29, Entries 20–22, RG 353, NARA.

18. At the April 1940 meeting of the Advisory Committee on Cultural Relations, participants first raised the possibility of expanding the membership of the committee. MacLeish and Leland headlined the expanded group that attended the July 1940 meeting; Wallace joined in February 1941. See Minutes of Meeting, General Advisory Committee of the Division of Cultural Relations of the Department of State, April 4–5, 1940; Minutes of Meeting, General Advisory Committee of the Division of Cultural Relations of the Department of State, July 9, 1940; and Minutes of Meeting, General Advisory Committee of the Division of Cultural Relations of the Department of State, September 17–18, 1941; all in Box 29, Entries 20–22, RG 353, NARA. It is notable that Wallace's participation in these discussions continued despite his public feud with the State Department over the way he ran the Bureau of Economic Warfare (BEW). Even though Cordell Hull pushed FDR to abolish the BEW entirely in mid-1943, the members of the Cultural Advisory Committee continued to welcome him to their meetings until that committee dissolved in 1944.

19. Minutes of Meeting, General Advisory Committee of the Division of Cultural Relations of the Department of State, September 17–18, 1941, Box 29, Entries 20–22, RG 353, NARA.

20. Ibid.

21. "Precis of the Discussion of the General Advisory Committee on the Future Cultural Relations Programs," Sep. 18, 1941; and Waldo G. Leland, Comments on "Precis..." March 12, 1942; both in Box B93, Papers of the American Council of Learned Societies, Manuscripts Division, LC.

22. These comments came from Harley Notter. Minutes of Meeting, General Advisory Committee of the Division of Cultural Relations of the Department of State, September 17–18, 1941, Box 29, Entries 20–22, RG 353, NARA.

23. Ibid.

24. Ibid.

25. Minutes of Meeting, General Advisory Committee of the Division of Cultural Relations of the Department of State, February 25–26, 1942, Box 29, Entries 20–22, RG 353, NARA.

26. On assigning control of the Interdepartmental Committee to the Cultural Division, see Sumner Welles, "Departmental Order 1047," April 15, 1942, Entry 718, RG 59, NARA; and Espinosa, *Inter-American Beginnings*, 161.

27. Minutes of Meeting, General Advisory Committee of the Division of Cultural Relations of the Department of State, February 25–26, 1942, Box 29, Entries 20–22, RG 353, NARA.

28. My arguments about the Open Door and the importance of the China Market follow, obviously, in the tradition of works such as Williams, *Tragedy*; LaFeber, *New Empire*; and McCormick, *China Market*.

29. Fairbank, *America's Cultural Experiment*, 9–38.

30. Minutes of Meeting, General Advisory Committee of the Division of Cultural Relations of the Department of State, November 5–6, 1941, Box 29, Entries 20–22, RG 353, NARA.

31. Fairbank, *America's Cultural Experiment*, 9–38.

32. Ibid.

33. Fairbank, *America's Cultural Experiment*, vii-ix.

34. Ibid.

35. Thomson, "The Permanent Cultural Relations Program as a Basic Instrumentality of American Foreign Policy," February 9, 1942, Folder 16, Box 225, MC 468, CU Historical Collection, UAR.

36. Minutes of Meeting, General Advisory Committee of the Division of Cultural Relations of the Department of State, February 25–26, 1942, Box 29, Entries 20–22, RG 353, NARA.

37. Minutes of Meeting, General Advisory Committee of the Division of Cultural Relations of the Department of State, September 17–18, 1941, Box 29, Entries 20–22, RG 353, NARA.

38. Minutes of Meeting, General Advisory Committee of the Division of Cultural Relations of the Department of State, September 17–18, 1941; Minutes of Meeting, General Advisory Committee of the Division of Cultural Relations of the Department of State, June 19–20, 1942; both in Box 29, Entries 20–22, RG 353, NARA.

39. Minutes of Meeting, General Advisory Committee of the Division of Cultural Relations of the Department of State, June 19–20, 1942, Box 29, Entries 20–22, RG 353, NARA.

40. Ibid.

41. Ibid.

42. Minutes of Meeting, General Advisory Committee of the Division of Cultural Relations of the Department of State, February 25–26, 1942, Box 29, Entries 20–22, RG 353, NARA.

43. Thomson, "The Permanent Cultural Relations Program as a Basic Instrumentality of American Foreign Policy," February 9, 1942, Folder 16, Box 225, MC 468, CU Historical Collection, UAR.

44. On Turner, see Ninkovich, *The Diplomacy of Ideas*, 66–67; and Turner, *The Great Cultural Traditions*.

45. "Tentative Agenda, General Advisory Committee," February 23–24, 1943, Fiche 176–171, *Post World War II Foreign Policy Planning*.

46. Welles to Thomson, February 22, 1943, Fiche 174–171, *Post World War II Foreign Policy Planning*; and Minutes of Meeting, General Advisory Committee of the Division of Cultural Relations of the Department of State, February 23–24, 1943, Box 29, Entries 20–22, RG 353, NARA.

47. General Advisory Committee of the Division of Cultural Relations of the Department of State, February 23–24, 1943, Box 29, Entries 20–22, RG 353, NARA.

48. Ibid.

49. Ibid.

50. On the geography of the American Century, see Smith, *American Empire*.

51. Walter Lippmann, "The State Department Trouble," *Washington Post*, September 16, 1943.

52. Neal Stanford, "Streamlining Wind Hits State Department," *Christian Science Monitor*, December 4, 1944.

53. Campbell and Herring, eds., *The Diaries of Edward R. Stettinius*, xiii–xxi.

54. Bob Considine, "New Secretary Jumps into State Department with Vigor—and Views," *Washington Post*, December 10, 1944.

55. FDR quoted in Johnson, "Edward R. Stettinius, Jr.," 210.

56. "Hull Details Changes," *New York Times*, January 16, 1944. For a graphic illustration of the two reorganizations of 1944, see the charts that accompany "State Dept. Revamped to Set Up 12 Divisions, Postwar Advisory Unit," *Washington Post*, January 16, 1944; and Bertram D. Hulen, "New State Department Set-up Is Under Way," *New York Times*, December 31, 1944.

57. "Secretary of State," *Washington Post*, November 28, 1944.

58. John MacCormac, "Hull to Take Reins over all Agencies in Economic Field," *New York Times*, September 3, 1943; and Neal Stanford, "Streamlining Wind Hits State Department," *Christian Science Monitor*, December 4, 1944.

59. "State Department," *Washington Post*, December 5, 1944.

60. General Advisory Committee to the Division of Cultural Relations of the Department of State, Minutes of Meeting, February 18–19, 1944, Fiche 180–185, *Post World War II Foreign Policy Planning*.

61. Minutes of the Meeting of the General Advisory Committee on Cultural Relations, June 28–29, 1944, Fiche 180–186, *Post World War II Foreign Policy Planning*.

62. Ibid.

63. Bertram D. Hulen, "New Men, New Set-up for State Department," *New York Times*, December 17, 1944; and "State Department," *Washington Post*, December 5, 1944.

64. Campbell and Herring, eds., *The Diaries of Edward R. Stettinius*, 169–170.

65. "New Foreign Affairs Team," *Christian Science Monitor*, December 5, 1944; and Arthur Krock, "State Department Shift," *New York Times*, December 6, 1944.

66. C. P. Trussell, "Grew is Aide of Stettinius in Wide Shift," *New York Times*, December 5, 1944; and "State Department Changes," *New York Times*, December 6, 1944.

Chapter 3

1. For example, in the most recent comprehensive synthesis of U.S. foreign and domestic policy during World War II—Kennedy's *Freedom from Fear*—the OWI appears only twice in the over 400 pages he devotes to the war. The standard study of the OWI remains Winkler, *Politics of Propaganda*. Three works that devote some attention to the OWI in the course of writing about the Voice of America are Shulman, *Voice of America*; Krugler, *Voice of America*; and Pirsein, *Voice of America*. Also containing important information on various aspects of OWI activities are Laurie, *Propaganda Warriors*; Koppes and Black, *Hollywood Goes to War*; and Savage, *Broadcasting Freedom*.

2. This quote comes from a letter Hull wrote to Davis in July 1942 shortly after the creation of the OWI. Initially, Hull seems to have ignored the decision to establish an autonomous propaganda bureau outside his control, but after sensing that it might undermine his authority he went on the war path. See Hull to Davis, July 8, 1942, Box 4, Entry 1, RG 208, NARA.

3. The literature on the Creel Committee is surprisingly thin. The standard work remains Vaughn, *Holding Fast the Inner Lines*; Axelrod, *Selling the Great War* is a thinly sourced, brief history; Brewer, *Why America Fights* contains an excellent chapter on the CPI. Also relevant are Mock and Larson, *Words that Won the War*, and Creel's memoir, *How We Advertised America*. On residual hostility toward the Creel Committee and its influence upon the origins of World War II propaganda, see Winkler, *The Politics of Propaganda*, 2–3, 8–9.

4. Axelrod, *Selling the Great War*, 218–219.

5. Brewer, *To Win the Peace*, 85.

6. The biographical information on MacLeish comes from Donaldson, *Archibald MacLeish*. See also my expanded take on MacLeish in "Archibald MacLeish Rediscovered."

7. On FDR's arm-twisting, see Drabeck and Ellis, eds., *Archibald MacLeish*, 130. The story about J. Parnell Thomas accusing MacLeish of being a "fellow traveler" in confirmation hearings comes from Donaldson, *Archibald MacLeish*, 295. On the importance of MacLeish's tenure at the Library of Congress, see Jones, "The Library of Congress Film Project." Gary, *Nervous Liberals*, has a more critical take, albeit one that also speaks to MacLeish's influence.

8. "Report from the Nation," April 27, 1942, Box 12, Entry 6E, RG 208, NARA.

9. "Description of the Organizational Breakdown and Function of the Units within the Office of Facts and Figures," March 11, 1941, Box 12, Entry 6E, RG 208; and OFF Bureau of Intelligence to OFF Director, Assistant Directors and Deputy Directors, February 25, 1942, Box 5, Entry 3D, RG 208; both in NARA.

10. OFF Bureau of Intelligence to OFF Director, Assistant Directors and Deputy Directors, February 25, 1942, Box 5, Entry 3D, RG 208, NARA.

11. Creel, *How We Advertised America*, 258–259.

12. On the connections between the CPI and the OWI, Winkler, *Politics of Propaganda*, mentions the CPI only in passing; Axelrod, *Selling the Great War*, surmises that World War II officials were familiar with the CPI example but admits that there is little documentation to this effect (217); Brewer, *Why America Fights*, documents similarities in the philosophical approach of the two agencies but does not provide examples of World War II propagandists who cited the CPI in approaching their work.

13. Brown, *Last Hero*, 7, 55–56, 164–167. See also the personal perspective of former Donovan assistant Corey Ford in *Donovan of OSS*. Other books on Donovan include Dunlop, *Donovan* and Troy, *Wild Bill and Intrepid*.

14. Brown, *Last Hero*, 168–215.

15. There is no outstanding biography of Robert Sherwood, partly because John Mason Brown died before completing the second volume of his two volume study. Nevertheless, Brown's partially completed *The Ordeal of a Playwright* takes the story up to 1941 and includes the text of *There Shall Be No Night*. The Norman Cousins quote comes from Cousins's introduction to this volume (p. 15). Also occasionally useful is Meserve, *Robert E. Sherwood*.

16. MacLeish to Davis, Eisenhower, Sherwood, and Cowles, "Basic Policy Statement on OWI Objectives," August 19, 1942, Box 4, Entry 1, RG 208, NARA. For one lengthy explication of the "strategy of truth" (a phrase that quickly achieved wide currency in propaganda circles), see Archibald MacLeish's address, "The Strategy of Truth," to the Annual Luncheon of the Associated Press on April 20, 1942. This address is reprinted in MacLeish, *Time to Act*, 21–31.

17. MacLeish to Donovan, December 1, 1941, Box 6, MacLeish Papers, LC.

18. Quoted in Ford, *Donovan of OSS*, 126.

19. Donaldson, *Archibald MacLeish*, 358–362; Winkler, *Politics of Propaganda*, 27–30. The OWI incorporated personnel and projects from four different existing agencies: The Office of Government Reports, the Division of Information in the Office of Emergency Management, the Foreign Information Service, and the Office of Facts and Figures. The last two agencies made a far greater contribution than the first two to the staff and structure of the OWI. The FIS transferred the largest number of

employees (over 400) to the OWI, while the OFF actually transferred the smallest number (112), although both agencies exerted a profound impact on the OWI approach to information policy. The Office of Government Reports, which was the oldest of the four and dated back to 1939, transferred some 200 employees, including its chief, Lowell Mellett, who went on to run the Bureau of Motion Pictures at the OWI. Mellett's group also brought a great deal of expertise in surveying public opinion. Meanwhile, the Division of Information at the Office of Emergency Management, which consisted mostly of lower-level paper pushers, left little lasting influence. Names and numbers of the employees of each of the four predecessor agencies can be found in U.S. Congress, House, Hearings Before the Subcommittee of the Committee on Appropriations, *National War Agencies Appropriation Bill for 1944*, Pt. 1, 78th Cong., 1st sess., 1943, 912–917; see also Winkler, *Politics of Propaganda*, 21–22.

20. MacLeish to Rosenman, March 24, 1942, in Winnick, ed., *Letters of Archibald MacLeish*, 310–311.

21. "Profile: Davis, Elmer…U. S. Administration," August 1943, Box 10, Entry 6E, RG 208, NARA; and Burlingame, *Don't Let Them Scare You*.

22. On Donovan's exile, see Brown, *The Last Hero*, 235–239; Ford, *Donovan of OSS*, 126–128; and Winkler, *The Politics of Propaganda*, 25–31.

23. The text of Executive Order 9182 can be found in "Executive Order on War News," *New York Times*, June 14, 1942; Creel quoted in Winkler, *Politics of Propaganda*, 35.

24. Davis's statement to Congress can be found in its original form in U.S. Congress, House, Hearings Before a Subcommittee of the Committee on Appropriations, *Second Supplemental National Defense Appropriation Bill for 1943*, 77th Cong., 2nd sess., 1942, 383–392; and in slightly expanded form in Davis and Price, *War Information and Censorship*.

25. Ibid.

26. Ibid.

27. MacLeish, *Time to Act*, 9.

28. MacLeish, *Time to Act*, 21–31.

29. Feller, "OWI on the Home Front"; and Barth to MacLeish, "Government Column or Newsletter," June 18, 1942, Box 7, Entry 1, RG 208, NARA; see attached memo from Elmer Davis expressing his disapproval of the idea.

30. On Hollywood and the OWI, see Koppes and Black, *Hollywood Goes to War*. Koppes and Black also discuss Hollywood's advocacy for intervention prior to World War II, as do Moser, "'Gigantic Engines of Propaganda'"; and Chambers, "The Movies and the Antiwar Debate." Most historians agree that money was the principal motivation behind Hollywood taking a pro-war stance. Since most films covered their costs through the domestic box office and then made their profits through overseas distribution, the collapse of the European market represented an especially grave threat to the motion picture industry.

31. U.S. Congress, House, Hearings Before the Subcommittee of the Committee on Appropriations, *National War Agencies Appropriation Bill for 1944*, Pt. 1, 78th Cong., 1st sess., 1943, 1047.

32. Souls to Lagemann, "Communications Facilities," March 29, 1944, Box 1, Entry 6B, RG 208, NARA.

33. On radiophoto, which is generally ignored in histories of the OWI, see "Historical Background of Radiophoto," n. d.; and "Historical Background of Operation Policy," November 19, 1942; both in Box 4, Entry 6A, RG 208, NARA.

34. Ibid.

35. "Work of the Book Section," April 30, 1943, Box 5, Entry 6B, RG 208, NARA.

36. Williamson to Barrett, August 28, 1944; "Distribution of U.S. Books Abroad," October 2, 1944; and "Work of the Book Section," April 30, 1943; all in Box 5, Entry 6B, RG 208, NARA.

37. "Distribution of U.S. Books Abroad," October 2, 1944, Box 5, Entry 6B, RG 208, NARA.

38. Williamson to Barrett, August 28, 1944, Box 5, Entry 6B, RG 208, NARA.

39. See Hawkins and Pettee, "OWI—Organization and Problems," in which the authors argue that "many of the fundamentals of propaganda were well understood twenty-five years ago, but an enormous amount of thought has since been put into the subject" (p. 31).

40. On the growth of the advertising industry, see Fox, *Mirror Makers*; Leach, *Land of Desire*; Marchand, *Advertising the American Dream*; and Lears, *Fables of Abundance*. In discussing the ways that policymakers adopted advertising models, I do not mean to suggest that they thought they could control perceptions of "America" in the world, but that, like advertisers, they approached the problem of image as a matter of measuring and then responding to the public's opinions.

41. "The Overseas Operations Branch," n. d., Box 1, Entry 6B, RG 208, NARA.

42. U.S. Congress, Senate, Hearings Before a Subcommittee of the Committee on Appropriations, *National War Agencies Appropriation Bill for 1944*, 78th Cong., 1st sess., 1943, 255–270. Notably, this relationship continued well into the Cold War, when the "War Advertising Council" morphed into the "Advertising Council," continuing to offer advice to the OWI's successors in the State Department. See Griffith, "The Selling of America" and Lykins, *From Total War to Total Diplomacy*.

43. Roper is now largely forgotten because of the hit to his reputation after his prediction in the hotly contested 1948 presidential election missed the mark by a whopping 12.3 percent. The information on Gallup and Roper comes from Fox, *Mirror Makers*, 181.

44. "Questions and Answers on Surveys Division Activities," n. d., Box 5, Entry 6A, RG 208, NARA. LaRoche's comment appears in U.S. Congress, Senate, Hearings Before a Subcommittee of the Committee on Appropriations, *National War Agencies Appropriation Bill for 1944*, 78th Cong., 1st sess., 1943, 265. Davis's statement to Congress appears in U.S. Congress, House, Hearings Before a Subcommittee of the Committee on Appropriations, *Second Supplemental National Defense Appropriation Bill for 1943*, 77th Cong., 2nd sess., 1942, 383–392.

45. Robert Sherwood, "Long-Range Directive," January 15, 1943, Box 4, Entry 6B, RG 208, NARA.

46. Ibid.

47. Ibid.

48. Elmer Davis, "The Office of War Information, 13 June 1942—15 September 1945, Report to the President," Box 13, Entry 6E, RG 208, NARA.

49. Davis to Sherwood, August 14, 1942, Box 6, Entry 1, RG 208, NARA.

50. Office of the Assistant Director to Branch Directors, Deputies Bureau Chiefs and Administrative Assistants, "British Imperialism" [Current Issues Memorandum #3] and India [Current Issues Memorandum #2], December 21, 1942, Box 2, Entry 6A; and "Minutes of the Committee on War Information Policy," August 12, 1942, Box 2, Entry 1; both in RG 208, NARA. For more on the U.S. propaganda dilemma in India during World War II, see Graham, "American Propaganda, the Anglo-American Alliance, and the 'Delicate Question' of Indian Self-Determination"; and Pullin, "'Noise and Flutter.'"

51. This sentence should not be misread as a critique of the American press for reporting on such stories. The point is simply that a free press creates certain dilemmas for propagandists concerned with the way their nation is perceived in the world.

52. "Minutes of the Office of Facts and Figures Meeting," March 17, 1942, Box 52; MacLeish to Roosevelt, January 19, 1942, Box 19; both in MacLeish Papers, LC. For the Goebbels quote in OWI files, see Cranston to Grover, January 13, 1942, Box 8, Entry 3D, RG 208, NARA.

53. Davis to Roosevelt, October 2, 1942, Box 1, Entry 1, RG 208, NARA; and Huse to Davis, Eisenhower, Cowles, MacLeish, and Sherwood, "Minutes of the [OWI] Board Meeting," November 14, 1942, Box 53, MacLeish Papers, LC.

54. Berry to Davis, "Summary and Suggestions on Negro Morale Problems," July 24, 1942; and "Blueprint of Program for Strengthening Negro Morale in War Effort," March 4, 1942; both in Box 8, Entry 1, RG 208, NARA. Berry's arguments received support in "Memorandum on Negro Morale," n. d., Box 1553, Entry 294, RG 208, NARA. The counter-argument is found in Starr to Lewis, October 22, 1942; Barnes to Eisenhower, September 28, 1942; both in Box 8, Entry 1, RG 208, NARA.

See also Barnes to Cowles, February 1, 1943, reel 1, part 1, *Records of the Office of War Information* (microfilm edition).

55. Starr to Bell, April 22, 1942, Box 6, Entry 3D; and [untitled memo], April 24, 1942, Box 3, Entry 7; both in RG 208, NARA. The OWI never really resolved this debate, eventually leading Berry to resign in frustration. Berry's resignation did not necessarily mean that Starr won the argument, however, because OWI leaders did acknowledge the need to actually do something about discrimination—not just talk about or discount it—even if they were not yet willing to challenge southern congressmen aggressively on Jim Crow.

56. Robert Sherwood, "Long-Range Directive," January 15, 1943, Box 4, Entry 6B, RG 208, NARA.

57. Eisenhower to McCloy, August 22, 1942, Reel 1, Part 1, *Records of the Office of War Information* (microfilm edition); Davis to FDR, October 2, 1942, Box 1, Entry 1; Cowles to Ball, November 28, 1942, Box 12A, Entry 20; Smith to Cranston, January 5, 1943, Box 1, Entry 1; and Davis to Grew, January 6, 1943, Box 1, Entry 1; all in RG 208, NARA.

58. For just one example of many, see Culbertson to Perry, January 20, 1942, 811.4016, Decimal File, 1940–1944, RG 59, NARA. This indifference to domestic racism began to change during the war, although the State Department initially focused only on the ways that reports of discrimination against Latinos in the United States undermined the Good Neighbor Policy. The contrast between State Department and OWI perceptions of domestic racism is the major focus of Hart, "Making Democracy Safe for the World."

59. "Memorandum on Negro Morale," n. d., Box 1553, Entry 294, RG 208, NARA.

60. The two most prominent examples of the now-large literature on what Mary Dudziak has termed "cold war civil rights" are Dudziak, *Cold War Civil Rights*; and Borstelmann, *The Cold War and the Color Line*. For the argument that this phenomenon originated during World War II rather than the Cold War, see Hart, "Making Democracy Safe for the World."

61. Eisenhower and MacLeish quoted in Winkler, *Politics of Propaganda*, 41–42.

62. "Explanation Given on Split in OWI," *New York Times*, April 13, 1943; "Impossible to Tell Full Truth, Say OWI Writers Who Quit," *Washington Post*, April 16, 1943; and Lewis Wood, "Feud within OWI Is Spreading Far," *New York Times*, April 18, 1943.

63. Lewis Wood, "Feud within OWI Is Spreading Far," *New York Times*, April 18, 1943.

64. On the Publications Bureau, see "Office of War Information, Overseas Branch, Bureau of Publications," n. d., Box 5, Entry 6A, RG 208, NARA; and U.S. Congress, House, Hearings Before the Subcommittee of the Committee on Appropriations, *National War Agencies Appropriation Bill for 1944*, Pt. 1, 78th Cong., 1st sess., 1943, 760–761, 1050–1051.

65. The controversy over *Negroes and the War* receives extensive coverage in Savage, *Broadcasting Freedom*, 124–135; and Winkler, *Politics of Propaganda*, 66–72.

66. The quotes about "racial equality" and a "philosophy that is alien to us" come from the comments of Democratic Congressman Leonard Allen of Louisiana, although Allen had plenty of company in race-baiting the OWI. For Allen's comments, see Subcommittee of the House Committee on Appropriations, *Hearings on National War Agencies Appropriation Bill for 1944*, 78th Cong., 1st sess., 1943, 1311.

67. Davis quoted in Winkler, *Politics of Propaganda*, 71; on the conflict with Congress in general, see Shulman, *Voice of America*, 95–98; Krugler, *Voice of America and the Domestic Propaganda Battles, 1945–1953*, 29–33; Meserve, *Robert E. Sherwood*, 176–182; Eisenhower, *President Is Calling*, Chapter 7; Barrett, *Truth Is Our Weapon*, Chapter 3; and Thomson, *Overseas Information Service*, Chapters 2–5.

68. The "moronic little king" episode receives excellent coverage in Winkler, *Politics of Propaganda*, 92–100; Shulman, *Voice of America*, 98–102; and Burlingame, *Don't Let Them Scare You*, 227–230. The most controversial excerpts from the broadcast can be found in "OWI Broadcasts Excerpts," *New York Times*, July 28, 1943.

69. William H. Stringer, "Allies Bend Every Effort to Drive Italy Out of the War," *Christian Science Monitor*, July 27, 1943; Ben W. Gilbert, "Broadcast Slur on Italian King is Repudiated by Roosevelt," *Washington Post*, July 28, 1943.

70. William L. Shirer, "Our Voice to Europe is Stilled," *Washington Post*, September 5, 1943. It is worth pointing out that Shirer did not address government propaganda trumpeting the alliance with Russia and its leader, Josef Stalin.

71. Arthur Krock, "OWI's Critics Stirred by Broadcast on Italy," *New York Times*, August 1, 1943.

72. Barnes, "Fighting with Information."

73. "Congress Regains Status, Taft Says," *New York Times*, July 7, 1943.

74. Taft quoted in Ford, *Donovan of OSS*, 126.

75. "18 Agencies Voted Nearly 3 Billions," *Washington Post*, June 19, 1943.

76. *Congressional Record*, 78th Cong., 1st sess., vol. 89, pt. 5, 6000.

77. State Department-Office of War Information Committee on Informational and Cultural Activities, "Draft of memorandum to be sent to State Department Heads of Missions and OWI Outpost Chiefs," April 24, 1945, Box 125, Entry 360, RG 208, NARA; and "Meeting of State Department-OWI Committee on Cultural Relations and Information," January 12, 1945, Box 1, Entry 1245, RG 59, NARA.

78. Ibid.

79. Office of War Information, Overseas Operations Branch, "Memorandum on Post-VE Propaganda," May 14, 1945, Box 2, Entry 1245, RG 59,

NARA; "Projection of America," January 5, 1945, Box 13, Entry 6E, RG 208; and "Draft Outline of a Directive for Projection of America," November 30, 1944, Box 13, Entry 6E, RG 208, NARA. State Department records (particularly Archibald MacLeish's Files in Entry 1245, RG 59, NARA) contain quite a bit of internal correspondence endorsing the long-range plans of the OWI.

80. On the fear that American actions would be perceived as imperialism—whether territorial, commercial, or political—see Office of War Information, Overseas Operations Branch, "Special Guidance on Long-Range Media for Europe," June 14, 1944, Box 3, Entry 6B, RG 208, NARA; and Cousins to Williamson, "Alice Curran's Review Board Memorandum," December 5, 1944, Box 13, Entry 6E, RG 208, NARA. The startling phrase "toward a new American imperialism" appears in a strategy memo on OWI propaganda in China. The goal of this "new" style of imperialism—that is, cultural imperialism—was to assuage "Chinese fears of the American colossus" by disentangling perceptions of the United States from perceptions of Great Britain, which the Chinese supposedly "regarded as the head and forefront of imperialism." As the memo candidly admits, "we cannot entirely dissociate ourselves from British imperialism, having so long shared its fruits in China, but we must not identify ourselves with it. We must avoid any underwriting of the *Status quo ante,* and make plain our independent position." See Office of War Information, Overseas Operations Branch, "Guidance for OWI Informational Work in Unoccupied China," October 24, 1944, Box 2, Entry 1245, RG 59, NARA.

81. "Draft Letter from Mr. Davis to the President," September 20, 1944, Box 10, Entry 6E, RG 208, NARA.

82. Ibid.

83. "Draft of letter from Messrs. Davis and Rockefeller to President," November 16, 1944, Box 10, Entry 6E, RG 208, NARA; and Davis to Manasco, June 16, 1944, Box 3, Entry 1, RG 208, NARA.

84. Klauber to Truman, August 17, 1945, Pt. 1, reel 3, *Records of the Office of War Information* (microfilm edition).

Chapter 4

1. [Notter], *Postwar Foreign Policy Preparation,* 67–78.

2. Official legend has it that Edward Gullion coined the term "public diplomacy" in 1965. However, as Nicholas J. Cull has demonstrated, the phrase actually dates back to the mid-19th century, and it was commonly used both during World War I and World War II. See Nicholas Cull, "'Public Diplomacy' before Guillon: The Evolution of a Phrase," http://uscpublicdiplomacy.org/pdfs/gullion.pdf (accessed August 16, 2012). In my view, the U.S. government's decision at the end of World War II to

combine cultural and educational exchanges with domestic and overseas information programs marked the beginnings of a unified approach to the practice of public diplomacy.

3. To make this argument is not to take a position on the loaded questions of what "caused," or who "started," the Cold War. On the relative strength of the United States compared to the Soviet Union, see Leffler, *Preponderance of Power.*

4. Block to Allen, September 8, 1948, Box 3, Entry 1559, RG 59, NARA. The two passages quoted here were excerpted from rhetorical questions that Block asked in the course of his memo to Allen. I have no doubt that Block meant these passages more as declarative statements than as open-ended questions, but readers can judge for themselves.

5. Minutes, Information Service Committee, January 4, 1945, Box 94, Entry 401–403, RG 353, NARA.

6. The title of this position changed from Assistant Secretary of State for Public and Cultural Relations to Assistant Secretary of State for Public Affairs at the time that Benton succeeded MacLeish.

7. The obituaries for Benton in the *New York Times* and the *Washington Post* on March 19, 1973 give the basic outline of his contributions to the advertising industry. See also Hyman, *Lives of William Benton*; and Fox, *Mirror Makers.*

8. Ibid.

9. U.S. Congress, House, Hearings before the Committee on Foreign Affairs, *Interchange of Knowledge and Skills between People of the United States and Peoples of Other Countries*, 79th Cong., 1st. sess., 1945, 5.

10. These concerns became even more acute after the Congressional Reorganization Act of 1946, which, according to Benton's harshest critic, Rep. John Taber (R-NY), prohibited appropriations for programs without specific legal authorization. See "House Group Kills Program of U.S. Broadcasts Abroad," *New York Times*, April 24, 1947.

11. U.S. Congress, House, Hearings before the Committee on Foreign Affairs, *Interchange of Knowledge and Skills between People of the United States and Peoples of Other Countries*, 79th Cong., 1st. sess., 1945, 4–9. On Taft's role in killing the bill, see Thomson, *Overseas Information Service*, 234, n. 11. Taft's involvement here is significant. Over the past decade, the practice of public diplomacy had always served as a symbol of Rooseveltian internationalism, and Taft was one of the last holdouts against the bipartisan embrace of Cold War internationalist ideologies in the United States.

12. U.S. Congress, House, Hearings before the Committee on Foreign Affairs, *Interchange of Knowledge and Skills between People of the United States and Peoples of Other Countries*, 79th Cong., 1st. sess., 1945, 139 and 121–129; and Ninkovich, *Diplomacy of Ideas*, 121. The charges about recreating the OWI within the State Department were actually quite

accurate, since Benton imported both theoretical precepts as well as many key staffers (such as Edward Barrett and Charles Hulten) from the OWI.

13. "Rep. Cox, 72, Fiery Foe of Truman Dies," *Los Angeles Times*, December 25, 1952; "Ex-Rep. John Taber Dies at 85," *New York Times*, November 23, 1965; "Styles Bridges Is Dead at 63," *New York Times*, November 27, 1961; "House Group Asks Free Hand on State," *Washington Post*, January 29, 1947; "Alien-Minded Seen," *New York Times*, May 9, 1947. The two legislators who distinguished themselves by getting into fistfights were Cox and Taber.

14. Not surprisingly, William Benton and his team paid particularly close attention to polling on this issue. For one example, see Russell to Benton, February 20, 1946, Box 6, Entry 1530, RG 59, NARA.

15. This highly revealing quote comes from the report put out by the House Appropriations Committee in 1947, explaining their decision to eliminate funding for public diplomacy from the State Department Budget. Excerpts from this report are in "Legislative History, International Information and Educational Activities," August 21, 1950, Box 65, Elsey Papers, HSTL.

16. U.S. Congress, House, Hearings before the Subcommittee of the Committee on Appropriations, *Department of State Appropriation Bill for 1948*, 80th Cong., 1st sess., 1947, 391–402.

17. Ibid., 408–411.

18. Ibid., 412–422; and "Legislative History, International Information and Educational Activities," August 21, 1950, Box 65, Elsey Papers, HSTL.

19. U.S. Congress, House, Subcommittee of the Committee on Foreign Affairs, *United States Information and Educational Exchange Act of 1947*, 80th Cong., 1st sess., 1947, 20–22.

20. H. Schuyler Foster of the State Department's Office of Public Opinion Studies used the term "public participation," although not in precisely this way, in a public address in 1961. See Foster, "The Role of the Public in U.S. Foreign Relations."

21. Although Kennan believed strongly in the importance of images and ideas in fighting the Cold War, he also harbored an astonishing degree of animosity toward public opinion and, more broadly, toward American pluralism. As Frank Costigliola points out, Kennan, in his famous "Long Telegram" of 1946, worried that a divided and confused public left the United States weak and vulnerable to Soviet exploitation. How? Through "penetration" of "labor unions, youth leagues, women's organizations, racial societies, religious societies...[and] liberal magazines." The communist threat, Kennan suggested, was the "point at which foreign and domestic policies meet." For these quotes, see Costigliola, "'Unceasing Pressure for Penetration,'" 1333–1334.

22. There has been little work on the Office of Public Opinion Studies or the Office of Public Affairs, of which it was a part. One recent exception is

Johnstone, "Creating a 'Democratic Foreign Policy,'" although this article focuses primarily on the Division of Public Liaison, a different entity within the Office of Public Affairs.

23. Harry S. Truman, Executive Order 9608, August 31, 1945, The American Presidency Project, http://www.presidency.ucsb.edu/ws/index.php?pid=60671 (accessed August 16, 2012). "A full and fair picture" became the motto of U.S. public diplomacy during the early Cold War.

24. "Principles Underlying the Conduct of United States Overseas Information Activities," December 29, 1945, Box 6, Entry 1530, RG 59, NARA.

25. For samples of Foster's scholarly output, see Foster and Friedrich, "Letters to the Editor"; Foster, "Pressure Groups and Administrative Agencies"; Foster, "How America Became Belligerent"; and Foster, "The Official Propaganda of Great Britain."

26. The polling firms Foster typically cited were the American Institute of Public Opinion (the Gallup poll), The Fortune Survey, The National Opinion Research Center (University of Denver), and the Office of Public Opinion Research (Princeton University/Hadley Cantril). Foster's reports can be found in various subsets of Entry 568, RG 59, NARA.

27. Foster, *Activism Replaces Isolationism*, 1–12.

28. See, for example, "Organization and Newspaper Opinion on the UN Genocide Convention," January 27, 1950, Box 23, Entry 568O, RG 59, NARA.

29. Foster, "The Role of the Public in U.S. Foreign Relations."

30. As Robert Beisner points out in *Dean Acheson* (p. 671, n. 23), the line about trying to "scare hell out of the country," although endlessly repeated over the years, appears to have originated in an un-footnoted passage from Goldman, *The Crucial Decade*, 59. Whether the quote is fabricated or not, there is little question that this was the strategy that the Truman administration pursued. See also Bostdorff, *Proclaiming the Truman Doctrine*, which reaches the same conclusion.

31. Discussion of the public relations strategy to accompany the Truman Doctrine comes from SWNCC, Subcommittee on Foreign Policy Information, February 28, 1947; Russell, "Memorandum on Genesis of President Truman's March 12 Speech," March 17, 1947; and Russell to Acheson, March 19, 1947; all in Box 3, Entry 1530, RG 59, NARA.

32. Ibid.

33. Ibid.

34. The Lippmann column that set off Russell was "Truman and Monroe," *Washington Post*, April 8, 1947; Russell's draft letter and Acheson's order to kill it are from April 8 & 10, 1947, respectively. They can be found, along with Russell's March 22, 1947 report to Acheson on public opinion

toward the Greek-Turkish aid bill, in Box 3, Entry 1530, RG 59, NARA. On Acheson's near fight with Lippmann, see Herring, *From Colony to Superpower*, 615–616.

35. One gets an excellent sense of the shift in public opinion toward the Soviet Union by reading Schuyler Foster's "Fortnightly Surveys of American Opinion." The period from 1944–1948 is covered in Box 11, Entry 568L, RG 59, NARA.

36. On the thinking of U.S. policymakers in deciding to pursue the Marshall Plan, see Hogan, *The Marshall Plan*, 26–53.

37. For an analysis of one portion of this campaign, see Wala, "Selling the Marshall Plan at Home."

38. State Department Policy Planning Staff, "Certain Aspects of the European Recovery Problem from the United States Standpoint," July 23, 1947, in Merrill, ed., *Documentary History*, Vol. 13, 216–218.

39. Dean Acheson, "The Requirements of Reconstruction," an Address before the Delta Council at Cleveland, MS, May 8, 1947, reprinted in *The Department of State Bulletin*, May 18, 1947: 991–994; and George Marshall, "European Initiative Essential to Economic Recovery," Commencement Address at Harvard University, Jun. 5, 1947, reprinted in *The Department of State Bulletin*, June 15, 1947: 1159–1160.

40. For a sampling of the reaction to Dean Acheson's Cleveland speech (particularly in relation to discussions of the Truman Doctrine), see "Initial Press and Radio Reaction to Under Secretary Acheson's Speech at Cleveland, Mississippi on May 8, 1947," May 15, 1947, in Merrill, ed., *Documentary History*, Vol. 13, 148–155.

41. For Lovett's statement, see "Report of Discussion with Robert A. Lovett," May 12, 1947, Vol. XII, Papers of the Council on Foreign Relations, Mudd Library.

42. On the decision to invite the Soviet Union to participate in the Marshall Plan, based on the assumption that Stalin would refuse, see Hogan, *Marshall Plan*, 35–53. For Stalin's reaction, see Leffler, *For the Soul of Mankind*, 65–68.

43. See, for example, Harold Callender, "France Is Stirred by Marshall Plan," *New York Times*, June 6, 1947.

44. "Department Information Program on the Marshall Plan," n. d. [but a penciled note indicates that it was circulated in September 1947], Box 3, Entry 1530, RG 59, NARA. This secret memo specifically proposed the creation of an independent public pressure group called the Citizens Committee on Foreign Reconstruction, suggesting several pages worth of prominent political, intellectual, and organizational leaders to serve on this committee. I have found no indication that it ever actually materialized, but the Committee for the Marshall Plan served the same purpose.

45. Ibid.

46. Ibid. For more specific information on public opinion, see also "Memorandum on U.S. Opinion on the European Recovery Program," December 18, 1947, Box 3, Entry 1530, RG 59, NARA.

47. The meeting between Graham and the representatives of the Office of Public Affairs is described in "Proposed Special Supplement by Washington Post on the Marshall Plan," August 18, 1947, Box 3, Entry 1530, RG 59, NARA.

48. My research in this paragraph comes from the ProQuest Historical Newspapers database. I searched for articles written by Kuhn on the Marshall Plan six months before and six months after August 18, 1947—the date of the meeting. This search also revealed reports in the *Post* on speeches that Kuhn gave to the Controllers Institute of America on December 16, 1947, and to the National Women's Democratic Club on January 5, 1948. There may well have been others, but these were the two written up in the *Post*.

49. The full scope of the Committee's work is laid out in "Report on the Activities of the Committee for the Marshall Plan to Aid European Recovery," April 5, 1948, Box 3, Acheson Papers, HSTL.

50. Acheson's work for the Committee for the Marshall Plan is addressed in Ferguson to Acheson, December 9, 1947; and Acheson to Ferguson, December 17, 1947; both in Box 3, Acheson Papers, HSTL. Acheson provides some retrospective reflection in *Present at the Creation*, 240–241; see also Beisner, *Dean Acheson*, 74–76.

51. Alger Hiss, "The Answers to Five Marshall Plan Questions," November 16, 1947, *New York Times Magazine*, reprinted in Committee for the Marshall Plan to Aid European Recovery, "What about the Marshall Plan," Box 4, Acheson Papers, HSTL.

52. Henry L. Stimson, "The Challenge to Americans," *Foreign Affairs*, October 1947, reprinted by Committee for the Marshall Plan to Aid European Recovery, Box 4, Acheson Papers, HSTL.

53. Acheson, *Present at the Creation*, 240.

54. Beisner, *Dean Acheson*, 76.

55. Whether the Soviet Union had, in fact, declared "psychological war" on the United States by January 1947 is certainly debatable. Stalin did not officially establish the Communist Information Bureau (Cominform) until that fall. The question of when the psychological Cold War officially started (or who started it) is less important here than this very revealing characterization of the potential potency of the Soviet message. See Hunt to Stone, January 10, 1947, Box 128, Entry 1559, RG 59, NARA.

56. "OIC Policy with Respect to the Soviet Anti-American Propaganda Campaign," July 25, 1947, Box 124, Entry 1559, RG 59, NARA.

57. The creation of the Cominform is discussed in OIC/OIE Staff Meeting Minutes, October 7, 1947, Box 119, Entry 1559, RG 59, NARA. It is also discussed in Selverstone, *Constructing the Monolith*, Chapter 4.

58. On the impact of the Cominform on U.S. information policy, see OIC/ OIE Staff Meeting Minutes, October 7, 1947, Box 119, Entry 1559, RG 59, NARA.

59. On the specifics of NSC-4 and some of the State Department's (largely unsuccessful) attempts to coordinate information policy with the other agencies involved, see Box 9, Entry 1559, RG 59, NARA.

60. On broader efforts to define the Soviet Union as Cold War foe, see Engerman, *Know Your Enemy*.

61. "U.S. Information Policy with Regard to Anti-American Propaganda," November 13, 1947; and Walter Bedell Smith to Secretary of State, November 15, 1947; both in Box 4, Entry 1530, RG 59, NARA.

62. U.S. Congress, House, Hearings before a Special Subcommittee of the Committee on Foreign Affairs, *United States Information and Educational Exchange Act of 1947*, 80th Cong., 1st sess., 1947, 1–3.

63. As Kenneth Osgood makes clear in *Total Cold War*, Eisenhower was a true believer in public diplomacy—especially the propaganda end—and he considerably expanded these programs as president.

64. Benton argued throughout 1947 that American "motives" might be "twisted" or "misrepresented into the charge...that we are militaristic and imperialistic." For one example, see U.S. Congress, House, Hearings before the Subcommittee of the Committee on Appropriations, *Department of State Appropriation Bill for 1948*, 80th Cong., 1st sess., 1947, 399. Some of the details of the "fact-finding" trip are contained in "The United States Information Service in Europe: Implementation by the Department of State of the recommendations contained in the Reports of the Committee on Foreign Relations (Smith-Mundt Congressional group), January 1948," Box 4, Entry 6H, RG 208, NARA. For the State Department's perspective on how the trips solidified support in Congress for Smith-Mundt, see OIE Staff Meeting, October 9, 1947; and OIE Staff Meeting, October 16, 1947; both in Box 119, Entry 1559, RG 59, NARA. The best example of a congressman who, upon returning from the trip, called for a stronger information program to amplify the economic effects of the Marshall Plan is Montana Democrat Mike Mansfield. In a meeting with Truman shortly after the trip, he urged accelerating the legislative timetable for both the Smith-Mundt Act and Marshall Plan aid. See "Memorandum from Mike Mansfield," n. d. [but clearly written upon his return from Europe], Box 4, Clifford Papers, HSTL. Krugler, *The Voice of America*, 65–72, also has a good account of the trip and its domestic impact.

65. George Allen, "U.S. Information Program," Address to Mount Holyoke College Institute of the United Nations, June 28, 1948, Box 2, Entry 1526, RG 59, NARA.

66. Ibid.

67. "Digest of Proceedings of the PAO Conference at The Hague, October 4–7, 1949," November 10, 1949, Box 113, Entry 1559, RG 59, NARA.

68. Marshall Andrews, "America Voice Radio Script is Criticized," *Washington Post*, March 6, 1948; and Neal Stanford, "Senate Hurricane of Criticism Sweeps on 'Voice of America'," *Christian Science Monitor*, May 27, 1948.

69. Ibid.

70. "'Voice' Had Comedy Touch, Says Writer," *Washington Post*, June 2, 1948; Neal Stanford, "Text of 'Know North America' Shows Congress Ire Not Entirely Justified," *Christian Science Monitor*, June 4, 1948; and "Hit State Department Negligence in 'Voice' Casts," *Chicago Daily Tribune*, June 16, 1948.

71. Samuel A. Tower, "Truman and Congress Rush 'Voice' Broadcast Inquiries," *New York Times*, May 28, 1948.

72. Allen to Marshall, June 10, 1948, Box 39, White House Central File, Confidential File, HSTL.

73. Ibid.

74. Edwards to Lehrbas, July 2, 1948, Box 119, Entry 1559, RG 59, NARA.

75. Lehrbas, Memorandum for Mr. Allen, July 4, 1948; Lehrbas, Memorandum for Mr. Allen, June 30, 1948; Edwards to Lehrbas, "Recent screening of Hollywood film *Fort Apache*," July 2, 1948; Edwards to Lehrbas, "Export of the American-made film *State of the Union*," July 2, 1948; and Edwards to Lehrbas, "Feature films sent abroad by motion picture industry," June 28, 1948; all in Box 119, Entry 1559, RG 59, NARA.

76. Ibid.

77. Ibid.

78. Hulten to Barrett, April 4, 1950, Box 53, Entry 1559, RG 59, NARA.

Chapter 5

1. The Truman administration's response to events in China throughout 1949 is nicely summarized and placed in broad context in "The Truman Administration During 1949: A Chronology," at http://www.trumanlibrary.org/chron/49chrono.htm (accessed August 17, 2012).

2. On the drafting of a domestic information strategy in response to the Chinese Revolution, see Russell to Jessup, "The Secretary's Press Conference Statement on China Following the Issuance of the White Paper," July 19, 1949; Swihart to Allen, "Distribution of the China White Paper," August 15, 1949; and Russell to Sargeant, "Policy Information Paper on China," January 4, 1950; all in Box 2, Entry 1530, RG 59, NARA.

3. Minutes of Meeting, General Advisory Committee of the Division of Cultural Relations of the Department of State, February 25–26, 1942, Box 29, Entries 20–22, RG 353, NARA.

4. "United States Information Policy with Regard to Anti-American Propaganda," July 20, 1948, Box 112, Entry 1559, RG 59, NARA.

5. "Meeting: Conference on Problems of United States Policy in China," October 6, 1949, Box 1, Entry 1526, RG 59, NARA.

6. Ibid.

7. Ibid.

8. White, *Rising Wind*.

9. "Record of Round-Table Discussion by Twenty-Four Consultants with the Department of State on 'Strengthening International Organizations,'" November 17–19, 1949, Box 40, Confidential File, White House Central File, HSTL.

10. Ibid.

11. Lodge quoted in Borstelmann, *Apartheid's Reluctant Uncle*, 142.

12. "Draft Speech for Mr. Howland Sargeant before Public Relations Society of America," December 5, 1949, Box 8, Sargeant Papers, HSTL; see also Draft Statement of Howland H. Sargeant, "International Information and Educational Exchange Activities," January 16, 1950, Box 112, Entry 1559, RG 59, NARA.

13. Ibid.

14. The text of NSC-68, classified until 1975, is now widely available in print and online. Its official publication was in *Foreign Relations of the United States: 1950*, Vol. I.

15. Bruce Cumings develops the argument about the shift from containment to rollback at considerable length in the introduction to *Origins of the Korean War*, Vol. 2.

16. Harry S. Truman, "Address on Foreign Policy at a Luncheon of the American Society of Newspaper Editors," April 20, 1950, at http://www.trumanlibrary.org/publicpapers/index.php?pid=715&st=&sti= (accessed August 17, 2012).

17. LaFeber, *America, Russia, and the Cold War*, 105.

18. Winnick, ed., *Letters of Archibald MacLeish*, 305.

19. Clearly, Korea qualified as a "war" in the sense that U.S. soldiers fought and died. Yet, the administration could not, after carefully defining the limits of the conflict, really treat this as a "time of war," with all the powers that designation bestowed. (It is worth remembering that Truman fired General Douglas MacArthur for insubordination in 1951 because MacArthur publicly criticized the idea of a limited war.)

20. On public opinion, propaganda, and the domestic climate of the Korean War, see Casey, *Selling the Korean War*.

21. "Statement by Senator William Benton (D. Conn.) before the subcommittee of the Senate Foreign Relations Committee which is considering S. Res. 243," July 5, 1950, Box 43, Entry 1559, RG 59, NARA.

22. There were actually two different manifestations of the Psychological Strategy Board under the Truman administration: First, the "National Psychological Strategy Board" under the direction of the State Department and then, after April 4, 1951, the reconstituted "Psychological Strategy Board" under an independent administrator. Essentially the same list of government departments participated in each group. For the

sake of convenience, I use "PSB" to refer to both, although events before April 4, 1951 took place under the former entity, while events after that date took place under the latter. The literature on the Psychological Strategy Board is surprisingly thin. Other than one chapter in Scott Lucas's *Freedom's War*, the only substantial examination of the PSB is Lilly, "The Psychological Strategy Board." Lilly, who worked as a Special Consultant to the Joint Chiefs of Staff during the early 1950s, prepared an extensive analysis of psychological warfare for the JCS that served as the basis for this study. His original report appears in Box 22, PSB Files, HSTL. Lilly's later study inexplicably contains numerous factual errors, although it may still be consulted with profit.

23. "Summary of psychological warfare activities during first month of hostilities," July 30, 1950, Box 18, Entry 1559, RG 59, NARA.

24. Stone to Barrett (July 19, 1950 memo from Brad Connors attached), July 27, 1950; and Stone to Barrett, "Summary of Psychological Warfare Activities—Korea," July 29, 1950; both in Box 18, Entry 1559, RG 59, NARA.

25. "Organization and Functions of the Director's Office and Staff of the Psychological Strategy Board," November 26, 1951, Box 25, PSB Files, HSTL.

26. Stone to Barrett, October 23, 1950, Box 10, Entry 1559, RG 59, NARA.

27. Glenn Fowler, "Edward W. Barrett, 79, ex-Journalism Dean, Dies," *New York Times*, October 5, 1989.

28. Neal Stanford, "U.S. Forms Strategy Unit to Prop Propaganda Effort," *Christian Science Monitor*, August 18, 1950. The other quotes come from Mary Hornaday, "'Voice' Awaits Funds to Hike Truth Drive," *Christian Science Monitor*, September 15, 1950; and Anthony Leviero, "U.S. Challenges the Soviet in Battle for Men's Minds," *New York Times*, December 10, 1951. See also Walter H. Waggoner, "Propaganda Body is Created by U.S.," *New York Times*, August 18, 1950.

29. On the Pentagon's objections see Stone, "Memorandum for Mr. Barrett, Subject: State Department Position on NSC-74," October 25, 1950; and Barrett to Acheson, December 11, 1950; both in Box 10, Entry 1559, RG 59, NARA.

30. Barrett, *Truth is Our Weapon*; and Oral History Interview with Edward W. Barrett, July 9, 1974, HSTL.

31. "Information Policy Objectives with Regard to Issues Arising from the Korean Situation," August 9, 1950, Box 19, Entry 1559, RG 59, NARA.

32. Stone, "Memorandum for Mr. Barrett, Subject: State Department Position on NSC-74," October 25, 1950, Box 10, Entry 1559, RG 59, NARA.

33. E. Fairbanks, "Notes on Information and Propaganda," January 24, 1951, Box 1, B File, Psychological Warfare, HSTL.

34. James Reston, "Cold War Agency Studied by Truman," *New York Times*, March 22, 1951; James Reston, "Truman is Shaking Up Staff and Duties of Security Unit," *New York Times*, April 3, 1951; and Ferdinand Kuhn, "Gray to Head Board for War of Ideas," *Washington Post*, June 29, 1951.

35. J. Y. Smith, "Gordon Gray, Former Secretary of U.S. Army, Dies at 73," *Washington Post*, November 27, 1982.

36. Charles W. McCarthy, "Organization and Functions of the Director's Office and Staff of the Psychological Strategy Board," n. d., Box 25, PSB Files, HSTL.

37. "Dr. Allen Accepts Strategy Position," *New York Times*, November 23, 1951; "Dr. Allen Slated for Chancellor of UCLA," *Los Angeles Times*, December 14, 1951; Harry Schwartz, "Admiral Kirk Gets Propaganda Post," *New York Times*, August 14, 1952; "A Job Worth Staying For," *New York Times*, December 18, 1951.

38. Lilly, "The Psychological Strategy Board," 370–382.

39. Gerald Horne makes the point about the lack of a Marshall Plan for Africa or the Middle East in "Who Lost the Cold War," 623.

40. Gray to Truman, February 22, 1952, Box 1, B File, Psychological Warfare, HSTL; and Charles W. McCarthy, "Organization and Functions of the Director's Office and Staff of the Psychological Strategy Board," n. d., Box 25, PSB Files, HSTL.

41. Nitze quoted in Lucas, *Freedom's War*, 132.

42. Eastman—the onetime running buddy of John Reed, one of the founders of the American Communist Party—had abandoned most of his authentically "liberal" principles some years before and would join the staff at William F. Buckley's *National Review* just a few years later. For the *New York Times* report on this meeting, see "Freedom Asked of Intellectuals," March 30, 1952. On the Committee for Cultural Freedom, more generally, see Scott-Smith, *Politics of Apolitical Culture*, and Saunders, *Cultural Cold War*.

43. Toner to Browne, April 3, 1952, Box 4, PSB Files, HSTL.

44. Ibid.

45. "A Positive Approach to the Peoples of MEA," September 23, 1952, Box 12; and "Preliminary Estimate of the Effectiveness of U.S. Psychological Strategy," May 5, 1952, Box 15; both in PSB Files, HSTL.

46. "Preliminary Estimate of the Effectiveness of U.S. Psychological Strategy," May 5, 1952, Box 15, PSB Files, HSTL.

47. Ibid.

48. On the complexities of U.S.-Indian relations in the postwar period, see Rotter, *Comrades at Odds*; and McMahon, *The Cold War on the Periphery*.

49. "Memorandum of Conversation (India)," January 17, 1952; and Chester Bowles, "A Progress Report from India," April 7, 1952; both in Box 7, PSB Files, HSTL.

50. There is no outstanding biography of Chester Bowles, although his own memoir, *Promises to Keep*, is quite good and well worth consulting.

51. Bowles to Allen, July 10, 1952, Box 7, PSB Files, HSTL.

52. Ibid.

53. Allen to Bowles, August 27, 1952, Box 7, PSB Files, HSTL.

54. Elliott to Browne, "Interview with Leo D. Hochstetter, Deputy Director of Information, Mutual Security Agency," September 26, 1952, Box 7, PSB Files, HSTL.

55. Ibid.

56. Korns "Memorandum for the Director," January 22, 1952, Box 7, PSB Files, HSTL.

57. Ibid.

58. On the Franco-American relationship in the Middle East in the context of the Algerian War, see Connelly, *Diplomatic Revolution*.

59. Sanger, Dunn, and Glidden, Special Paper, "The French Position in the Middle East," October 29, 1952, Box 12, PSB Files, HSTL.

60. "A Positive Approach to the Peoples of NEA," September 23, 1952; and Memorandum for the Record, "Informal Report by Assistant Secretary of State, Henry A. Byroade, on His Recent Trip to the Middle East"; both in Box 12, PSB Files, HSTL.

61. The State Department Arabists who authored these reports all spoke Arabic and boasted academic expertise in what the British call "Oriental Studies." Yet Harold W. Glidden, the most famous of the group, is best remembered as the author of an infamous study of "Arab emotions" that first appeared in the *American Journal of Psychiatry* and today often pops up in readers on Orientalism. See Harold W. Glidden, "The Arab World," *American Journal of Psychiatry* 128 (February 1972): 984–988.

62. Davis to Taylor, July 8, 1952; and "A Positive Approach to the Peoples of NEA," September 23, 1952; both in Box 12, PSB Files, HSTL.

63. "A Positive Approach to the Peoples of NEA," September 23, 1952, Box 12, PSB Files, HSTL.

64. For the argument that public diplomacy helped to create the "third world" as an ideological entity, see Jason C. Parker, "Crisis Management and Missed Opportunities: U.S. Public Diplomacy and the Creation of the Third World, 1947–1950," in Osgood and Etheridge, eds., *The United States and Public Diplomacy*.

Chapter 6

1. "Public Comment on Communists in the State Department," March 14, 1950, Box 20, Entry 568N, RG 59, NARA.

2. The best biography of McCarthy remains Oshinsky, *Conspiracy So Immense*. My narrative of McCarthy's rise closely follows that of Oshinsky.

3. Quoted in Schrecker, *Many are the Crimes*, 243.

4. This hostility and scrutiny did not stop with the creation of the USIA in 1953. Despite the effort to neutralize McCarthy's attacks by removing public diplomacy from the State Department and installing it in a separate agency, these sorts of criticisms continued, periodically, all the way up to the demise of the USIA in the 1990s when another conservative

Republican senator, Jesse Helms from North Carolina, again targeted the messages disseminated by U.S. public diplomats. Helms's crusade to dismantle the USIA brought everything full circle, as public diplomacy moved back into the State Department, where it has remained, largely neglected, ever since.

5. "Won't Turn Back on Hiss, Acheson Says," *Los Angeles Times*, January 26, 1950; and William R. Conklin, "Hiss is Sentenced to Five Year Term; Acheson Backs Him," *New York Times*, January 26, 1950.

6. William Moore, "Acheson Under New Assault as Pal of Hiss," *Chicago Tribune*, January 25, 1950; "Acheson Censured on Support of Hiss," *New York Times*, January 27, 1950; "Oust Acheson, Legislature in Texas Urges," *Chicago Tribune*, February 2, 1950; and Willard Edwards, "Won't Quit Hiss—Acheson," *Chicago Tribune*, January 26, 1950. For more on the linkage of homosexuality and communism, as well as efforts to tie this connection to Acheson's purported effeminacy (such as McCarthy's famous branding of Acheson's social circle as the "lace handkerchief crowd"), see Johnson, *Lavender Scare*; and Cuordileone, *Manhood and American Political Culture*. On the reaction of the Office of Public Opinion Studies, see Box 20, Entry 568N, RG 59, NARA.

7. Oshinsky, *Conspiracy So Immense*, 72–84.

8. It has often been noted that there was McCarthyism before there was McCarthy (for one example see Schrecker, *Many are the Crimes*, 241), so it would be fair to say that in Wheeling McCarthy found his "ism."

9. Regarding McCarthy's progression from 205 (which at one point became 207) to 57 to 81: The first figure came from a letter that Secretary of State James Byrnes wrote to Congress in 1946 acknowledging the presence of 205 potential security risks (not members of the Communist Party) in the State Department. McCarthy had no idea how many of these people had left or been fired in the intervening years, or how many of them had been deemed security risks because of political affiliations, as opposed to various allegedly "blackmailable" offenses, such as gambling or homosexuality. Moreover, cases like these had prompted the creation of the Loyalty-Security Board the following year, leading to further crackdowns in subsequent years. McCarthy arrived at the figure of 57 in the same way—taking it from a different list of 108 cases that had been investigated by Congress in 1947 and 1948. Of the original 108 potential "security risks" (again, not "Communists") identified by Congressional investigators, 57 had been cleared and remained in the Department as of 1948. By 1950, that number was down to the low forties. For a thorough explication of the confusing genesis of all these numbers see the report "McCarthy versus the State Department," prepared by Duke University sociologist Hornell Hart, in Merrill, ed., *Documentary History*, Vol. 25, 269–304.

10. Merrill, ed., *Documentary History*, Vol. 25, 44–50.

11. One need only compare the coverage of McCarthy from the *Chicago Tribune* to the *New York Times* or the *Washington Post* to get a sense of the dynamic that I describe here.

12. For approximately six months starting in February 1950, the Office of Public Opinion Studies issued daily reports entitled "Public Comment on Communists in the State Department." These reports provide an incredible range of reaction to McCarthy's charges and the subsequent investigations, including the various sentiments described in this paragraph. For the quote from the *Philadelphia Inquirer*, see the report from March 3, 1950, Box 20, Entry 568N, RG 59, NARA.

13. McCarthy quoted in Oshinsky, *Conspiracy So Immense*, 108, 196.

14. Harold B. Hinton, "M'Carthy Charges Spy for Russia has a Top State Department Post," *New York Times*, February 21, 1950; and William S. White, "M'Grath, Hoover Refuse Senate Bid for Loyalty Files," *New York Times*, March 28, 1950. Although Lattimore had more than a tangential connection to public diplomacy, having served two years as the Director of Pacific Operations for the OWI during the war, his work there formed only a small part of McCarthy's case. On Lattimore's tenure at the OWI, see William S. White, "Assails Lattimore," *New York Times*, March 31, 1950. McCarthy did introduce a letter Lattimore wrote at the OWI that, according to McCarthy, was meant to purge all of Chiang Kai-shek's allies in the OWI.

15. Willard Edwards, "Point 4 Head Named as Red, Senate Told," *Chicago Tribune*, April 28, 1950.

16. "U.S. Radio Voice under Quiz of Sen. McCarthy," *Chicago Tribune*, April 29, 1951.

17. On the *Amerasia* case, see Klehr, *Amerasia Spy Case*.

18. "Voice of America Handling of McCarthy Story," August 3, 1950, Box 43, Entry 1559, RG 59, NARA.

19. Taber to Barrett, July 27, 1950, Box 65, Elsey Papers, HSTL.

20. See, for example, "Freeing the Satellites," *Washington Post*, August 28, 1952; and Oshinsky, *Conspiracy So Immense*, 242.

21. On this, I disagree somewhat with Kenneth Osgood's argument in *Total Cold War*, 46–55. Osgood argues that in one speech Eisenhower "lambast[ed]" Truman's lack of commitment to the war of ideas, but my research suggests that Eisenhower never offered any specific suggestions about what the United States should do differently. At one point, he actually suggested that the role of the Voice of America should be fairly "limited." See Robert C. Albright, "Ike Rejects Delegation Contest Deal," *Washington Post*, June 8, 1952. For a few examples in which Eisenhower obliquely calls for a stronger propaganda program, see W. H. Lawrence, "Eisenhower and Stevenson Agree on Principles but Differ on Details," *New York Times*, August 24, 1952; and Harrison E. Salisbury, "Pravda Sees War Eisenhower's Aim," *New York Times*, August 30, 1952. While Eisenhower held a deep commitment to psychological warfare and he did

expand every aspect of the U.S. effort, this was not clear from the campaign.

22. Krugler, *Voice of America*, 197–198; and Cull, *Cold War and the United States Information Agency*, 81–84.

23. Oshinsky, *Conspiracy So Immense*, 243–250.

24. Ibid., 250–251.

25. Ibid., 267–268.

26. Edward Ranzal, "M'Carthy Sifting Voice of America," *New York Times*, February 13, 1953.

27. On the "Loyal Underground," see Krugler, *Voice of America*, 185–196; and Oshinsky, *Conspiracy So Immense*, 269–276. The entire run of *Tribune* coverage of the hearings is worth reading. These quotes come from Willard Edwards, "Voices Tell Pro-Red Policy in Voice of U.S.," *Chicago Tribune*, February 14, 1953.

28. Willard Edwards, "Voice of America Boss Quits; Quiz Blamed," *Chicago Tribune*, February 19, 1953; and C. P. Trussell, "Dr. Compton Quits as Head of 'Voice,'" *New York Times*, February 19, 1953.

29. The quote from the Dulles order is from Krugler, *Voice of America*, 194. The State Department leaked the existence of this memo to the press without mentioning the previous directive that it duplicated. See C. P. Trussell, "Voice Must Drop Works of Leftists," *New York Times*, February 20, 1953. For more on the sequence of directives, see Cull, *Cold War and the United States Information Agency*, 88. On the suspension of Alfred H. Morton, see Ferdinand Kuhn, "'Voice Chief is Suspended for Ignoring Ban on Reds," *Washington Post*, February 25, 1953. The story of the State Department suspending Morton after McCarthy got wind of his memo comes from Oshinsky, *Conspiracy So Immense*, 278.

30. C. P. Trussell, "Dr. Compton Quits as Head of 'Voice,'" *New York Times*, February 19, 1953. The fact that the State Department publicly rescinded three separate orders in one week after McCarthy complaints also perpetuated this idea. The newspaper quotes come from William S. White, "McCarthy Poses an Administration Problem," *New York Times*, February 22. 1953; and Joseph and Stewart Alsop, "Showdown with McCarthy Near," *Washington Post*, February 22, 1953.

31. Willard Edwards, "Halt Building of Two Voice Transmitters," *Chicago Tribune*, February 17, 1953; "Deliberate Waste Charged to Voice," *New York Times*, February 17, 1953; and "'Voice' Suicide's Record Clear, M'Carthy Finds," *Chicago Tribune*, March 8, 1953.

32. C. P. Trussell, "State Department Voids Curb in McCarthy Study of 'Voice,'" *New York Times*, February 21, 1953; and Willard Edwards, "Voice Sneered at U.S., Fired Red Foe Says," *Chicago Tribune*, February 21, 1953.

33. Willard Edwards, "Voice Aid Called Prayers Drivel, Probers Told," *Chicago Tribune*, March 3, 1953; and Oshinsky, *Conspiracy So Immense*, 272–274.

34. C. P. Trussell, "'Voice' Aide Sees McCarthy Aiming at 'My Public Neck,'" *New York Times*, March 4, 1953; and "Offers Proof of Scheme to Destroy Voice," *Chicago Tribune*, March 5, 1953.

35. William Moore, "Books of 250 Red Suspects in U.S. Libraries," *Chicago Tribune*, May 7, 1953; and Oshinsky, *Conspiracy So Immense*, 276–278.

36. "Call Official Back to U.S. for McCarthy Quiz," *Chicago Tribune*, April 8, 1953; "Finds 'Anti-Red' U.S. Aid Wrote Pro-Red Plays," *Chicago Tribune*, April 9, 1953; "M'Carthy Aids Get Going Over by Britishers," *Chicago Tribune*, April 20, 1953; Drew Pearson, "McCarthy's Men Get Attention," *Washington Post*, April 22, 1953; "Two McCarthy Probers Spike Smearers' Lies," *Chicago Tribune*, April 25, 1953; "British Press Pokes Fun at M'Carthy Investigators," *New York Times*, April 26, 1953; and Nat McKitterick, "Mr. Cohn and Mr. Schine Needed no Press Agent," *Washington Post*, April 26, 1953.

37. William Moore, "Browder Jeers at Red Probe; Hurls Insults," *Chicago Tribune*, March 25, 1953; and C. P. Trussell, "Browder, M'Carthy Clash at Hearing," *New York Times*, March 25, 1953.

38. "Survey Lists Authors U.S. Bans Abroad," *Washington Post*, June 23, 1953.

39. Walter Sullivan, "U.S. Purges Libraries it Runs in Germany," *New York Times*, June 11, 1953; and "Survey Lists Authors U.S. Bans Abroad," *Washington Post*, June 23, 1953.

40. "U.S. Purge in Germany," *New York Times*, June 12, 1953; Joseph and Stewart Alsop, "U.S. Book-Burning is Cowardly," *Washington Post*, June 14, 1953; C. P. Trussell, "Some Books Literally Burned after Inquiry, Dulles Reports," *New York Times*, June 16, 1953; Anthony Leviero, "Eisenhower Backed on Book Ban Talk," *New York Times*, June 17, 1953; and Laurence Burd, "Ike Condemns Red Literature Critical of U.S.," *Chicago Tribune*, June 18, 1953. Roughly a week later, Eisenhower reversed course again and denounced "zealots" who tried to censor the free exchange of ideas. Again, he declined to provide specifics. See Gladwin Hill, "Eisenhower Assails 'Zealots' and Backs Freedom of Ideas," *New York Times*, June 27, 1953.

41. Roland Sawyer, "America Drops Restrictions on Library Books," *Christian Science Monitor*, July 9, 1953.

42. Anthony Leviero, "Eisenhower Moves to Limit State Department to Policy," *New York Times*, June 2, 1953.

43. Partisan politics, the systematic oppression of the left, and a political culture rooted in anti-intellectualism, have all served as standard explanations for the "witch hunt" of the late 1940s and early 1950s. Yet, with the notable exception of the literature on communist spy networks in the United States, few scholars have examined the possibility that McCarthyism really was on some level a response to the infiltration or potential infiltration of "foreign" ideologies. Perhaps fearful of validating the hysterical accusation that all forms of progressive politics fed into the

international communist conspiracy, historians have not spent a lot of time looking at McCarthyism as a response to real fears rather than, or as well as, an anti-progressive crusade ginned up for political gain. The standard work on McCarthyism is Schrecker, *Many Are the Crimes*. Schrecker treats McCarthyism as part of a systematic effort to crush the left in America. So does Lieberman, *The Strangest Dream*. Oshinsky, *A Conspiracy so Immense*, and Fried, *Nightmare in Red*, both look at issues of partisan politics. Richard Hofstadter's classic study, *Anti-intellectualism in American Life*, analyzes McCarthyism as just the latest manifestation of an enduring tradition in American political culture. For a sampling of the literature on domestic spy networks, which is far more sympathetic to the movement that McCarthy represented, if not necessarily to the man himself, see Weinstein and Vassiliev, *The Haunted Wood*; and Haynes and Klehr, *Venona*.

Epilogue

1. Dean Acheson, transcript of Princeton Seminar, July 8–9, 1953, Acheson Papers, HSTL.
2. "A Study of USIA Operating Assumptions," December 1954, Vol. 5, p. C-2, Box 82, "Reports," USIA Historical Collection, RG 306, NARA. This report has been published as Bogart, *Premises for Propaganda*.
3. Ibid., pp. C-11 & C-13.

BIBLIOGRAPHY

Archival Collections

Harry S. Truman Library, Independence, MO (HSTL)

    Harry S. Truman Papers

        White House Central File (WHCF); Confidential File

        WHCF; Official File

        WHCF; President's Personal File

        Staff Member and Office Files (SMOF); Files of Charles W. Jackson

        SMOF; Files of Charles Murphy

        SMOF; Files of Clark M. Clifford

        SMOF; Files of Philleo Nash

        SMOF; Psychological Strategy Board Files

    Dean Acheson Papers

    George Elsey Papers

    Bryn J. Hovde Papers

    Charles M. Hulten Papers

    Howland H. Sargeant Papers

    Charles Thayer Papers

    Francis Wilcox Papers

    Oral History Interviews

    Papers of the Presidents Committee on Civil Rights

Library of Congress, Washington, DC (LC)

    Papers of the American Council of Learned Societies

    Papers of Waldo Leland

    Papers of Henry Luce

    Papers of Archibald MacLeish

Papers of Leo Pasvolsky
Papers of Arthur Sweetster
National Archives, College Park, MD (NARA)
   RG 44—Office of Government Reports
      Entry 171, Records of the Bureau of Intelligence
   RG 59—Records of the Department of State
     Central File (Decimal File), 1945–1949
     Entries 568J-568O, Office of Public Opinion Studies
     Entry 1245, Archibald MacLeish Chronological File
     Entry 1374, Office of Public Affairs, Information Memorandums
     Entry 1454, Office Files of Edward W. Barrett
     Entry 1526, Assistant Secretary of State for Public Affairs, Subject File
     Entry 1527, Top Secret Files of Howland H. Sargeant
     Entry 1530, Subject Files of Francis H. Russell
     Entry 1559, Records Relating to International Information Activities,
       1938–1953
     Entry 1587, Miscellaneous Records of the Bureau of Public Affairs
     Entry UD60, Division of Cultural Cooperation
   RG 208—Records of the Office of War Information
     Entry 1, Records of the Director
     Entry 3D, Records of the OFF
     Entry 5, Decimal File of the Director
     Entries 6A-6H, Records of the Historian
     Entry 7, Subject File of the OFF
     Entries 20–27, Domestic Operations Branch
     Entries 82–84, Deputy Director for Labor and Civilian Welfare
     Entry 222, News Bureau
     Entry 294, Bureau of Motion Pictures
     Entry 360, Director of Overseas Operations
   RG 229—Records of the Office of Inter-American Affairs
     Entry 1, Central Files
     Entry 10, Immediate Office of the Coordinator
     Entry 15, Minutes of the Meetings of Subsidiary Corporations
     Entry 21, Advertising Division
     Entry 127, Department of Press and Publications
   RG 306—Records of the United States Information Agency
     Entry 1001, U. S. Advisory Commission on Information
     Entry 1048, Office of Research and Intelligence
     Entry 1051, Subject Files, 1952–1955
     Historical Collection, Lawson File
     Historical Collection, Bureau of Programs
     Historical Collection, Reports and Studies
   RG 353—Records of Interdepartmental and Intradepartmental Committees
     Entry 13, History and Development of the Council
     Entry 14, Subject File

Entries 20–31, Interdepartmental Committee on Scientific and Cultural
    Cooperation
Entries 401–403, Information Committee
Entries 428–445, Social Policy and Cultural Affairs
Seeley G. Mudd Manuscript Library, Princeton, NJ (Mudd Library)
    Papers of the Council on Foreign Relations
    Papers of John Foster Dulles
    Papers of George Frost Kennan
University of Arkansas Libraries, Special Collections Division, Fayetteville, AR (UAR)
    MC 468—Bureau of Educational and Cultural Affairs Historical Collection

Newspapers

Chicago Tribune
Christian Science Monitor
Los Angeles Times
New York Times
Philadelphia Inquirer
Washington Post

Microfilm/Microfiche Collections

*Post World War II Foreign Policy Planning: State Department Records of Harley A.
    Notter, 1939–1945.* Bethesda, MD: Congressional Information Service, Inc., 1987.
Culbert, David H., ed. *Information Control and Propaganda: Records of the Office
    of War Information.* Frederick, MD: University Publications of America, 1987.

Congressional Hearings

U.S. Congress. House. Committee on Appropriations. *Second Supplemental
    National Defense Appropriation Bill for 1943.* 77th Cong., 2nd sess., 1942.
U.S. Congress. House. Committee on Foreign Affairs. *International Office of
    Education.* 79th Cong., 1st sess., 1944.
U.S. Congress. House. Committee on Foreign Affairs. *World Freedom of Press
    and Radio.* 78th Cong., 2nd sess., 1944.
U.S. Congress. House. Committee on Foreign Affairs. *Interchange of Knowledge
    and Skills Between People of the United States and People of Other Countries.*
    79th Cong., 1st & 2nd sess., 1945 and 1946.
U.S. Congress. House. Committee on Foreign Affairs. *Membership and Partici-
    pation by the United States in the United Nations Educational, Scientific, and
    Cultural Organization.* 79th Cong., 2nd sess., 1946.
U.S. Congress. House. Committee on Foreign Affairs. *United States Information
    and Educational Exchange Act of 1947.* 80th Cong., 1st sess., 1947.
U.S. Congress. House. Subcommittee of the Committee on Appropriations.
    Department of State Appropriations Bill. For the following years:
        1943 (77th Cong., 2d sess., 1942)
        1944 (78th Cong., 1st sess., 1943)

    1945 (78th Cong., 2d sess., 1944)
    1946 (79th Cong., 1st sess., 1945)
    1947 (79th Cong., 2d sess., 1946)
    1948 (80th Cong., 1st sess., 1947)
    1949 (80th Cong., 2d sess., 1948)
    1950 (81st Cong., 1st sess., 1949)
    1951 (81st Cong., 2nd sess., 1950)
    1952 (82nd Cong., 1st sess., 1951)
    1953 (82nd Cong., 2nd sess., 1952)
    1954 (83rd Cong., 1st sess., 1953)

U.S. Congress. House. Subcommittee of the Committee on Appropriations. *National War Agencies Appropriation Bill.* For the following years:
    1944 (78th Cong., 1st sess., 1943)
    1945 (78th Cong., 2nd sess., 1944)

U.S. Congress. Senate. Committee on Foreign Relations. *Expanded International Information and Education Program.* 81st Cong., 2nd sess., 1950.

U.S. Congress. Senate. Subcommittee of the Committee on Appropriations. *Departments of State, Justice, Commerce, and the Judiciary.* For the following years:
    1943 (77th Cong., 2d sess., 1942)
    1944 (78th Cong., 1st sess., 1943)
    1945 (78th Cong., 2d sess., 1944)
    1946 (79th Cong., 1st sess., 1945)
    1947 (79th Cong., 2d sess., 1946)
    1948 (80th Cong., 1st sess., 1947)
    1949 (80th Cong., 2d sess., 1948)
    1950 (81st Cong., 1st sess., 1949)
    1951 (81st Cong., 2nd sess., 1950)
    1952 (82nd Cong., 1st sess., 1951)
    1953 (82nd Cong., 2nd sess., 1952)
    1954 (83rd Cong., 1st sess., 1953)

U.S. Congress. Senate. Subcommittee of the Committee on Appropriations. *National War Agencies Appropriation Bill.* For the following years:
    1944 (78th Cong., 1st sess., 1943)
    1945 (78th Cong., 2nd sess., 1944)

U.S. Congress. Senate. Subcommittee of the Committee on Foreign Relations. *Overseas Information Programs of the United States.* 82nd Cong., 2nd sess., and 83rd Cong., 1st and 2nd sess., 1953 and 1954.

Additional Published Government Documents

Addresses and Statements by the Honorable Cordell Hull: In Connection with His Trip to South America to attend the Inter-American Conference for the Maintenance of Peace held at Buenos, Aires, Argentina, December 1–23, 1936. Department of State Publication 1019, Conference Series No. 31. Washington, DC: U.S. Government Printing Office, 1937.

Congressional Record, various volumes. Washington, DC: U.S. Government
  Printing Office.

Espinosa, J. Manuel. *Inter-American Beginnings of U. S. Cultural Diplomacy,*
  1936–1948. Washington, DC: U.S. Department of State, 1976.

Fairbank, Wilma. *America's Cultural Experiment in China, 1942–1949.* Washington,
  DC: U.S. Department of State, 1976.

Foster, H. Schuyler. "The Role of the Public in U.S. Foreign Relations." Address
  Made Before the Foreign Policy Association of New Orleans, New Orleans,
  LA. Washington, DC: U.S. Government Printing Office, 1961.

Hanson, Haldore. *The Cultural Cooperation Program, 1938–1943.* Washington,
  DC: U.S. Government Printing Office, 1944.

Hull, Cordell. *Opening Address to the Inter-American Conference for the Main-*
  tenance of Peace. State Department Publication 959. Washington, DC: U.S.
  Government Printing Office, 1936.

International Information and Educational Exchange Program. *Semiannual*
  Report of the Secretary of State to Congress.

Reports #s 1–11, 1948–1953

Kellerman, Henry J. *Cultural Relations as an Instrument of U.S. Foreign Policy:*
  The Educational Exchange Program between the United States and Germany,
  1945–1954. Washington, DC: U.S. Department of State, 1978.

Merrill, Dennis, ed. *Documentary History of the Truman Presidency.* 35 Vols.
  Washington, DC: University Press of America, 1995–2002.
    Vol. 8: *The Truman Doctrine and the Beginning of the Cold War*
    Vol. 13: *Establishing the Marshall Plan, 1947–1948.*
    Vol. 25: *President Truman's Confrontation with McCarthyism*
    Vol. 27: *The Point Four Program: Reaching Out to Help the Less*
      Developed Countries.
    Vol. 35: *The United Nations, 1945–1953: The Development of a World*
      Organization.

[Notter, Harley A.] *Postwar Foreign Policy Preparation, 1939–1945.* Department of
  State Publication 3580. Washington, DC: U.S. Government Printing Office,
  1949.

Report of the Delegation of the United States of America to the Inter-American
  Conference for the Maintenance of Peace, Buenos Aires, Argentina, December
  1–23, 1936. Department of State Publication 1088. Conference Series No. 33.
  Washington, DC: U.S. Government Printing Office, 1937.

[Rowland, Donald W.] *History of the Office of the Coordinator of Inter-American*
  Affairs. Washington, DC: U.S. Government Printing Office, 1947.

U.S. Department of State. *Foreign Relations of the United States.* Washington,
  DC: U.S. Government Printing Office, [the following volumes].
    1945.Vol. 1: General: The United Nations.
    1947.Vol. 4: Eastern Europe; The Soviet Union.
    1945–1950. Emergence of the Intelligence Establishment.
    1950.Vol. 1: National Security; Foreign Economic Policy.

Books and Articles

Acheson, Dean. *Present at the Creation: My Years in the State Department.*
    New York: W. W. Norton & Company, 1969.
Adams, Walter and John A. Garraty. *Is the World Our Campus?* East Lansing:
    Michigan State University Press, 1960.
Almond, Gabriel A. *The American People and Foreign Policy.* New York: Frederick
    A. Praeger, 1960.
Anderson, Benedict. *Imagined Community: Reflections on the Origin and Spread
    of Nationalism.* Rev. ed. New York: Verso, 2006.
Anderson, Carol. *Eyes off the Prize: The United Nations and the African American
    Struggle for Human Rights, 1945–1955.* Cambridge: Cambridge University Press,
    2003.
Arndt, Richard T. *The First Resort of Kings: American Cultural Diplomacy in the
    Twentieth Century.* Washington, DC: *Potomac Books,* 2005.
Arndt, Richard T. and David Lee Rubin. *The Fulbright Difference.* New
    Brunswick, NJ: Transaction, 1996.
Axelrod, Alan. *Selling the Great War: The Making of American Propaganda.*
    New York: Palgrave Macmillan, 2009.
Barnes, Joseph. "Fighting with Information: OWI Overseas." *Public Opinion
    Quarterly* 7 (Spring 1943): 34–45.
Barrett, Edward W. *Truth is Our Weapon.* New York: Funk & Wagnalls
    Company, 1953.
Beard, Charles A. *The Idea of National Interest: An Analytical Study in American
    Foreign Policy.* New York: The MacMillan Company, 1934.
Beard, Charles A. *The Open Door at Home: A Trial Philosophy of National Interest.*
    New York: The MacMillan Company, 1935.
Becker, David G. and Richard L. Sklar, eds. *Postimperialism and World Politics.*
    Westport, CT: Praeger, 1999.
Becker, William H. and William M. McClenahan, Jr. *The Market, the State, and
    the Export-Import Bank of the United States, 1934–2000.* New York: Cambridge
    University Press, 2003.
Beisner, Robert L. *Dean Acheson: A Life in the Cold War.* New York: Oxford
    University Press, 2006.
Beisner, Robert L. *From the Old Diplomacy to the New, 1865–1900.* 2d ed. Arling-
    ton Heights, IL: Harlan Davidson, 1986.
Bell, Daniel. *The Coming of Post-industrial Society: A Venture in Social Forecast-
    ing.* New ed. New York: Basic Books, 1999.
Bell, Jonathan. *The Liberal State on Trial: The Cold War and American Politics in
    the Truman Years.* New York: Columbia University Press, 2004.
Belmonte, Laura Ann. *Selling the American Way: U.S. Propaganda and the Cold
    War.* Philadelphia: University of Pennsylvania Press, 2008.
Bemis, Samuel Flagg. *The Latin American Policy of the United States.* New York:
    Harcourt, Brace, and Company, 1943.

Berghahn, Volker R. *America and the Intellectual Cold Wars in Europe: Shepard Stone Between Philanthropy, Academy, and Diplomacy.* Princeton, NJ: Princeton University Press, 2001.

Berkovitch, Nitza. *From Motherhood to Citizenship: Women's Rights and International Organization.* Baltimore, MD: The Johns Hopkins University Press, 1999.

Bernays, Edward L. *Crystallizing Public Opinion.* New York: Liveright Publishing, 1923.

Bernays, Edward L. *The Engineering of Consent.* Norman, University of Oklahoma Press, 1955.

Bernays, Edward L. *Propaganda.* New York: Liveright Publishing, 1928.

Bernays, Edward L. *Public Relations.* Norman: University of Oklahoma Press, 1952.

Bernhard, Nancy E. "Clearer than Truth: Public Affairs Television and the State Department's Domestic Information Campaigns, 1947–1952," *Diplomatic History* 21 (Fall 1997): 545–568.

Bernard, Nancy E.. *U.S. Television News and Cold War Propaganda, 1947–1960.* New York: Cambridge University Press, 1999.

Bernstein, Barton J., ed. *Politics and Policies of the Truman Administration.* Chicago: Quadrangle Books, 1970.

Bernstein, Barton J., ed. *Towards a New Past.* New York: Pantheon Books, 1968.

Bird, Kai. *The Color of Truth: McGeorge Bundy and William Bundy: Brothers in Arms.* New York: Simon & Schuster, 1998.

Blum, John Morton, ed. *The Price of Vision: The Diary of Henry A. Wallace, 1942–1946.* Boston: Houghton Mifflin Company, 1973.

Blum, John Morton. *V Was for Victory: Politics and American Culture During World War II.* New York: Harcourt Brace Jovanovich, Inc., 1976.

Bogart, Leo. *Premises for Propaganda: The United States Information Agency's Operating Assumptions in the Cold War.* New York: The Free Press, 1976.

Bohlen, Charles E. *The Transformation of Foreign Policy.* New York: W. W. Norton, 1969.

Boli, John and George M. Thomas, eds. *Constructing World Culture: International Nongovernmental Organizations Since 1875.* Stanford, CA: Stanford University Press, 1999.

Borgwardt, Elizabeth. *A New Deal for the World: America's Vision for Human Rights.* Cambridge, MA: Harvard University Press, 2005.

Borstelmann, Thomas. *Apartheid's Reluctant Uncle: The United States and Southern Africa during the Cold War.* New York: Oxford University Press, 1993.

Borstelmann, Thomas. *The Cold War and the Color Line: American Race Relations in the Global Arena.* Cambridge, MA: Harvard University Press, 2001.

Bostdorff, Denise M. *Proclaiming the Truman Doctrine: The Cold War Call to Arms.* College Station: Texas A&M University Press, 2008.

Bowles, Chester. *Promises to Keep: My Years in Public Life, 1941–1969.* New York: Harper & Row Publishers, 1971.

Boyer, Paul. *By the Bomb's Early Light: American Thought and Culture at the Dawn of the Atomic Age*. New York: Pantheon Books, 1985.

Brands, H. W. *The Specter of Neutralism: The United States and the Emergence of the Third World, 1947–1960*. New York: Columbia University Press, 1989.

Brewer, Susan. *To Win the Peace: British Propaganda in the United States during World War II*. Ithaca, NY: Cornell University Press, 1997.

Brewer, Susan. *Why America Fights: Patriotism and War Propaganda from the Philippines to Iraq*. New York: Oxford University Press, 2009.

Brinkley, Alan. *The End of Reform: New Deal Liberalism in Recession and War*. New York: Alfred A. Knopf, 1995.

Brinkley, Alan. *The Publisher: Henry Luce and His American Century*. New York: Vintage, 2011.

Brown, Anthony Cave. *The Last Hero: Wild Bill Donovan*. New York: Times Books, 1982.

Brown, John Mason. *The Ordeal of a Playwright: Robert E. Sherwood and the Challenge of War*. New York: Harper & Row, Publishers, 1970.

Burlingame, Roger. *Don't Let Them Scare You: The Life and Times of Elmer Davis*. Philadelphia: J. B. Lippincott Company, 1961.

Byrnes, James F. *Speaking Frankly*. New York: Harper & Brothers Publishers, 1947.

Campbell, Thomas M. and George C. Herring, eds. *The Diaries of Edward R. Stettinius, Jr., 1943–1946*. New York: Franklin Watts, Inc., 1975.

Cantril, Hadley. *Gauging Public Opinion*. Princeton, NJ: Princeton University Press, 1947.

Cantril, Hadley and Gordon W. Allport. *The Psychology of Radio*. New York: Harper & Brothers, 1935.

Casey, Steven. *Cautious Crusade: Franklin D. Roosevelt, American Public Opinion, and the War against Nazi Germany*. New York: Oxford University Press, 2001.

Casey, Steven. *Selling the Korean War: Propaganda, Politics, and Public Opinion in the United States, 1950–1953*. New York: Oxford University Press, 2008.

Chace, James. *Acheson: The Secretary of State Who Created the American World*. New York: Simon & Schuster, 1998.

Chadwin, Mark Lincoln. *The Hawks of World War II*. Chapel Hill: The University of North Carolina Press, 1968.

Chambers, John Whiteclay. "'All Quiet on the Western Front' (1930): The Antiwar Film and the Image of the First World War." *Historical Journal of Film, Radio and Television* 14 (Fall 1994): 377–411.

Chambers, John Whiteclay, ed. *The Eagle and the Dove: The American Peace Movement and United States Foreign Policy, 1900–1922*. 2nd ed. Syracuse, NY: Syracuse University Press, 1991.

Chambers, John Whiteclay. "The Movies and the Antiwar Debate in America, 1930–1941." *Film & History* 36 (No. 1, 2006): 44–57.

Cobbs, Elizabeth Anne. *The Rich Neighbor Policy: Rockefeller and Kaiser in Brazil*. New Haven, CT: Yale University Press, 1992.

Cohen, Lizabeth. *Making a New Deal: Industrial Workers in Chicago, 1919–1939*. New York: Cambridge University Press, 1990.

Cohen, Warren I. *America's Response to China: A History of Sino-American Relations*. 5th ed. New York: Columbia University Press, 2010.

Cole, Wayne S. *America First: The Battle against Intervention, 1940–1941*. Madison: University of Wisconsin Press, 1953.

Cole, Wayne S. *Roosevelt & the Isolationists, 1932–1945*. Lincoln: University of Nebraska Press, 1983.

Cole, Wayne S. *Senator Gerald P. Nye and American Foreign Relations*. Minneapolis: University of Minnesota Press, 1962.

Connelly, Matthew J. *A Diplomatic Revolution: Algeria's Fight for Independence and the Origins of the Post-Cold War Era*. New York: Oxford University Press, 2002.

Costigliola, Frank. *Awkward Dominion: American Political, Economic, and Cultural Relations with Europe, 1919–1933*. Ithaca, NY: Cornell University Press, 1984.

Costigliola, Frank. "The Nuclear Family: Tropes of Gender and Pathology in the Western Alliance." *Diplomatic History* 21 (Spring 1997): 163–183.

Costigliola, Frank. *Roosevelt's Lost Alliances: How Personal Politics Helped Start the Cold War*. Princeton, NJ: Princeton University Press, 2011.

Costigliola, Frank. "'Unceasing Pressure for Penetration': Gender, Pathology, and Emotion in George Kennan's Formation of the Cold War." *The Journal of American History* 83 (March 1997): 1309–1339.

Creel, George. *How We Advertised America*. New York: Harper & Brothers, 1920.

Creel, George. *Rebel at Large: Recollections of Fifty Crowded Years*. New York: G. P. Putnam's Sons, 1947.

Cull, Nicholas J. *The Cold War and the United States Information Agency: American Propaganda and Public Diplomacy, 1945–1989*. New York: Cambridge University Press, 2008.

Cull, Nicholas J. *The Decline and Fall of the United States Information Agency: American Public Diplomacy, 1989–2001*. New York: Palgrave Macmillan, 2012.

Cull, Nicholas J. *Selling War: The British Propaganda Campaign against American "Neutrality" during World War II*. New York: Oxford University Press, 1995.

Culver, John C. and John Hyde, *American Dreamer: The Life and Times of Henry A. Wallace*. New York: W. W. Norton & Company, 2000.

Cumings, Bruce. "The American Century and the Third World." *Diplomatic History* 23 (Spring 1999): 355–370.

Cumings, Bruce. *The Origins of the Korean War*. 2 vols. Princeton, NJ: Princeton University Press, 1981 & 1990.

Cumings, Bruce. *The Korean War: A History*. New York: Modern Library, 2010.

Cumings, Bruce. "'Revising Postrevisionism,' or, The Poverty of Theory in Diplomatic History." *Diplomatic History* 17 (Fall 1993): 539–569.

Cuordileone, K. A. *Manhood and American Political Culture in the Cold War*. New York: Routledge, 2005.

Curti, Merle. *American Philanthropy Abroad: A History*. New Brunswick, NJ: Rutgers University Press, 1963.

Curti, Merle and Kendall Birr. *Prelude to Point Four: American Technical Missions Overseas, 1838–1938*. Madison: The University of Wisconsin Press, 1954.

Dallek, Robert. *Franklin D. Roosevelt and American Foreign Policy*. New York: Oxford University Press, 1979.

Davis, Elmer and Byron Price. *War Information and Censorship*. Washington, DC: American Council on Public Affairs, 1943.

DeBenedetti, Charles. *The Peace Reform in American History*. Bloomington: Indiana University Press, 1980.

de Grazia, Victoria. *Irresistible Empire: America's Advance through Twentieth-Century Europe*. Cambridge, MA: Harvard University Press, 2005.

Del Pero, Mario. "The United States and 'Psychological Warfare' in Italy, 1948–1955." *Journal of American History* 87 (March 2001): 1304–1334.

Denning, Michael. *The Cultural Front: The Laboring of American Culture in the Twentieth Century*. New York: Verso, 1997.

Divine, Robert A. *The Reluctant Belligerent: American Entry Into World War II*. 2d ed. New York: Alfred A. Knopf, 1979.

Divine, Robert A. *Second Chance: The Triumph of Internationalism in America during World War II*. New York: Atheneum, 1967.

Dizard, Wilson. *Inventing Public Diplomacy: The Story of the U.S. Information Agency*. Boulder, CO: Lynne Rienner, 2004.

Dizard, Wilson. *Strategy of Truth: The Story of the U.S. Information Service*. Washington, DC: Public Affairs Press, 1961.

Doenecke, Justus. *Anti-Intervention: A Bibliographical Introduction to Isolationism and Pacifism from World War I to the Early Cold War*. New York: Garland Publishers, 1987.

Doherty, Thomas. *Cold War, Cool Medium: Television, McCarthyism, and American Culture*. New York: Columbia University Press, 2003.

Doherty, Thomas. *Projections of War: Hollywood, American Culture, and World War II*. New York: Columbia University Press, 1993.

Donaldson, Scott. *Archibald MacLeish: An American Life*. Boston: Houghton Mifflin Company, 1992.

Dower, John W. *War Without Mercy: Race and Power in the Pacific War*. New York: Pantheon Books, 1986.

Drabeck, Bernard A. and Helen E. Ellis, eds. *Archibald MacLeish: Reflections*. Amherst: The University of Massachusetts Press, 1986.

Dudziak, Mary L. *Cold War Civil Rights: Race and the Image of American Democracy*. Princeton, NJ: Princeton University Press, 2000.

Duggan, Stephen. *A Professor at Large*. Freeport, NY: Books for Libraries Press, 1972.

Duggan, Stephen. *The Two Americas: An Interpretation*. New York: C. Scribner's Sons, 1934.

Dunlop, Richard. *Donovan: America's Master Spy*. Chicago: Rand McNally & Company, 1982.

Eisenberg, Carolyn. *Drawing the Line: The American Decision to Divide Germany, 1944–1949*. New York: Cambridge University Press, 1996.

Eisenhower, Milton S. *The President Is Calling*. Garden City, NY: Doubleday & Company, Inc., 1974.

Ekbladh, David. *The Great American Mission: Modernization and the Construction of an American World Order*. Princeton, NJ: Princeton University Press, 2010.

Engerman, David C. *Know Your Enemy: The Rise and Fall of America's Soviet Experts*. New York: Oxford University Press, 2011.

Engerman, David C., Nils Gilman, Mark H. Haefele, and Michael E. Latham, eds. *Staging Growth: Modernization, Development, and the Global Cold War*. Amherst: University of Massachusetts Press, 2003.

Fejes, Fred. "The Office of the Coordinator of Inter-American Affairs (OCIAA) and the Origins of United States Cultural Diplomacy." Conference Paper #71. New York: Columbia University-New York University Consortium, 1993.

Feller, A. H. "OWI on the Home Front." *The Public Opinion Quarterly* 7 (Spring 1943): 55–65.

Ferrell, Robert H, ed. *The American Secretaries of State and Their Diplomacy*.
   Vol. XIV, E. R. Stettinius, Jr., by Richard L. Walker and James F. Byrnes, by George Curry. New York: Cooper Square Publishers, Inc., 1965.
   Vol. XV, *George Marshall*, by Robert H. Ferrell. New York: Cooper Square Press, 1966.
   Vol XVI, *Dean Acheson*, by Gaddis Smith. New York: Cooper Square Publishers, Inc., 1972.

Foglesong, David S. *America's Secret War Against Bolshevism: U.S. Intervention in the Russian Civil War, 1917–1920*. Chapel Hill: The University of North Carolina Press, 1995.

Foglesong, David S. *The American Mission and the "Evil Empire": The Crusade for a "Free Russia" since 1881*. New York: Cambridge University Press, 2007.

Ford, Corey, *Donovan of OSS*. Boston: Little, Brown and Company, 1970.

Foster, H. Schuyler, Jr. *Activism Replaces Isolationism: U. S. Public Attitudes, 1940–1975*. Washington, DC: Foxhall Press, 1983.

Foster, H. Schuyler, Jr. "How America Became Belligerent: A Quantitative Study of War News, 1914–17." *The American Journal of Sociology* 40 (January 1935): 464–475.

Foster, H. Schuyler, Jr., and Carl J. Friedrich. "Letters to the Editor as a Means of Measuring the Effectiveness of Propaganda." *The American Political Science Review* 31 (February 1937): 71–79.

Foster, H. Schuyler, Jr. "The Official Propaganda of Great Britain." *The Public Opinion Quarterly* 3 (April 1939): 263–271.

Foster, H. Schuyler, Jr. "Pressure Groups and Administrative Agencies." *Annals of the American Academy of Political and Social Science* 221 (May 1942): 21–28.

Fousek, John. *To Lead the Free World: American Nationalism and the Cultural Roots of the Cold War*. Chapel Hill: The University of North Carolina Press, 2000.

Fox, Stephen. *The Mirror Makers*. New York: William Morrow and Company, Inc., 1984.

Frankel, Charles. *The Neglected Aspect of Foreign Affairs: American Educational and Cultural Policy Abroad*. Washington, DC: The Brookings Institution, 1965.

Fraser, Steve and Gary Gerstle, eds. *The Rise and Fall of the New Deal Order, 1930–1980*. Princeton, NJ: Princeton University Press, 1989.

Fried, Richard M. *Nightmare in Red: The McCarthy Era in Perspective*. New York: Oxford University Press, 1990.

Fried, Richard M. *The Russians Are Coming! The Russians Are Coming! Pageantry and Patriotism in Cold-War America*. New York: Oxford University Press, 1998.

Gaddis, John Lewis. "The Emerging Post-Revisionist Synthesis on the Origins of the Cold War." With responses by Lloyd C. Gardner, Lawrence Kaplan, Warren F. Kimball, and Bruce R. Kuniholm. *Diplomatic History* 7 (Summer 1983): 171–204.

Gaddis, John Lewis. *George F. Kennan: An American Life*. New York: Penguin Press, 2011.

Gaddis, John Lewis. *Strategies of Containment: A Critical Appraisal of Postwar American National Security Policy*. New York: Oxford University Press, 1982.

Gardner, Lloyd C. *Approaching Vietnam: From World War II through Dienbienphu*. New York: W. W. Norton & Company, 1988.

Gardner, Lloyd C. *Architects of Illusion: Men and Ideas in American Foreign Policy, 1941–1949*. Chicago: Quadrangle Books, 1970.

Gardner, Lloyd C. *Economic Aspects of New Deal Diplomacy*. Madison: University of Wisconsin Press, 1964.

Gardner, Lloyd C., ed. *Redefining the Past: Essays in Diplomatic History in Honor of William Appleman Williams*. Corvallis, OR: Oregon State University Press, 1986.

Gardner, Lloyd C. *Safe for Democracy: The Anglo-American Response to Revolution, 1913–1923*. New York: Oxford University Press, 1984.

Gardner, Lloyd C. *Spheres of Influence: The Great Powers Partition Europe, from Munich to Yalta*. Chicago: Ivan R. Dee, 1993.

Gary, Brett. *The Nervous Liberals: Propaganda Anxieties from World War I to the Cold War*. New York: Columbia University Press, 1999.

Gellman, Irwin F. *Good Neighbor Diplomacy: United States Policies in Latin America, 1933–1945*. Baltimore, MD: The Johns Hopkins University Press, 1979.

Gellman, Irwin F. *Secret Affairs: Franklin Roosevelt, Cordell Hull, and Sumner Welles*. Baltimore, MD: Johns Hopkins University Press, 1995.

Gienow-Hecht, Jessica C. E. "*Shame on US?* Academics, Cultural Transfer, and the Cold War—A Critical Review." *Diplomatic History*. 24 (Summer 2000): 465–528.

Gienow-Hecht, Jessica C. E. *Sound Diplomacy: Music and Emotions in Transatlantic Relations*. Chicago: University of Chicago Press, 2009.

Gienow-Hecht, Jessica C. E. *Transmission Impossible: American Journalism as Cultural Diplomacy in Postwar Germany, 1945–1955.* Baton Rouge: Louisiana State University Press, 1999.

Gilman, Nils. *Mandarins of the Future: Modernization Theory in Cold War America.* Baltimore, MD: Johns Hopkins University Press, 2003.

Glendon, Mary Ann. *A World Made New: Eleanor Roosevelt and the Universal Declaration of Human Rights.* New York: Random House, 2001.

Goldman, Eric F. *The Crucial Decade—and After: America, 1945–1960.* New York: Vintage Books, 1961.

Gould-Davies, Nigel. "Rethinking the Role of Ideology in International Politics during the Cold War." *Journal of Cold War Studies* 1 (Winter 1999): 90–109.

Graebner, Norman A. *An Uncertain Tradition: American Secretaries of State in the Twentieth Century.* New York: McGraw-Hill, 1961.

Graham, Sarah Ellen. "American Propaganda, the Anglo-American Alliance, and the 'Delicate Question' of Indian Self-Determination." *Diplomatic History* 33 (April 2009): 223–260.

Gramsci, Antonio. *Selections from the Prison Notebooks.* Edited and Translated by Quintin Hoare and Geoffrey Nowell Smith. New York: International Publishers, 1971.

Grandin, Greg. *Empire's Workshop: Latin America, the United States, and the Rise of the New Imperialism.* New York: Metropolitan Books, 2006.

Green, David. *The Containment of Latin America: A History of the Myths and Realities of the Good Neighbor Policy.* Chicago: Quadrangle Books, 1971.

Griffith, Robert. "The Selling of America: The Advertising Council and American Politics, 1942–1960." *Business History Review* 57 (Autumn 1983): 388–412.

Guinsburg, Thomas N. *The Pursuit of Isolationism in the United States Senate from Versailles to Pearl Harbor.* New York: Garland Publishers, 1982.

Hahn, Peter L. and Mary Ann Heiss. *Empire and Revolution: The United States and the Third World since 1945.* Columbus: Ohio State University Press, 2001.

Hall, Stuart. "Gramsci's "Relevance for the Study of Race and Ethnicity." *The Journal of Communitarian Inquiry* 10 (Issue 2, 1986): 5–27.

Hamby, Alonzo L. *For the Survival of Democracy: Franklin Roosevelt and the World Crisis of the 1930s.* New York: Free Press, 2004.

Hamby, Alonzo L. *Man of the People: A Life of Harry S. Truman.* New York: Oxford University Press, 1995.

Hart, Justin. "Archibald MacLeish Rediscovered: The Poetry of U. S. Foreign Policy." *Historically Speaking* 8 (January/February 2007): 20–22.

Hart, Justin. "'Foreign Relations, Domestic Affairs': The Role of the 'Public' in the Origins of U.S. Public Diplomacy." In Kenneth L. Osgood and Brian Ethridge, eds. *The United States and Public Diplomacy: New Directions in Cultural and International History.* Leiden: Martinus Nijhoff Publishers, 2010: 195–223.

Hart, Justin. "'In Terms of Peoples Rather Than Nations': World War II Propaganda and Conceptions of U.S. Foreign Policy." In G. Kurt Piehler and Sidney Pash, eds. *The United States and the Second World War: New*

Perspectives on Diplomacy, War and the Home Front. New York: Fordham University Press, 2010: 68–98.

Hart, Justin. "Making Democracy Safe for the World: Race, Propaganda, and the Transformation of U. S. Foreign Policy during World War II." *Pacific Historical Review* 73 (February 2004): 49–84.

Hartz, Louis. *The Liberal Tradition in America: An Interpretation of American Political Thought Since the Revolution.* New York: Harcourt, Brace & World, Inc., 1955.

Hawkins, Lester G. and George S. Pettee. "OWI—Organization and Problems." *Public Opinion Quarterly* 7 (Spring 1943): 15–33.

Hawley, Ellis W. *The New Deal and the Problem of Monopoly: A Study in Economic Ambivalence.* Princeton, NJ: Princeton University Press, 1966.

Haynes, John Earl and Harvey Klehr. *Venona: Decoding Soviet Espionage in America.* New Haven, CT: Yale University Press, 1999.

Henderson, John W. *The United States Information Agency.* New York: Frederick A. Praeger, Publishers, 1969.

Herring, George. *From Colony to Superpower: U.S. Foreign Relations since 1776.* New York: Oxford University Press, 2008.

Hilderbrand, Robert C. *Power and the People: Executive Management of Public Opinion in Foreign Affairs, 1897–1921.* Chapel Hill: The University of North Carolina Press, 1981.

Hixson, Walter L. *George F. Kennan: Cold War Iconoclast.* New York: Columbia University Press, 1989.

Hixson, Walter L. *Parting the Curtain: Propaganda, Culture, and the Cold War, 1945–1961.* New York: St. Martin's, 1997.

Hofstadter, Richard. *The Age of Reform: From Bryan to F.D.R.* New York: Alfred A. Knopf, 1955.

Hofstadter, Richard. *Anti-intellectualism in American Life.* New York: Alfred A. Knopf, 1963.

Hogan, Michael J., ed. *The Ambiguous Legacy: U. S. Foreign Relations in the American Century.* New York: Cambridge University Press, 1999.

Hogan, Michael J. *A Cross of Iron: Harry S. Truman and the Origins of the National Security State, 1945–1954.* New York: Cambridge University Press, 1998.

Hogan, Michael J. *Informal Entente: The Private Structure of Cooperation in Anglo-American Economic Diplomacy, 1918–1928.* Columbia: University of Missouri Press, 1977.

Hogan, Michael J. *The Marshall Plan: America, Britain, and the Reconstruction of Western Europe, 1947–1952.* New York: Cambridge University Press, 1987.

Holsti, Ole R. *Public Opinion and American Foreign Policy.* Ann Arbor, MI: University of Michigan Press, 1996.

Horne, Gerald. "Who Lost the Cold War? Africans and African Americans." *Diplomatic History* 20 (October 1996): 613–626.

Horten, Gerd. *Radio Goes to War: The Cultural Politics of Propaganda during World War II.* Berkeley: University of California Press, 2002.

Hull, Cordell. *The Memoirs of Cordell Hull*. 2 vols. New York: The Macmillan Company, 1948.

Hunt, Michael H. *Ideology and U.S. Foreign Policy*. New Haven, CT: Yale University Press, 1987.

Hunt, Michael H. "The Long Crisis in U.S. Diplomatic History: Coming to Closure," *Diplomatic History* 16 (Winter 1992): 115–140.

Huxley, Julian. *UNESCO: Its Purpose and Its Philosophy*. Washington, DC: Public Affairs Press, 1947.

Hyman, Sydney. *The Lives of William Benton*. Chicago: The University of Chicago Press, 1969.

Inman, Samuel Guy. *Inter-American Conferences, 1826–1954*. Edited by Harold Eugene Davis. Gettysburg, PA: Times & News Publishing Co., for The University Press of Washington, DC, and the Community College Press, 1965.

Iriye, Akira. *Across the Pacific: An Inner History of American-East Asian Relations*. New York: Harcourt, Brace, & World, 1967.

Iriye, Akira. *After Imperialism: The Search for a New Order in the Far East, 1921–1931*. Cambridge, MA: Harvard University Press, 1965.

Iriye, Akira. *Cultural Internationalism and World Order*. Baltimore: The Johns Hopkins University Press, 1997.

Iriye, Akira. *Global Community: The Role of International Organizations in the Making of the Contemporary World*. Berkeley: University of California Press, 2002.

Irwin, Douglas A. and Randall S. Kroszner. "Interests, Institutions, and Ideology in Securing Policy Change: The Republican Conversion to Trade Liberalization after Smoot-Hawley." *Journal of Law and Economics* 42 (October 1999): 643–673.

Isaacson, Walter and Evan Thomas. *The Wise Men: Six Friends and the World They Made*. New York: Simon & Schuster, Inc., 1986.

Jacobson, Mark R. "'Minds Then Hearts': U.S. Political and Psychological Warfare during the Korean War." Ph.D. diss., Ohio State University, 2005.

Johnson, David K. *The Lavender Scare: The Cold War Persecution of Gays and Lesbians in the Federal Government*. Chicago: University of Chicago Press, 2004.

Johnson, Robert David. *Congress and the Cold War*. New York: Cambridge University Press, 2005.

Johnson, Walter. "Edward R. Stettinius, Jr." In Norman A. Graebner, ed. *An Uncertain Tradition: American Secretaries of State in the Twentieth Century*. New York: McGraw-Hill Book Company, Inc., 1961: 210–222.

Johnson, Walter and Francis J. Colligan. *The Fulbright Program: A History*. With a Foreword by J. W. Fulbright. Chicago: The University of Chicago Press, 1965.

Johnstone, Andrew. "Creating a 'Democratic Foreign Policy': The State Department's Division of Public Liaison and Public Opinion, 1944–1953." *Diplomatic History* 35 (June 2011): 483–503.

Jonas, Manfred. *Isolationism in America, 1935–1941.* Ithaca, NY: Cornell University Press, 1966.

Jones, Janna. "The Library of Congress Film Project: Film Collecting and a United State(s) of Mind." *The Moving Image* 6 (Fall 2006): 30–51.

Kaplan, Amy and Donald Pease, eds. *Cultures of United States Imperialism.* Durham, NC: Duke University Press, 1993.

Kaufman, Burton I. *The Korean War: Challenges in Crisis, Credibility, and Command.* 2nd ed. New York: McGraw-Hill, 1997.

Kennan, George F. *American Diplomacy, 1900–1950.* Chicago: The University of Chicago Press, 1951.

Kennan, George F. *Memoirs: 1925–1963.* 2 vols. Boston, MA: Little, Brown, and Company, 1967 & 1972.

Kennedy, David M. *Freedom from Fear: The American People in Depression and War, 1929–1945.* New York: Oxford University Press, 1999.

Kimball, Warren F. *Forged In War: Roosevelt, Churchill, and the Second World War.* New York: William Morrow and Company, Inc., 1997.

Kimball, Warren F. *The Juggler: Franklin Roosevelt as Wartime Statesman.* Princeton, NJ: Princeton University Press, 1991.

Kepley, David R. *The Collapse of the Middle Way: Senate Republicans and the Bipartisan Foreign Policy, 1948–1952.* New York: Greenwood Press, 1988.

Klehr, Harvey. *The Amerasia Spy Case: Prelude to McCarthyism.* Chapel Hill: University of North Carolina Press, 1996.

Knock, Thomas J. *To End All Wars: Woodrow Wilson and the Quest for a New World Order.* New York: Oxford University Press, 1992.

Koppes, Clayton R. "The Good Neighbor Policy and the Nationalization of Mexican Oil: A Reinterpretation." *Journal of American History* 79 (June 1982): 62–81.

Koppes, Clayton R. and Gregory D. Black. *Hollywood Goes to War: How Politics, Profits and Propaganda Shaped World War II Movies.* Berkeley: University of California Press, 1987.

Kraske, Gary E. *Missionaries of the Book: The American Library Profession and the Origins of American Cultural Diplomacy.* Westport, CT: Greenwood, 1985.

Krenn, Michael L. *Black Diplomacy: African Americans and the State Department, 1945–1969.* New York: M. E. Sharp, 1998.

Krenn, Michael L. *Fallout Shelters for the Human Spirit: American Art and the Cold War.* Chapel Hill: University of North Carolina Press, 2005.

Krugler, David F. *The Voice of America and the Domestic Propaganda Battles, 1945–1963.* Columbia: University of Missouri Press, 2000.

Kuehl, Warren F. "Midwestern Newspapers and Isolationist Sentiment." *Diplomatic History* 3 (Summer 1979): 283–306.

Kuisel, Richard. *Seducing the French: The Dilemma of Americanization.* Berkeley, CA: University of California Press, 1993.

LaFeber, Walter. *America, Russia, and the Cold War, 1945–2006.* 10th ed. New York: McGraw-Hill, 2006.

LaFeber, Walter. *Inevitable Revolutions*. New York: W. W. Norton & Company, 1983.

LaFeber, Walter. *The New Empire: An Interpretation of American Expansion, 1860–1898*. Ithaca, NY: Cornell University Press, 1963.

LaFeber, Walter. "Roosevelt, Churchill, and Indochina: 1942–1945." *The American Historical Review* 80 (December 1975): 1277–1295.

Lasswell, Harold D. *Propaganda Technique in the World War*. New York: Peter Smith, 1938.

Latham, Michael E. *Modernization as Ideology: American Social Science and 'Nation Building' in the Kennedy Era*. Chapel Hill: The University of North Carolina Press, 2000.

Lauren, Paul Gordon. *Power and Prejudice: The Politics and Diplomacy of Racial Discrimination*. Boulder, CO: Westview Press, 1988.

Laurie, Clayton D. *The Propaganda Warriors: America's Crusade Against Nazi Germany*. Lawrence: University Press of Kansas, 1996.

Laves, Walter H. C. and Charles A. Thomson. *UNESCO: Purpose, Progress, Prospects*. Bloomington: Indiana University Press, 1957.

Lawrence, Mark Atwood. *Assuming the Burden: Europe and the American Commitment to War in Vietnam*. Berkeley: University of California Press, 2005.

Leach, William. *Land of Desire: Merchants, Power, and the Rise of a New American Culture*. New York: Pantheon Books, 1993.

Lears, T. J. Jackson. *Fables of Abundance: A Cultural History of Advertising in America*. New York: Pantheon Books, 1994.

Leffler, Melvyn P. *For the Soul of Mankind: The United States, the Soviet Union, and the Cold War*. New York: Hill and Wang, 2008.

Leffler, Melvyn P. *A Preponderance of Power: National Security, the Truman Administration, and the Cold War*. Stanford, CA: Stanford University Press, 1992.

Lerner, Daniel. *Psychological Warfare Against Nazi Germany: The Sykewar Campaign, D-Day to VE-Day*. Cambridge, MA: The M.I.T. Press, 1971.

Leuchtenburg, William E. *Franklin D. Roosevelt and the New Deal, 1932–1940*. New York: Harper & Row, Publishers, 1963.

Levin, N. Gordon, Jr. *Woodrow Wilson and World Politics: America's Response to War and Revolution*. New York: Oxford University Press, 1968.

Lewis, David Levering. *W.E.B. Du Bois: The Fight for Equality and the American Century, 1919–1963*. New York: Henry Holt and Company, 2000.

Lieberman, Robbie. *The Strangest Dream: Communism, Anti-communism and the U.S. Peace Movement, 1945–1963*. Syracuse, NY: Syracuse University Press, 2000.

Lilly, Edward P. "The Psychological Strategy Board and Its Predecessors: Foreign Policy Coordination, 1938–1953." In Gaetano L. Vincitorio, ed. *Studies in Modern History*. New York: St. John's University Press, 1968: 337–382.

Livingston, James. *Pragmatism, Feminism, and Democracy: Rethinking the Politics of American History*. New York: Routledge, 2001.

Louis, Wm. Roger. *Imperialism at Bay: The United States and the Decolonization of the British Empire, 1941–1945.* New York: Oxford University Press, 1978.

Lucas, Scott. *Freedom's War: The American Crusade against the Soviet Union.* New York: New York University Press, 1999.

Lundestad, Geir. *The United States and Western Europe Since 1945: From "Empire" by Invitation to Transatlantic Drift.* New York: Oxford University Press, 2003.

Lykins, Daniel L. *From Total War to Total Diplomacy: The Advertising Council and the Construction of the Cold War Consensus.* Westport, CT: Praeger, 2003.

MacLeish, Archibald. *A Time to Act.* Boston: Houghton Mifflin Company, 1943.

MacLeish, Archibald. *A Time to Speak.* Boston: Houghton Mifflin Company, 1940.

Maier, Charles. *Among Empires: American Ascendancy and Its Predecessors.* Cambridge, MA: Harvard University Press, 2006.

Maier, Charles. "Marking Time: The Historiography of International Relations." In *The Past Before Us: Contemporary Historical Writing in the United States,* edited by Michael Kammen. Ithaca, NY: Cornell University Press, 1980: 355–390, with responses in *Diplomatic History* 5 (Fall 1981): 353–382.

Maier, Charles. "The Politics of Productivity: Foundations of American International Economic Policy after World War II." *International Organization* 31 (Autumn 1977): 607–633.

Manela, Erez. *The Wilsonian Moment: Self-Determination and the International Origins of Anticolonial Nationalism.* New York: Oxford University Press, 2007.

Marchand, Roland. *Advertising the American Dream: Making Way for Modernity: 1920–1940.* Berkeley: University of California Press, 1985.

Markowitz, Norman D. *The Rise and Fall of the People's Century: Henry A. Wallace and American Liberalism, 1941–1948.* New York: The Free Press, 1973.

May, Elaine Tyler. *Homeward Bound: American Families in the Cold War Era.* Rev. ed. New York: Basic Books, 2008.

Mayer, Arno J. *Wilson vs. Lenin: Political Origins of the New Diplomacy, 1917–1918.* Cleveland, OH: The World Publishing Company, 1964.

McCormick, Thomas. *China Market: America's Quest for Informal Empire, 1893–1901.* Chicago: Quadrangle Books, 1967.

McCullough, David. *Truman.* New York: Simon & Schuster, 1992.

McEnaney, Laura. *Civil Defense Begins at Home: Militarization Meets Everyday Life in the Fifties.* Princeton, NJ: Princeton University Press, 2000.

McKenzie, Brian Angus. *Remaking France: Americanization, Public Diplomacy, and the Marshall Plan.* New York: Berghahn Books, 2005.

McMahon, Robert J. *The Cold War on the Periphery: The United States, India, and Pakistan.* New York: Columbia University Press, 1994.

McMahon, Robert J. *Colonialism and Cold War: The United States and the Struggle for Indonesian Independence, 1945–49.* Ithaca, NY: Cornell University Press, 1981.

McMahon, Robert J. *Dean Acheson and the Creation of an American World Order*. Washington, DC: Potomac Books, 2009.

McMurray, Ruth Emily and Muna Lee. *The Cultural Approach: Another Way in International Relations*. Chapel Hill: University of North Carolina Press, 1947.

Mecham, J. Lloyd. *The United States and Inter-American Security: 1889–1960*. Austin: The University of Texas Press, 1961.

Meserve, Walter J. *Robert E. Sherwood: Reluctant Moralist*. New York: Pegasus, 1970.

Meyerhoff, Arthur E. *The Strategy of Persuasion: The Use of Advertising Skills in Fighting the Cold War*. New York: Coward-McCann, 1965.

Milward, Alan S. *The Reconstruction of Western Europe, 1945–1951*. London: Methuen, 1984.

Miscamble, Wilson D. *George F. Kennan and the Making of American Foreign Policy, 1947–1950*. Princeton, NJ: Princeton University Press, 1992.

Miscamble, Wilson D. *From Roosevelt to Truman: Potsdam, Hiroshima, and the Cold War*. New York: Cambridge University Press, 2007.

Mitrovich, Gregory. *Undermining the Kremlin: America's Strategy to Subvert the Soviet Bloc, 1947–1956*. Ithaca, NY: Cornell University Press, 2000.

Mock, James R. and Cedric Larson. *Words that Won the War: The Story of the Committee on Public Information, 1917–1919*. Princeton: Princeton University Press, 1939.

Morgenthau, Hans J. *Politics among Nations: The Struggle for Power and Peace*. New York: Alfred A. Knopf, 1948.

Morgenthau, Hans J. *Scientific Man vs. Power Politics*. Chicago: University of Chicago Press, 1946.

Moser, John. "'Gigantic Engines of Propaganda': The 1941 Senate Investigation of Hollywood." *The Historian* 63 (No. 4, 2001): 731–753.

Myrdal, Gunnar. *An American Dilemma: The Negro Problem and Modern Democracy*. 2 vols. New York: Harper & Brothers Publishers, 1944.

Ninkovich, Frank. *The Diplomacy of Ideas: U. S. Foreign Policy and Cultural Relations, 1938–1950*. New York: Cambridge University Press, 1981.

Nye, Joseph. *Soft Power: The Means to Success in World Politics*. New York: Public Affairs, 2004.

Offner, Arnold A. *Another Such Victory: President Truman and the Cold War, 1945–1953*. Stanford, CA: Stanford University Press, 2002.

Osgood, Kenneth. *Total Cold War: Eisenhower's Secret Propaganda Battle at Home and Abroad*. Lawrence: University Press of Kansas, 2006.

Osgood, Kenneth. and Brian C. Etheridge, eds. *The United States and Public Diplomacy: New Directions in Cultural and International History*. Leiden: Martinus Nijhoff Publishers, 2010.

Osgood, Kenneth and Andrew K. Frank. *Selling War in a Media Age: The Presidency and Public Opinion in the American Century*. Gainesville: University Press of Florida, 2011.

Oshinsky, David M. *A Conspiracy So Immense: The World of Joe McCarthy*. New York: Free Press, 1983.

Ostrower, Gary. *The United Nations and the United States*. New York: Twayne Publishers, 1998.

Parker, Jason C. *Brother's Keeper: The United States, Race, and Empire in the British Caribbean, 1937–1962*. New York: Oxford University Press, 2008.

Parry-Giles, Shawn J. *The Rhetorical Presidency, Propaganda, and the Cold War, 1945–1955*. Westport, CT: Praeger, 2002.

Paterson, Thomas G. *On Every Front: The Making of the Cold War*. New York: W. W. Norton, 1979.

Patterson, David S. *Toward a Warless World : The Travail of the American Peace Movement, 1887–1914*. Bloomington: Indiana University Press, 1976.

Pease, Stephen E. *Psywar: Psychological Warfare in Korea, 1950–1953*. Harrisburg, PA: Stackpole Books, 1992.

Pells, Richard. *Not Like Us: How Europeans Have Loved, Hated and Transformed American Culture since World War II*. New York: Basic Books, 1997.

Pierpaoli, Paul G. *Truman and Korea: The Political Culture of the Early Cold War*. Columbia: University of Missouri Press, 1999.

Pirsein, Robert William. *The Voice of America: A History of the International Broadcasting Activities of the United States Government, 1940–1962*. New York: Arno Press, 1979.

Plummer, Brenda Gayle. *Rising Wind: Black Americans and U.S. Foreign Affairs, 1935–1960*. Chapel Hill: The University of North Carolina Press, 1996.

Polanyi, Karl. *The Great Transformation: The Political and Economic Origins of Our Time*. Boston: Beacon Press, 1965.

Potter, David M. *People of Plenty: Economic Abundance and the American Character*. Chicago: The University of Chicago Press, 1954.

Puddington, Arch. *Broadcasting Freedom: The Cold War Triumph of Radio Free Europe and Radio Liberty*. Lexington: University of Kentucky Press, 2000.

Pullin, Eric D. "'Noise and Flutter': American Propaganda Strategy and Operation in India during World War II." *Diplomatic History* 34 (April 2010): 275–299.

Qing, Simei. *From Allies to Enemies: Visions of Modernity, Identity, and U.S.-China Diplomacy, 1945–1960*. Cambridge, MA: Harvard University Press, 2007.

Rawnsley, Gary D., ed. *Cold War Propaganda in the 1950s*. New York: St. Martin's, 1999.

Reeves, Thomas C. *The Life and Times of Joe McCarthy*. New York: Stein and Day, 1982.

Reynolds, David. *Rich Relations: The American Occupation of Britain*. London: Harper Collins, 1995.

Richmond, Yale. *Cultural Exchange & the Cold War: Raising the Iron Curtain*. University Park: The Pennsylvania State University Press, 2003.

Rivas, Darlene. *Missionary Capitalist: Nelson Rockefeller in Venezuela*. Chapel Hill: The University of North Carolina Press, 2002.

Robin, Ron. *The Making of the Cold War Enemy: Culture and Politics in the Military-Intellectual Complex.* Princeton, NJ: Princeton University Press, 2001.

Rodgers, Daniel T. *Atlantic Crossings: Social Politics in a Progressive Age.* Cambridge, MA: Harvard University Press, 1998.

Rofe, Simon J. *Franklin Roosevelt's Foreign Policy and the Welles Mission.* New York: Palgrave Macmillan, 2007.

Rosenberg, Emily S. *Spreading the American Dream: American Economic and Cultural Expansion, 1890–1945.* New York: Hill and Wang, 1982.

Rossiter, Clinton and James Lare, eds. *The Essential Lippmann: A Political Philosophy for Liberal Democracy.* New York: Random House, 1963.

Rotter, Andrew J. *Comrades at Odds: The United States and India, 1947–1964.* Ithaca, NY: Cornell University Press, 2000.

Rupp, Leila J. *Worlds of Women: The Making of an International Women's Movement.* Princeton, NJ: Princeton University Press, 1997.

Ryan, David and Victor Pungong, eds. *The United States and Decolonization: Power and Freedom.* New York: St. Martin's Press, 2000.

Saunders, Frances Stonor. *The Cultural Cold War: The CIA and the World of Arts and Letters.* New York: The New Press, 1999.

Savage, Barbara Dianne. *Broadcasting Freedom: Radio, War, and the Politics of Race.* Chapel Hill: The University of North Carolina Press, 1999.

Schaffer, Howard B. *Chester Bowles: New Dealer in the Cold War.* Cambridge, MA: Harvard University Press, 1993.

Schmidt, Oliver Matthias Arnol. "Civil Empire by Co-optation: German-American Exchange Programs as Cultural Diplomacy." Ph.D. diss., Harvard University, 1999.

Schoultz, Lars. *Beneath the United States.* Cambridge, MA: Harvard University Press, 1998.

Schrecker, Ellen. *Many are the Crimes: McCarthyism in America.* New York: Little, Brown, 1998.

Schulzinger, Robert. *The Wise Men of Foreign Affairs: The History of the Council of Foreign Relations.* New York: Columbia University Press, 1984.

Schumpeter, Joseph A. *Capitalism, Socialism, and Democracy.* 3d ed. New York: Harper & Brothers Publishers, 1950.

Schurmann, Franz. *The Logic of World Power: An Inquiry into the Origins, Currents, and Contradictions of World Politics.* New York: Pantheon Books, 1974.

Schwartz, Thomas Alan. *America's Germany: John J. McCloy and the Federal Republic of Germany.* Cambridge, MA: Harvard University Press, 1991.

Scott-Smith, Giles. *Networks of Empire: The US State Department's Foreign Leader Program in the Netherlands, France and Britain 1950–1970.* Brussels: Peter Lang, 2008.

Scott-Smith, Giles. *The Politics of Apolitical Culture: The Congress for Cultural Freedom, the CIA, and Postwar American Hegemony.* New York: Routledge, 2002.

Scott-Smith, Giles and Hans Krabbendam, eds., *The Cultural Cold War in Western Europe, 1945–1960*. London: Frank Cass, 2003.

Selverstone, Marc J. *Constructing the Monolith: The United States, Great Britain, and International Communism, 1945–1950*. Cambridge, MA: Harvard University Press, 2009.

Sherry, Michael S. *In the Shadow of War: The United States Since the 1930s*. New Haven, CT: Yale University Press, 1995.

Sherwin, Martin J. *A World Destroyed: Hiroshima and the Origins of the Arms Race*. New York: Vintage Books, 1987.

Shrecker, Ellen. *Many Are the Crimes: McCarthyism in America*. New York: Little, Brown, 1998.

Shulman, Holly Cowan. *The Voice of America: Propaganda and Democracy, 1941–1945*. Madison: The University of Wisconsin Press, 1990.

Simpson, Christopher, ed. *Universities and Empire: Money and Politics in the Social Sciences during the Cold War*. New York: The New Press, 1998.

Sklar, Martin J. *The Corporate Reconstruction of American Capitalism, 1890–1916: The Market, the Law, and Politics*. New York: Cambridge University Press, 1988.

Smith, Neil. *American Empire: Roosevelt's Geographer and the Prelude to Globalization*. Berkeley: University of California Press, 2003.

Sorenson, Thomas. *The Word War: The Story of American Propaganda*. New York: Harper & Row, 1968.

Sproule, J. Michael. *Propaganda and Democracy: The American Experience of Media and Mass Persuasion*. New York: Cambridge University Press, 1997.

Spykman, Nicholas John. *America's Strategy in World Politics*. New York: Harcourt, Brace and Company, 1942.

Starr, Paul. *The Creation of the Media: Political Origins of Modern Communications*. New York: Basic Books, 2004.

Steele, Richard W. *Propaganda in an Open Society: The Roosevelt Administration and the Media, 1933–1941*. Westport, CT: Greenwood Press, 1985.

Stephanson, Anders. *Kennan and the Art of Foreign Policy*. Cambridge, MA: Harvard University Press, 1989.

Stuart, Graham H. *American Diplomatic and Consular Practice*. 2nd ed. New York: Appleton-Century-Crofts, 1952.

Stuart, Graham H. *The Department of State: A History of Its Organization, Procedure, and Personnel*. New York: The Macmillan Company, 1949.

Stueck, William W. *The Korean War: An International History*. Princeton, NJ: Princeton University Press, 1995.

Stueck, William W. *Rethinking the Korean War: A New Diplomatic and Strategic History*. Princeton, NJ: Princeton University Press, 2002.

Stueck, William W. *The Road to Confrontation: American Policy Toward China and Korea, 1947–1950*. Chapel Hill: University of North Carolina Press, 1981.

Susman, Warren. *Culture as History: The Transformation of American Society in the Twentieth Century*. New York: Pantheon Books, 1984.

Sweeney, Michael S. *Secrets of Victory: The Office of Censorship and the American Press and Radio in World War II*. Chapel Hill: University of North Carolina Press, 2001.

Thomson, Charles A. and Walter H. C. Laves. *Cultural Relations and U.S. Foreign Policy*. Bloomington: Indiana University Press, 1963.

Thomson, Charles A. H. *Overseas Information Service of the United States Government*. New York: Arno Press, 1972.

Thorne, Christoper. *Allies of a Kind: The United States, Great Britain, and the War Against Japan, 1941–1945*. New York: Oxford University Press, 1978.

Trachtenberg, Marc. *A Constructed Peace: The Making of the European Settlement, 1945–1963*. Princeton, NJ: Princeton University Press, 1999.

Troy, Thomas F. *Wild Bill and Intrepid: Donovan, Stephenson, and the Origin of CIA*. New Haven, CT: Yale University Press, 1996.

Trumpbour, John. *Selling Hollywood to the World: U.S. and European Struggles for Mastery of the Global Film Industry, 1920–1950*. New York: Cambridge University Press, 2002.

Turner, Ralph E. *The Great Cultural Traditions*. 2 vols. New York: McGraw-Hill Book Company, Inc., 1941.

Tye, Larry. *The Father of Spin: Edward L. Bernays and the Birth of Public Relations*. New York: Henry Holt, 1998.

Vaughn, Stephen. *Holding Fast the Inner Lines: Democracy, Nationalism, and the Committee on Public Information*. Chapel Hill: The University of North Carolina Press, 1980.

von Eschen, Penny M. *Race Against Empire: Black Americans and Anticolonialism, 1937–1957*. Ithaca, NY: Cornell University Press, 1996.

von Eschen, Penny M. *Satchmo Blows Up the World: Jazz Ambassadors Play the Cold War*. Cambridge, MA: Harvard University Press, 2004.

Wagnleitner, Reinhold. *Coca-Colonization and the Cold War: The Cultural Mission of the United States in Austria after the Second World War*. Chapel Hill: University of North Carolina Press, 1994.

Wagnleitner, Reinhold and Elaine Tyler May, eds. *"Here, There and Everywhere": The Foreign Politics of American Popular Culture*. Hanover, NH: University Press of New England, 2000.

Wala, Michael. "Selling the Marshall Plan at Home: The Committee for the Marshall Plan to Aid European Recovery." *Diplomatic History* 10 (July 1986): 247–265.

Walker, J. Samuel. *Henry A. Wallace and American Foreign Policy*. Westport, CT: Greenwood, 1976.

Watt, D. Cameron. *Succeeding John Bull: America in Britain's Place, 1900–1975*. Cambridge: Cambridge University Press, 1984.

Weinstein, Allen and Alexander Vassiliev. *The Haunted Wood: Soviet Espionage in America—the Stalin Era*. New York: Random House, 1999.

Welles, Benjamin. *Sumner Welles: FDR's Global Strategist*. New York: St. Martin's Press, 1997.

Welles, Sumner. *The Time for Decision*. New York: Harper & Brothers Publishers, 1944.

White, Graham and John Maze. *Henry A. Wallace: His Search for a New World Order*. Chapel Hill: The University of North Carolina Press, 1995.

White, Walter. *A Rising Wind*. Garden City, NY: Doubleday, Doran, 1945.

Whitfield, Stephen J. *The Culture of the Cold War*. 2nd ed. Baltimore, MD: Johns Hopkins University Press, 1996.

Williams, William Appleman. *The Contours of American History*. New York: W. W. Norton, 1988.

Williams, William Appleman. *The Roots of the Modern American Empire: A Study of the Growth and Shaping of Social Consciousness in a Marketplace Society*. New York: Random House, 1969.

Williams, William Appleman. *The Tragedy of American Diplomacy*. New ed. New York: W. W. Norton & Company, 2009.

Wiltz, John E. *In Search of Peace: The Senate Munitions Inquiry, 1934–1936*. Baton Rouge: Louisiana State University Press, 1963.

Wiltz, John E. *From Isolation to War, 1931–1941*. Arlington Heights, IL: Harlan Davidson, 1968.

Winkler, Alan M. *The Politics of Propaganda: The Office of War Information, 1942–1945*. New Haven, CT: Yale University Press, 1978.

Winkler, Jonathan Reed. *Nexus: Strategic Communications and American Security in World War I*. Cambridge, MA: Harvard University Press, 2008.

Winnick, R. H., ed. *Letters of Archibald MacLeish, 1907 to 1982*. Boston: Houghton Mifflin Company, 1983.

Wood, Bryce. *The Making of the Good Neighbor Policy*. New York: Columbia University Press, 1961.

Woods, Randall Bennett. *Fulbright: A Biography*. New York: Cambridge University Press, 1995.

INDEX

—————

·